GERMAN ACHIEVEMENTS IN AMERICA:

Rudolf Cronau's Survey History

Edited by
Don Heinrich Tolzmann

HERITAGE BOOKS
2012

HERITAGE BOOKS

AN IMPRINT OF HERITAGE BOOKS, INC.

Books, CDs, and more—Worldwide

For our listing of thousands of titles see our website
at
www.HeritageBooks.com

Published 2012 by
HERITAGE BOOKS, INC.
Publishing Division
100 Railroad Ave. #104
Westminster, Maryland 21157

Cover illustration:
Constantin Grebner, *Die Deutschen* (1902)

International Standard Book Numbers
Paperbound: 978-0-7884-0167-1
Clothbound: 978-0-7884-9294-5

Table of Contents

Editor's Preface

In 1909, Rudolf Cronau's **Drei Jahrhunderte deutschen Lebens in Amerika** appeared, and was clearly one of the major German-American histories published before the First World War. (1) A prolific author, Cronau (1855-1939) had come to America in 1880 after attending the art academy in Düsseldorf. His aim was to write articles dealing with the American Wild West for the noted German periodical, **Die Gartenlaube**. He, hence, traveled extensively throughout the U.S., but especially in the West.

After writing about the West for the German press, Cronau also began to write for the German-American press, and supported himself as well by lecturing on a wide variety of topics drawn from his various travels in Germany and America.

In the 1880s, he then began to publish his work in book form, several of which dealt with his travels in the West. (2) His works also reflected his artistic interests and education, and were usually richly illustrated.

In 1908, the 300th anniversary of the arrival of the first German settlers in America at Jamestown, Virginia, was celebrated. (3) This became the occasion for the publication of several major German-American histories by Cronau, Albert B. Faust, Max Heinrici, and Georg von Bosse. Faust's work, the only one which was published in English, went on to become the standard basic history, which was updated in 1927, and continues to be reprinted. (4) However, each of the three other German-language works are of value, as each provides a somewhat different approach and coverage. The value in Cronau's work was that, although it was not encyclopedic like Faust's work, it provided a well-written general survey. A special value was that it surpasses all the other histories in terms of the numerous quality illustrations it contains. However, as it was in German it was, of course, only accessible to the German-American community.

In 1916, Cronau then decided to publish a German-American history in the English language, but he decided not to translate his extensive 1909 work, but rather to compile a concise compendium, based on his previous work. The occasion for the publication of this work was the First World War, a time in which German-Americans and the German heritage would become the targets of the Anti-German Hysteria. (5) Of course, in such a time, the topic of German-American history would become obscured.

Cronau obviously felt that it was necessary to bring out a work which would provide some basic information on German-American history. Such a work was intended not only for German-Americans, so that they could become more informed about their history, and then inform others, but was also intended for the general public at large, so that all Americans would become informed about the role German-Americans had played in American history.

The result was this handy historical compendium of German-American history, which is profusely illustrated. Then, as now, it provides a concise introduction to German-American history, from the beginnings up to the time of the First World War. It also provides information on the influence German-Americans have had in numerous areas - from politics, agriculture, industry, commerce, physical education, science, publishing, literature, music, to the arts, etc.

Given Cronau's background, this work is especially good for the arts, music, and literature. And, it also contains a chapter on the role of German-American women, which few other works at that time did. Of special interest, in consideration of the time the book was written, is Cronau's final chapter dealing with "The Future Mission of the German Element in America." A selective bibliography has been added for those interested in reading further in German-American history.

It is hoped that this work will prove to be as useful now as it originally was for all those interested in some of the basic facts regarding German-American history.

Notes

1. Rudolf Cronau, **Drei Jahrhunderte deutschen Lebens in Amerika.** (Berlin: Dietrich Reimer, 1909).

2. For bio-bibliographical information regarding Cronau, see Robert E. Ward, **A Bio-Bibliography of German-American Writers, 1670-1970.** (White Plains, NY: Kraus, 1985), pp. 57-58.

3. Regarding this aspect of German-American history, see Don Heinrich Tolzmann, ed., **The First Germans in America, With A Biographical Directory of New York Germans.** (Bowie, MD: Heritage Books, Inc., 1992).

4. For a discussion of the writing of German-American history, see Don Heinrich Tolzmann, ed., **Germany and America (1450-1700):** **Julius Friedrich Sachse's History of the German Role in the Discovery, Exploration, and Settlement of the New World.** (Bowie, MD: Heritage Books, Inc., 1991), pp. 16-28.

5. For references to sources dealing with the First World War, see Don Heinrich Tolzmann, **German-Americana: A Bibliography.** (Metuchen, NJ: Scarecrow Pr., 1975), pp. 87-96.

To the millions of children, born by German parents and raised in German American homes, the Hope and Future of our United States, this book is dedicated by

THE AUTHOR.

WORKS BY THE SAME AUTHOR

Geschichte der Solinger Klingenindustrie (Stuttgart, 1885).

Von Wunderland zu Wunderland. Landschafts- und Lebensbilder aus den Staaten und Territorien der Union (2 Vol., Leipzig, 1886).

Fahrten im Lande der Sioux Indianer (Leipzig, 1886).

Geschichte, Wesen und Praxis der Reklame (Ulm, 1887).

Im wilden Westen. Eine Künstlerfahrt durch die Prairien und Felsengebirge der Union (Braunschweig, 1890).

Amerika, die Geschichte seiner Entdeckung von der ältesten bis auf die neueste Zeit (2 Vol., Leipzig, 1890-92).

America, historia de su descubrimiento desde los tiempos primitivos hasta los mas modernos (3 Vol. Barcelona, 1892).

Illustrative Cloud Forms for the Guidance of Observers in the Classification of Clouds (U. S. Publication No. 112. Washington, D. C., 1897).

Our Wasteful Nation. The Story of American Prodigality and the Abuse of Our National Resources (New York, 1908).

Drei Jahrhunderte deutschen Lebens in Amerika (Berlin, 1909).

Do We Need a Third War for Independence? (New York, 1914).

The British Black Book (New York, 1915).

England a Destroyer of Nations (New York, 1915).

Our Hyphenated Citizens. Are They Right or Wrong? (New York, 1916).

INTRODUCTION.

THE great world war which has plunged the European nations into endless misery, suffering and death, has brought great embarrassment also to all American citizens of German descent.

No protection was needed heretofore by them against misrepresentation or attacks upon their good name. Now, however, the great European Conflict, sowing in unprecedented manner the seed of discord, unloosening envy, calumny and prejudice, compels them constantly to parry most unwarranted insinuations launched by men who ought to know better, yet apparently find delight in questioning the loyalty of the German Americans toward the land of their adoption.

If there be any one inclined to lend an ear to these most despicable and baseless insinuations, let him inform himself through these pages of the glorious past of the German Element in America, of its well-nigh endless record of achievements and sacrifices on behalf of the nation, of its enduring patriotism, when others failed of their duty or knew not where to turn.

The descendants of Germans in this country may justly be proud of the fact that their ancestors were among the first American pioneers; that they were the makers of true American homes, and that they participated in laying the foundations upon which the entire present-day structure of our United States has been reared.

That the reverent love which the Germans bear the land of their birth in no way tends to diminish the loyalty which they owe to the country of their adoption, is a fact which no fair-minded man requires to be proven, but of which this record bears ample witness. In defense of the Constitution, for the preservation of liberty and the rights of man they will stand firm and unafraid as of yore.

May this book help to set aright the opinion of our American people with regard to their German fellow-citizens, and may it inspire our young generation to emulate the industry, enterprise and patriotism which distinguished the men and women of whom it tells.

Mediaeval Germany and the Causes of

German Emigration.

Far beyond the Atlantic, occupying the greater part of central Europe, lies a country dear to all Americans of German descent. It is known as a land of romantic scenery, where the most beautiful of rivers, the Rhine, sweeps through vineclad mountains; where gray old churches and majestic cathedrals point heavenward; where in crumbling castles, sombre forests and silent valleys cling thousands of legends and fairy tales. It is praised as the home of science; as the birthplace of eminent philosophers and poets, whose names are known throughout the world. It is hailed as the land of great artists, sculptors and composers; as the cradle of most important inventions, that gave new impulse to mankind. Americans of German origin cherish it as the land of their ancestors, as the "Old Fatherland," and when speaking of it, they feel longing tugging at their heartstrings.

Reminiscences of the past are then revived. Noble heroes, none greater known to history, arise before their minds: Hermann the Cheruskan, the Emperors Karl and Otto the Great, Frederick Barbarossa, Rudolf and Maximilian, who, during the middle ages, made Germany the most prosperous and powerful empire in Europe.

Under the sceptre of such brilliant rulers beautiful castles and palaces, imposing churches and cathedrals arose everywhere. Villages and cities sprang into existence and became the homes of able craftsmen, who united into powerful guilds. Enterprising merchants opened commerce with all countries of Europe and the Orient. Many of these merchant-princes became famous for their wealth. As for instance the Fuggers of Augsburg, who amassed a fortune amounting to more than 60 Million Gulden; then the Welsers, who were able to advance to Emperor Charles V. a loan of twelve tons of gold.

These merchants, however, were not lost in selfishness. Proud of their native cities, they contributed freely to their beauty and importance. And so the German cities of the Middle Ages gained steadily in splendor and influence. To further their interests, many of these cities combined to form powerful federations. The cities of Southern Germany for

9

instance founded the "Schwaebische Staedtebund;" the cities of Northern Germany the "Hansa," which, embracing 85 cities, became the most famous of all.

Emperors, princes and magistrates vied with one another in beautifying their cities. To impress foreigners with the cities' importance and wealth, the entrance gates as well as the town halls, proud symbols of self-government, were adorned with magnificent portals, colonades and sculpture work. The great show pieces of these buildings were, however, the state or banquet halls, on which often enormous sums were lavished. Here were to be found exquisite carvings in wood, costly tapestries and paintings. From the ceilings hung elaborate chandeliers and models of merchant vessels or men-of-war. The ornaments of the fire places bore the coat of arms of the city or of such families, which had played in the history of the community important roles. Richly carved closets and chests contained the treasures of the city: beautiful dishes, bowls and cups of ebony, ivory, crystal, silver and gold. And over all this splendor rays of sunshine, breaking through beautiful windows of stained glass, cast a bewitching light.

In the public squares, fronting these city halls, arose magnificent fountains, topped with the figures of the city patrons or famous knights or kings.

While thus the rulers and magistrates beautified all public buildings and squares, the burghers did their best to complete the picture. The innate sense for art accomplished wonders in many cities of Germany. Loving their homes, the citizens adorned the front of their houses with carvings and allegorical paintings. Even such inconspicuous objects as weather-vanes and door-knockers became in the hands of skilled craftsmen specimens of genuine art. However, these efforts to beautify the exterior of the houses, were not accomplished to the neglect of the interior. Wealthy families took pride in artistic furniture, beautiful carpets, precious objects of crystal and silver, and in paintings and etchings of famous masters.

This period of prosperity and culture was also a time of great ecclesiastic architecture. Especially the architects of the 11th, 12th and 13th centuries created cathedrals, which in bold construction and sublime beauty surpass everything hitherto and since accomplished. The cathedrals of Worms, Speyer, Mayence, Frankfort on the Main, Ulm, Strassburg, Cologne and other cities rank among the greatest masterpieces of Romanic and Gothic art.

The Middle Ages were also a period in which great German poets, artists, inventors and reformers flourished. Then it was, that one of the masterpieces of the world's literature, the "Nibelungenlied," was written. Then it was, that Walter von der Vogelweide, Wolfram von Eschenbach, Heinrich von

Offterdingen, Frauenlob and many others wrote the most inspiring poems in praise of womanhood. It was also the time of Albrecht Duerer, Hans Holbein, Lucas Cranach, Stephan Lochner, Peter Vischer and other artists, who belong to the greatest of the great. Berthold Schwarz invented gunpowder, causing thereby a thorough revolution in warfare. Johannes Gutenberg, by inventing movable type, made the art of printing the most effective means for distributing knowledge and enlightenment throughout the world. The astronomers Kopernikus and Kepler opened new vistas by establishing the fact, contrary to the teachings of the Bible, that the sun does not move around the earth, but is a center, around which the earth and many other planets revolve.

Another imposing figure of these great times was Martin Luther, who gave to his people not only the German Bible, but with it, a literary language. Whereas, up to his time, every German writer had written in the dialect with which he was familiar, the language used by Luther in his translation of the Bible became the common one in all Germany, proving the most powerful factor toward forming national unity and in establishing a national literature.

In view of all these facts we may well ask, why people abandoned such a glorious land and emigrated to far distant countries of which they knew nothing and where their future was uncertain?

In history we find the answer.

The reformation, initiated by Luther, resulted, unfortunately, in conflict among religious creeds and was followed by the most overwhelming calamity that ever befell any country. Beginning in 1618 and lasting till 1648, the so-called Thirty Years' War swept over Germany like a hurricane, ruining it beyond recognition. Hundreds of cities and villages were burned by Spanish, Italian, Hungarian, Dutch and Swedish soldiers, who made Germany their battleground. Of the 17 million inhabitants of Germany 13 millions were killed or swept away through starvation and the pest. In Bohemia the population was diminished from 3,000,000 to 780,000. In Saxony, during the two years 1631 and 1632, 943,000 persons were slaughtered or died through sickness and want. In Würtemberg over 500,000 lost their lives. The Palatinate, having had a population of 500,000, suffered a loss of 457,000. In some parts of Thuringia ninety per cent. of all the people perished. Agriculture, commerce, industries and the arts were annihilated. Of many villages nothing remained but their names. According to the chronicles of these times, one could wander for many miles without seeing a living creature except wolves and ravens. It was during those dreadful years that Alsace and Lorraine, two of the richest countries of Germany, were stolen by France.

The terrors of all these calamities were not forgotten, when, at the end of the 17th and at the beginning of the 18th centuries, the "most Christian king" Louis XIV. of France ordered his generals to raid the countries along the Rhine and to make them one vast desert.

In obeying this cruel command the French armies destroyed everything that had survived the ravages of the Thirty Years' War. Dozens of cities were laid in ashes. Villages without number went up in flames. The ruins of hundreds of beautiful castles on the Rhine, Moselle and Neckar, among them Heidelberg, are lasting reminders of the years when the demons of rape and devastation held sway.

Besides such calamities, many German countries suffered from oppression by their own princes, who tried to ape the splendor of the court of Louis XIV., and indulged in brilliant festivals, the cost of which had to be borne by the people. And in accordance with the old motto "cujus regio, egus religio" ("Who governs the people, gives them also their religion") these princes quite often forced their subjects to change their faith according to their own belief. The Palatines, for instance, were compelled to change their faith several times. From Catholics they had to become Protestants, then Reformed, later on Lutherans and finally Catholics once more.

In 1756 the long suffering inhabitants of Germany were overrun again by the furies of war, when France, Russia, Poland, Sweden, Saxony and Austria sought to divide the kingdom of Frederick the Great.

The desperate struggle, then ensuing, is known as the Seven Years' War. Only 42 years later it was followed by the onslaught of that monstrous adventurer Napoleon I., by whom Germany was humiliated as never before. The whole country was subjected to systematic plundering. The imperial crown of Germany was trodden into the dust. The German states were torn apart and given by Napoleon as presents to his favorites, who made the German cities resound with gay life, at the burghers' expense.

Under the burden of all these sufferings many inhabitants of Germany despaired of a future in their native country and resolved to emigrate to America, hoping that there they would enjoy not only better material existence, but also freedom of worship. The report, that William Penn had thrown open his grant of land, Pennsylvania, as a place of refuge to all who suffered persecution on account of their religious faith, served as a special inducement for many Germans, to emigrate to that part of the New World.

Germans Predecessors of the Puritans.

Long before the Puritans, glorified in our Colonial History, thought of emigrating to America, Germans had already landed in several parts of the New World. At the very time when the British "Heroes of the Sea," the Hawkins, Drake, Cavendish, Morgan and others were engaged in abominable slave trade and in plundering the Spanish Colonies, numerous German mechanics, artisans, traders and miners busied themselves with all kinds of useful work.

As early as 1538, **Johann Cromberger,** a German, established a printing office in the City of Mexico, and issued numerous books, that bear the notice "Impressa en la gran ciudad de Mexico en casa de Juan Cromberger."

From the Colonial history of Venezuela we know, that the German explorers, who came to that country in 1528 to 1546, also brought a printing press with them. Besides, they took with them fifty miners, to explore the mountains of Venezuela.

Among the first English settlers, who came with Captain John Smith to Virginia, were also a number of German craftsmen, who had been procured by the British Colonial Office, at Captain Smith's suggestion "to send to Germany and Poland for laborers."

German traders also appeared in different parts of North America. Soon after Henry Hudson had discovered the noble river which now bears his name, a German, **Hendrick Christiansen** of Kleve, became the explorer of that stream. Attracted by its beauty and grandeur, he undertook eleven expeditions to its shores. He also built the first houses on Manhattan Island, 1613, and laid the foundations of the trading stations New Amsterdam and Fort Nassau, the present cities of New York and Albany. In what light Christiansen was regarded by his contemporaries, may be learned from a passage in the "Historisch Verhael" of the Dutch chronicler Nicolas Jean de Wassenaer, who wrote: "New Netherland was first explored by the honorable Hendrick Christiansen of Kleve. . . . . Hudson, the famous navigator, was also there."

A few years after this enterprising German had been killed by an Indian, another German, **Peter Minnewit** or **Minuit,** became Director-General of New Netherland, the colony established by the Dutch at the mouth of the Hudson River. Minnewit was born in Wesel, a city on the lower

THE PURCHASE OF MANHATTAN ISLAND FROM THE INDIANS, BY PETER MINNEWIT.
(After a Painting by Alfred Fredericks for the Title Guarantee and Trust Co., New York).

Rhine. Not much is known of his earlier life, but it is stated, that he was a Protestant and for some time held the position of deacon in the Reformed Church.

When, during the Thirty Years' War, the countries of the Lower Rhine and of Westfalia, Ditmarsen, Friesland and Holstein were being ravaged by Spanish soldiers, Minnewit, like many other Protestants fled to Holland, to escape certain death. In Amsterdam Minnewit entered the service of a trading company, for which he made several trips to the East Indies and South America. These voyages were so successful, that the leaders of the "Dutch West India Company" selected Minnewit as a director-general for her colony, New Netherland. They entrusted him with almost absolute power. Minnewit arrived in New Amsterdam on May 4, 1626. To secure title for the colony, one of his first acts was the closing of a bargain with the Manhattan Indians, by which, in exchange for such trinkets as colored cloth, beads, kettles and small looking glasses to the value of 60 guilders, or $24, the whole of Manhattan Island, containing about 22,000 acres, became the property of the Dutch.

NEW AMSTERDAM AT THE TIME OF PETER MINNEWIT.
(From an Old Engraving.)

By dealing fairly with the Indians Minnewit won their good will. From them New Netherland had nothing to fear. But the colony had dangerous neighbors, the English in Massachusetts, who started a number of settlements there and who claimed the whole Atlantic coast as far south as the 40th degree. To protect New Netherland against an attack by

15

these steadily encroaching neighbors, Minnewit erected a fort at the south end of Manhattan Island.

Under the able management of this German, the trading station developed successfully. While in 1624 the output in furs amounted to 25,000 guilders, the export increased within a few years to 130,000 guilders.

Minnewit remained at his post till 1631. Soon afterwards he became the founder and first director of New Sweden, a Swedish colony at the mouth of the Delaware River. Unfortunately this energetic man lost his life in the West Indies during a hurricane. He had set sail with two vessels to open up trade relations with these islands.

His successor in New Sweden was a German nobleman, **Johann Printz von Buchau,** a giant in body and energy. During his regime, which lasted from 1643 to 1654, the colony New Sweden became very successful and thereby aroused the jealousy of the Dutch, who, while Buchau was on a trip to Europe, attacked the colony and annexed it to New Netherland. In 1664 it fell a prey to the English together with all of New Netherland. As is well known, the English now named the colony New York, in honor of the king's brother, the Duke of York.

When this event took place, the colony already had among her citizens numerous Germans, of whom several held responsible positions in the Dutch West Indian Trading Company. There were also German physicians, lawyers and merchants. One of the latter, **Nicholaus de Meyer,** a native of Hamburg, became in 1676 burgomaster of New York.

To the most prominent men of that period belonged also **Augustin Herrman.** a surveyor, who made the first reliable maps of the colonies of Maryland and Virginia.

The unknown interior of the latter colony was first explored by a young German scholar, **Johann Lederer.** who, born in Hamburg, came to Jamestown in 1668. Here he made the acquaintance of Governor Berkeley of Virginia, who sent him to explore the mountains in the western part of the colony, in the hope of finding a passage to the Indian Ocean, which was believed to be just beyond the western slopes of the Appalachian Mountains. During the years 1669 and 1670 Lederer made three expeditions to the west and southwest. It seems that he traversed not only Virginia, but also a part of South Carolina. But in spite of the most heroic efforts it was impossible for him to cross the many parallel ridges of the Appalachian Mountains. When he had succeeded in scaling one, he saw from its summit in the distance other still higher ones. To cross them was impossible because of insufficient outfit and provisions.

Lederer's itinerary, written in Latin, abounds in highly interesting descriptions of the country and the different Indian tribes he encountered. These notes were translated by Governor Talbot of Maryland into English. Printed in 1672 in London, they constitute one of the most valuable documents in the history of the exploration of our North American continent.

Franz Daniel Pastorius and the Settlers of Germantown.

What Plymouth Rock is to Anglo-Americans, Germantown is to Americans of German descent: a spot consecrated by history, a spot where every American should stand with uncovered head!

At Plymouth Rock we cherish the memory of the Puritan Pilgrims; in Germantown that of those pious Mennonites, who, after their arrival in Philadelphia, broke ground for the first permanent German settlement in North America.

There is no chapter in our colonial history, which in general interest and elevating character surpasses the story of that little town, which to-day is one of the suburbs of William Penn's famous "City of Brotherly Love." Like the Puritans, the Mennonites, followers of the reformer Menno Simon, had been subjected to so many restrictions and persecution, that they gladly accepted the invitation of Penn, to settle in his American domain. The first group of Mennonites, which crossed the ocean, came from Crefeld, a city of the lower Rhine. Numbering 33 persons, they landed, after a voyage of 73 days in the good ship "Concord," in Philadelphia October 6, 1683. They were received by William Penn and **Franz Daniel Pastorius,** a young lawyer from Frankfort on the Main, who had hurried to America in advance of the Mennonites, in order to prepare everything for their arrival.

The first problem was to select a suitable location for the future town of the Mennonites. After due search they decided upon a tract near the Schuylkill River, two hours above Philadelphia. Here they broke ground on October 24.

For the first year the life of the settlers was but one continuous struggle against the vast wilderness, whose depths no white man had ever penetrated. Trees of enormous size, hundreds of years old, and almost impenetrable brushwood had to be removed to win a clearing for the little houses. The trials of the settlers, who by occupation were weavers and not accustomed to hard work, were often so great, that it took the combined persuasion of Pastorius and Penn, to encourage the Mennonites to persist in the bitter fight against the cruel wilderness. But when at last the work was done, Germantown was well worth looking at. A street 60 feet wide and planted with peach-trees on both sides, divided the village in two parts. Every house was surrounded by a three-acre garden, in whose virgin soil flowers and vegetables grew in such abundance, that the settlers raised not only enough for their own use, but were also able to provide the market of Philadelphia.

Special care was given to the cultivation of flax and grape-vine. The flax was of importance, as the Mennonites continued in their profession as weavers with such success, that the linen and other woven goods from Germantown became famous for quality. As the inhabitants of Germantown came from the Rhine, their hearts were open to blissful enjoyment of life, and wine was appreciated as the means to drive away all grief and sorrow. Before long the windows and entrances of the houses were surrounded by heavy grapevines.

Certainly it was a happy idea, when Pastorius, in designing an official seal for the town, selected the clover, the leaves of which were to represent the grape-vine, the flax blossom and the weavers' shuttle. These were surrounded by the Latin motto: "Vinum, Linum et Textrinum" (Vine, Linen and Weaving). With this he indicated, that culture of the grapes, flax-growing and the textile industries were the principal occupations in Germantown. At the same time it indicated the mission of the German in America, to promote agriculture, manufacture and enjoyment of life.

Happy hours these German Pilgrims must have had in Germantown, when at eventide, after the day's work had been done, they sat on the benches by the doors, listening to the cooing of the doves, and enjoying the fragrant odor of the manifold flowers, the seeds of which they had brought with them from their native home.

While attending to their daily work, the inhabitants of Germantown did not neglect their intellectual life. Pastorius, this true shepherd of his flock, was its center. He established a school and arranged also an evening class, in which he imparted freely of his great wisdom to all who were eager to enrich their knowledge.

When Germantown was incorporated as a town, Pastorius was of course elected its first burgomaster. How deeply rooted in his heart was the love of his old Fatherland and his countrymen, is indicated by a "Greeting to Posterity," which he wrote on the first page of the "Grund- und Lager-buch," the first official document of Germantown. Translated from the Latin it reads as follows: "Hail Posterity! Hail to you, future generations in Germanopolis! May you never forget that your ancestors, of their own free will, left the beloved land, which bore and nourished them — ah! for those hearths and homes! — to live the rest of their days in the forests of Pennsylvania, in the lonely wilderness, with less care and anxiety, but still after the German fashion, like brothers. May you also learn, how arduous a task it was, after crossing the Atlantic Ocean, to plant the German race in this part of North America. And, dear descendants, where we have set an example of righteousness, follow our footsteps! But where we have turned from the straight and narrow path, forgive us! May the perils which we encountered, make you wise! Farewell, Posterity! Farewell, my German Kin! Farewell, forever and ever!''

Undoubtedly Pastorius was also the author of a document, by which the inhabitant of Germantown set an everlasting monument to themselves.

The importation of negro slaves from Africa to America had been practised by the English and Dutch since the 16th century. Slaves were sold to the English colonies without disapproval of the Puritans and Quakers, who claimed to be defenders of human rights. The Germans, however, who had suffered so much in their own fatherland, regarded in just appreciation of the personal rights of others the traffic in human flesh as a heavy crime against the teachings of Christ. For this reason they drew up on February 18, 1688, a protest against slavery, the first ever written in any language. This remarkable document reads as follows:

"This is to ye Monthly Meeting held at Richard Warrel's. These are the reasons why we are against the traffick of men Body, as followeth: Is there any that would be done or handled at this manner? to be sold or made a slave for all the time of his life? How fearfull and fainthearted are many on sea when they see a strange vessel, being afraid it should be a Turk, and they should be taken and sold for slaves into Turckey. Now what is this better done as Turcks doe? Yea rather is it worse for them, which say they are Christians; for we hear that ye most part of such Negers are brought hither against their will and consent; and that many of them are stollen. Now, tho' they are black, we cannot conceive there is more liberty to have them slaves, as it is to have other white ones. There is a saying, that we shall doe to all men, like as we will be done our selves; making no difference of what generation, descent or colour they are. And those who steal or robb men, and those who buy or purchase them, are they not all alike? Here is liberty of conscience, which is right and reasonable; here ought to be likewise liberty of ye body, except of evildoers, which is another case. But to bring men hither, or to robb and sell them against their will, we stand against. In Europe there are many oppressed for conscience sake; and here there are those oppressed which are of a black colour. And we, who know that men must not commit adultery, some doe commit adultery in others, separating wifes from their husbands and giving them to others; and some sell the children of those poor creatures to

20

other men. Oh! doe consider well this things, you who doe it; if you would be done at this manner? and if it is done according to Christianity? You surpass Holland and Germany in this thing. This makes an ill report in all those countries of Europe, where they hear off, that ye Quackers doe here handel men like they handel there ye cattel. And for that reason some have no mind or inclination to come hither, and who shall maintaine this your cause or plaid for it? Truly we can not do so, except you shall inform us better hereoff, that Christians have liberty to practise this things. Pray! What thing on the world can be done worse towards us, then if men should robb or steal us away, and sell us for slaves to strange countries, separating housbands from their wifes and children. Being now this is not done at that manner, we will be done at, therefore we contradict and are against this traffick of menbody. And we who profess that it is not lawful to steal, must likewise avoid to purchase such things as are stollen but rather help to stop this robbing and stealing if possible; and such men ought to be delivered out of ye hands of ye Robbers and sett free as well as in Europe. Then is Pennsylvania to have a good report, instead it hath now a bad one for this sacke in other countries. Especially whereas ye Europeans are desirous to know in what manner ye Quackers doe rule in their Province; and most of them doe look upon us with an envious eye. But if this is done well, what shall we say is done evill?

If once these slaves (which they say are so wicked and stubborn men) should joint themselves, fight for their freedom and handel their masters and mastrisses as they did handel them before, will these masters and mastrisses tacke the sword at hand and warr against these poor slaves, like we are able to believe, some will not refuse to doe? Or have these Negers not as much right to fight for their freedom, as you have to keep them slaves?

Now consider well this thing, if it is good or bad? and in case you find it to be good to handel these blacks at that manner, we desire and require you hereby lovingly, that you may inform us here in, which at this time never was done, that Christians have such a liberty to do so, to the end we shall be satisfied in this point, and satisfie lickewise our good friends and acquaintances in our natif country, to whose it is a terrour or fairfull thing that men should be handeld so in Pennsilvania.

This is from our Meeting at Germantown held ye 18. of the 2. month 1688. to be delivered to the monthly meeting at Richard Warrel's.

> gerret hendericks
> derick op de graeff
> Francis Daniell Pastorius
> Abraham op Den graeff."

This protest was submitted at several meetings of the Quakers, who, however, found the question too important to take action upon, since this question stood in intimate relation with other affairs. The document, set up by the humble inhabitants of Germantown, however, compelled the Quakers to think. Becoming aware that the traffic in human beings did not harmonize with Christian religion, they introduced in 1711 "an act to prevent the importation of Negroes and Indians into the province," and later on they declared against slave trade. But as the Government found such laws inadmissible, the question dragged along, until 150 years later this black spot on the escutcheon of the United States was eradicated.

Pastorius, the noble leader of Germantown, departed this life about Christmas of 1719, much deplored by his many friends, who, like William Penn, respected him as "an upright and courageous, moderate and wise man, a shining example to his countrymen."

AN OLD GERMAN PRINTING PRESS.
(In the Museum of the Historical Society of Pennsylvania.)

A few years after Pastorius' death another remarkable person made Germantown his home: **Christoph Saur,** a native of Westphalia. Being a printer, he published here in 1739 the first newspaper in German type, and also in 1743 the first German Bible in America. This antedated, by forty years, the printing of any other Bible in America, in another European language. Besides Saur published numerous other volumes, among them many textbooks for schools. To him is due also the founding of the Germantown Academy, which still exists.

Germantown deserves credit also as the place, where **Wilhelm Rittenhaus** established in 1690 the first paper mill in America. So the name of Germantown is connected with many events of great importance in American history. No one who intends to give a true idea of the origin and development of American culture, can omit to mention Germantown and its founders.

The great success of the Mennonites inspired many other German sectarians to follow their example and emigrate to the Western hemisphere. Among them were the Tunker or Dunkards, whose cloister Ephrata in Pennsylvania became famous as a seat of learning. It had its own printing press, paper mill and book bindery, and published in 1749 the "Märtyrer Spiegel," a folio volume of 1514 pages, the greatest literary undertaking of the American colonies.

Furthermore, there were the Herrnhuter or Moravians, the founders of Bethlehem, Nazareth and other settlements in Pennsylvania and Ohio. Many of these Moravians devoted themselves to missionary work among the Indians. Some of these devout emissaries, for instance **Christian Friedrich Post, Johann Heckewelder** and **David Zeisberger** performed most valuable work among the Delawares, Mohicans and other tribes.

The Salzburgers, driven from their homes in the Alps in 1731, established in Georgia a flourishing colony, named Ebenezer. Other German sectarians founded Zoar and Harmony in Ohio, Economy in Pennsylvania, Bethel and Aurora in Missouri, Amana in Iowa, and other colonies, many of which created world-wide attention because of their successful application of communistic ideas.

THE SEAL OF GERMANTOWN.

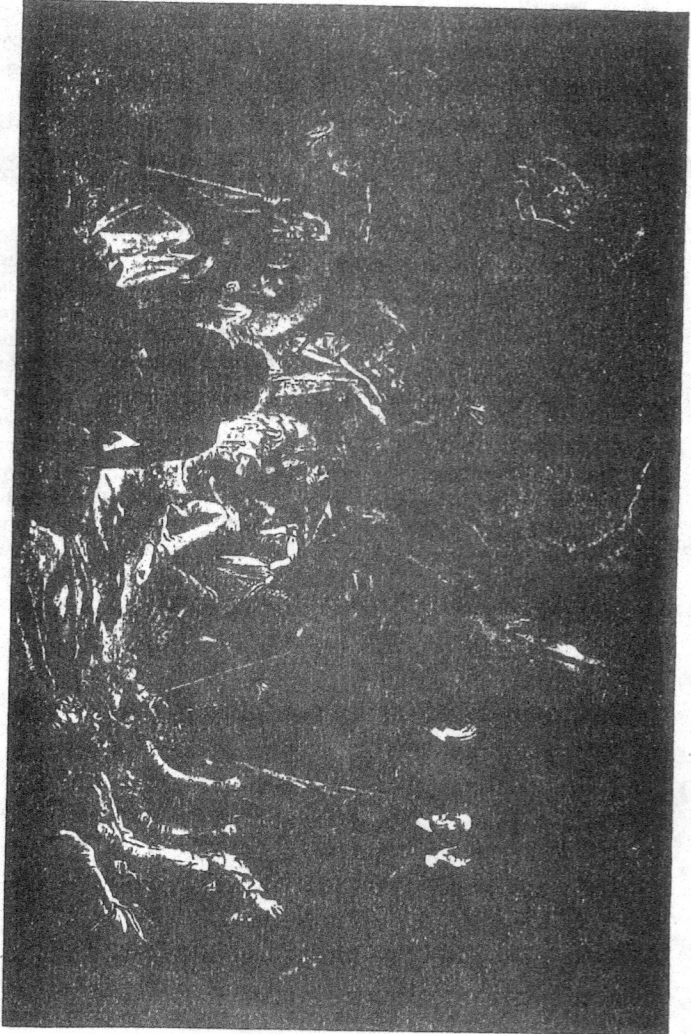

THE MORAVIAN MISSIONARY DAVID ZEISBERGER PREACHING TO THE INDIANS.
(After a Painting by Christian Schüssele)

The Coming of the Palatines.

Of all the German states which suffered from the terrors of the Thirty Years' War and the raids of the French, the Palatinate fared worst. During the first catastrophe one hundred and forty-seven towns and villages were wiped out of existence, so that nothing remained but their almost forgotten names. Everything which escaped the ravages of that dreadful war, was destroyed by the soldiers of the "most Christian King" Louis XIV. of France. In utter despair, the few thousand survivors of the carnage and plundering resolved to give up their homes and emigrate to any country, where they would be free from the terrors of war.

The first Palatines to emigrate were 55 Lutherans. Under the leadership of their minister, **Josua von Kocherthal,** they arrived in New York in the winter of 1708. Upon the western shore of the Hudson they established a settlement, which they called Neuburg, from which the present city of Newburgh takes its name. —

In the following year the Rhine became the scene of an extraordinary event. Vast fleets of boats and rafts glided down the river, all crowded with unhappy people, who carried their few belongings with them in bundles and boxes.

How many thousand persons there were, is not exactly known. Estimates vary from 15,000 to 30,000. The fugitives went to Holland and from there to London, to beg the British government for transportation to America. Several thousand were sent to Ireland; several hundred to Virginia, Carolina and New England; and more than 3,000 to New York. The latter embarked in ten vessels in January, 1710.

The voyage across the ocean took several months; the last boat did not arrive in New York before July. Accommodations and food on the vessels were so poor that 470 of the emigrants perished during the trip; 250 more died on Governor's Island, where the Palatines were kept in quarantine for many weeks without any apparent reason.

Furthermore, the government, instead of granting the Palatines the same privileges that other emigrants received, treated them as serfs, who ought to make good by their labor for everything the government had done for them. So the Palatines were settled along the shores of the Hudson, where we now find Germantown and Saugerties. Here they were forced to raise hemp for cordage, and to manufacture tar and pitch, so that the government would no longer be obliged to buy these much-needed objects for ship-building from other countries.

Unfortunately, the contract for supplying the Palatines with all necessities of life was given to Robert Livingston, a perfect type of those disreputable men, who came to America only to get rich quickly. In Albany he had been made Town Clerk and Secretary for Indian Affairs. Later on to these offices were added those of Collector of Excise and Quit Rents, Clerk of Peace and Clerk of the Court of Common Pleas. A born grafter, he associated himself secretly with the famous pirate Captain Kidd, and thereby added greatly to his fortune.

When in 1701 he could not account for large sums, said to have passed through his hands, he was deprived of his offices and his estates were confiscated. However, upon going to London he obtained from the Queen a restoration of his offices, returned to New York in 1709, became, through bribery, a member of Assembly and secured a repeal of the act confiscating his estates.

Such was the history of the gentleman, into whose care the unfortunate Palatines were given. Naturally, they fared badly. While they almost starved to death, the bills, handed by Livingston to the government, ran to enormous sums. From November 10, 1710, to September, 1712, they amounted to 76,000 pounds sterling!

During the severe winter of 1712-13 the distress of the Palatines became unbearable. They had neither food nor clothing. Suffering from hunger and cold, their clamor became so heartrending that the Indians, who dwelt in the neighborhood, came to their assistance, and presented them with a stretch of land in the valley of the Schoharie River, whereto the Palatines might emigrate.

Seeing no other course before them, the Palatines resolved to escape to this place. They started in March, 1713. As no roads existed and deep snow covered the ground, the trip was exhausting. The fugitives had neither wagons nor animals for the transportation of the sick, the aged, the women and children. All belongings had to be carried upon the back. And, of course, there was nothing to eat. If the Indians had not helped, the Palatines would certainly have perished.

Hardly ever were settlements started under greater difficulties than these in the Schoharie Valley. Rough logs furnished the material for the huts. Clothes were made from the skins of wild animals. As no one possessed a plough, the settlers were obliged to dig furrows into the ground with their knives. They then sowed the only bushel of wheat they had bought in Schenectady with their last money. As they had no mill, the first harvest was crushed between stones.

After toiling for several years, the Palatines, never giving up hope, began to look for a better future, when suddenly came the news, that the governor had ceded their land to some speculators, among them Livingston, with whom the Palatines must come to an agreement. That the land had been given to the Palatines by the Indians, and that by the right of first settlement they had an indisputable claim, the governor would not acknowledge. Furious about their escape, he molested the Palatines so persistently that the majority decided to move again. Several hundred quitted the inhospitable colony of New York forever, and went to Pennsylvania. Others moved to the valley of the Mohawk River, occupying a strip of land which was donated to them by the Mohawk Indians.

The first settlement there became known as the German Flats. But in the course of time the Palatines founded many other villages and towns, some of which betray their German origin by their names, as Mannheim, Oppenheim, Frankfort, Palatine, Herkimer, Palatine Bridge, New Paltz Landing and Palatine Church. —

The Palatines who had been brought to Carolina, Virginia and New England also founded numerous villages and towns, whose original German names, however, became so distorted later, that to-day they can hardly be recognized. —

Through a strange irony of fate the Palatines, who had emigrated from Germany to escape the brutalities of the French, were compelled to again face the same enemies in America. It was during the years 1754 to 1763, when the French, assisted by their Indian allies, the Ottawas, Hurons, Miamis, Shawnees and Illinois, made frequent raids from Canada and the Ohio Valley on the settlements of the Palatines, who in fact had been placed by the government as outposts on the frontier against the French and Indians.

In assisting the Germans in the defense of the frontier the government was always so tardy that the Germans often resorted to drastic demonstrations to compel the authorities to do their duty. In November, 1755, when the Palatine settlements in Pennsylvania had been raided, several hundred Germans marched to Philadelphia, to demand measures of defense. They brought with them a number of bodies of friends murdered, mutilated and scalped, and displayed them at the doors of the assembly hall. This gruesome exhibition created great sensation, yet the government did not call the militia before spring of the next year for the protection of the suffering settlements. Many members of this militia were Palatines. They were also largely represented among the "Royal Americans," a regiment of 4000 Germans of Pennsylvania and Maryland, which under the able command of

Henry Bouquet, a native of Switzerland, in the wars against the French and Indians won a glorious record.

Out of the ranks of the Palatine colonists came many vigorous men, who gained renown in American history. As for instance **Konrad Weiser, Peter Zenger, and Nicholas Herchheimer,** who, like all their countrymen, served this country devotedly in times of peace, and gladly gave their lives for it in times of war.

Their descendants, reinforced by large numbers of Palatines, who arrived during the 18th and 19th centuries, number at present many hundred thousands, a valuable army of diligent, industrious and contented people. Where energy and persistence are needed, where experience, mechanical or artistic abilities are required, the Palatines take no second place. We find them engaged in all trades, in the fields, the orchards and vineyards, and always devoted to the place which gives them support. None of their beautiful farms in the Schoharie and Mohawk valleys, or in Pennsylvania, ever had to be abandoned because of exhausted soil, as was the case with so many thousands of Yankee-farms in the New England States. Like all other German immigrants that settled in America, the Palatines took great care to uphold and increase the fruitfulness of their farms, and the good name and credit of their business, in order that they might pass them on to their children and grandchildren as valuable inheritances.

Besides their diligence and industriousness, the Palatines in America have also preserved their genuine Rhenish cheerfulness, their love for poetry, music and song. Some of their poets rank among the best our country has produced. Their singing-societies are of the first order, while their festivals are brimful of harmless fun and rejoicing.

What virtues they brought with them from the Fatherland they have preserved and transmitted with great success and to their own honor from generation to generation. And so the Palatines will live in the history of America; and future generations will celebrate the great influx of the Palatines in 1710 as an event which became a blessing to this nation.

The Life of the German Settlers in Colonial Times.

To take a glimpse at the life of the early pioneers in America is certainly interesting. It will be remembered that the British government purposely placed many of these Germans at the most exposed parts of the "frontier," where their settlements would serve as outposts and as protection against the French and their Indian allies. In this way the Germans in the valleys of the Mohawk, of the Susquehanna, Shenandoah and Wyoming and at the Blue Mountains formed the vangard of civilization.

For their own safety's sake these settlers were compelled to place their log houses close together, so that in case of danger they could be better protected. The intervals between the houses were closed with palisades, ten or twelve feet high. Sometimes these rude fortresses were surrounded by deep ditches. In the center of the village stood a very strong blockhouse, which served as a place of refuge in case of extreme danger. It had mostly two or three stories, the upper projecting over the lower. The heavy walls were pierced by numerous loop-holes. In greatly exposed villages there were three or four such strongholds at the corners of the village, so that the gunfire of the defenders could sweep in every direction.

The ever present danger compelled the settlers to keep constant guard. Every man was obliged to perform sentinel duty at times. As soon as the scouts noticed any danger they gave signals, the meaning of which was understood by all. In case of siege, all men and boys had to hurry to their respective posts at the stockade. The women assisted in loading guns, in casting bullets, in providing the men with food and water, in taking care of the wounded, besides looking after the children and cattle.

As the very existence of the whole settlement depended upon preparedness, it was every man's duty to keep his arms and ammunition in perfect condition and ready to be used at a moment's notice. Skill in the use of weapons was highly valued and encouraged. Even small boys were allowed to carry guns and hunting-knives. Bows and arrows and tomahawks they handled with an Indian's dexterity. Racing, jump-

DEFENDING A SETTLEMENT.
(After an Old Engraving.)

ing, swimming, climbing, wrestling and all other physical exercises, the knowledge of which could be helpful in the hard struggle for existence, were encouraged. Challenges for shooting and fighting-matches were frequently exchanged between neighboring settlements, and when these contests were fought out, enthusiastic spectators were never wanting.

As the population of Germany during the 17th and 18th centuries supported itself mainly by agriculture, naturally the majority of German emigrants consisted of farmers. Of their splendid qualities the accounts of many travellers and statesmen bear testimony. When the famous French botanist André Michaux visited North America, he was surprised at the fine condition of the German farms. In mentioning them he says: "The superior culture of the fields and the better condition of the fences indicate that here are settlements of Germans. Everything breathes comfort and well-being, the reward of diligence and intelligent work. These Germans live under much better conditions than the American descendants of the English, Scotch and Irish; they are not so much given to strong drink and have not that restless spirit, which frequently induces settlers of other nationality to move, for the most trifling reasons, to distances of perhaps hundreds of miles in search of more fertile land."

In still more enthusiastic terms Dr. Benjamin Rush, Surgeon general at the time of the Revolution, spoke after passing through all the colonies. In 1789 he published "An Account

THE FIRST HOME.

of the Manners of the German Inhabitants of Pennsylvania." In this classic little essay Rush, who has justly been called the Tacitus of the German-Americans, enumerates the particulars, in which the German farmers differed from most of the others. "In settling a tract of land they always provide large

31

and suitable accommodations for their horses and cattle, before they lay out much money in building a house for themselves. The first house is small and built of logs. It generally lasts through the lifetime of the first settler and hence, they have a saying, that a son should always begin his improvements, where his father left off."

"They always prefer good land, or that land on which there are great meadows. By giving attention to the cultivation of grass, they often in a few years double the value of an old farm, and grow rich on farms, on which their predecessors, of whom they purchased them, had nearly starved."

"In clearing new land they do not simply girdle or belt the trees, and leave them to perish in the ground, as is the custom of their English or Irish neighbors; they generally cut them down and burn them. Underbrush and bushes they pull out by the roots. The advantage is that the land is fit for cultivation the second year."

"They feed their horses and cows well, thereby practicing economy, for such animals perform twice the labor or yield twice the amount of the less well fed. A German horse is known in every part of the state."

"The German farmers are also great wood-economists. They do not waste it in large fire-places, but burn it in stoves, using about one-fourth to one-fifth* as much. Their houses are made very comfortable by these stoves, around which the family can get more equal chance than when burning their faces and freezing their backs before open fire-places."

"The Germans live frugally in regard to diet, furniture and dress. They eat sparingly of boiled meat, but use large quantities of all kinds of vegetables. They use few distilled spirits (whiskey and rum), preferring cider, beer, wine, and simple water. In their homespun garments they are likewise economical. When they use European articles of dress, they prefer those of best quality and highest price. They are afraid to get into debt, and seldom purchase anything without paying cash for it."

"Kitchen gardening the Germans introduced altogether. Their gardens contain useful vegetables at every season of the year. Pennsylvania is indebted to the Germans for the principal part of her knowledge of horticulture. The work of the gardens is generally done by the women of the family. Hired help is procured only in harvest time. The favorable influence of agriculture, as conducted by the Germans, in extending the most happiness, is manifested by the joy expressed at the birth of a child. No dread of poverty or distrust of Providence from an increasing family depress the spirits of this industrious and frugal people."

"In their children they produce not only the habits of labor but a love of it."

"When a young man asks the consent of his father to marry the girl of his choice he does not inquire so much whether she be rich or poor, or whether she possess any personal or mental accomplishments, but whether she be industrious, and acquainted with the duties of a good housewife."

Ennumerating other good qualities of the Germans, Rush says: "They are no strangers to the virtue of hospitality. The hungry or benighted traveller is always sure to find a hearty welcome under their roofs. They are extremely kind and friendy as neighbors."

As stated in former chapters, there were also among the German immigrants many mechanics, who found everywhere remunerative work for their skill and reliability. The conditions, prevailing in the colonies, were very favorable, as the practice of the different professions was not, as in Europe, restricted by the rules of guilds. Such corporations had not yet been started. In fact, they were impossible, as in the thinly settled and very extensive colonies all had to rely upon their own abilities. As in the solitude of the wilderness the farmer had of necessity to be a "Jack of all trades," so in the villages and cities such craftsmen were most welcome, who could be helpful in many different ways. As Gottlieb Mittelberger, a German teacher visiting Pennsylvania in 1750, stated in one of his letters: "No profession is restrained by the laws of guilds. Every one can make his living according to his choice. He may carry on ten different trades, and nobody will hinder him."

A splendid type of such many-sided men was **Christopher Saur,** the famous printer at Germantown. Of him Pastorius speaks in his notes: "He is a very ingenious man, who learned about thirty different professions without the help of an instructor. He came here as a tailor; but now he is a printer, apothecary, surgeon, botanist, watchmaker, carpenter, bookbinder and newspaper man. He made all his tools for printing; he also makes paper, wire, lead, etc."

Such ingenious craftsmen were the very first in starting many industries in America, which flourish to-day. The earliest iron-works on record were operated by miners from Siegen, Germany, who on invitation of Governor Spotswocd established a settlement Germanna at the Rapidan River in Virginia in 1714. Two lears later **Thomas Ruetter** or **Rutter** from Germantown, Pa., founded the first ironworks in Pennsylvania at the Matawny Creek, Berks County. The first hammer-works and smelting furnaces were constructed in 1750 by **Johannes Huber.** His furnace, located in Lancaster County, Pa., bore the inscription:

"Johann Huber ist der erste deutsche Mann
Der das Eisenwerk vollführen kann."

In 1757 he sold his works to a German Baron, **Friedrich Wilhelm von Stiegel,** a genuine "captain of industry."

Engaging large numbers of German smiths and other workmen, he started the town of Mannheim, where he made iron stoves, wagons and many other things.

Perhaps the greatest of all American industrials of the 18th century was **Peter Hasenclever,** born in 1716 in Remscheid, a city in Rhenish Prussia, famous for her iron-industry. Having been informed, that North America was rich in iron and forests and that the English government was compelled to import annually more than 40,000 tons of rod-iron, he submitted plans to work these mines and, by manufacturing rod-iron, make England independent of other countries. As his propositions were favored, he emigrated to New York in 1765 and established numerous smelting and stamping works, forges and other factories in the neighborhood of the German Flats in the Mohawk Valley. From his native home he imported 550 miners and smiths, for whom he built 200 houses. By damming several creeks he provided cheap and constant water power; by constructing good roads and bridges he also procured means for communication.

Within a few years the establishment grew to a most promising seat of industry, with all prospects for a bright future. But unfortunately the English partners of Hasenclever, living in London, were dishonest people. Leading a very luxurious life, they burdened the establishment with such heavy debts, that Hasenclever, in spite of all efforts, was unable to prevent its bankruptcy. To save his good name he went to England and instituted proceedings against his partners. The lawsuit dragged along for twenty years, but was decided after Hasenclever's death in favor of his heirs, to whom the accused party had to pay one million Thalers indemnity.

Another enterprising German of the 18th century was **Johann Jacob Faesch,** owner of the Mount Hope forges. During the war for independence he supplied the American army with large quantities of cannon and ammunition. Other Germans furnished her with splendid guns, with which the Minute Men worked great havoc in British lines. The bored rifles in particular, made by German gun-smiths in Lancaster, Pa., were highly prized in all colonies.

The first glass-factory was started in 1738 near Salem, N. J., by **Kaspar Wüster,** a native of Heidelberg. His name became corrupted to Wistar. That the manufacture of glass was exclusively in the hands of Germans, is proved by a letter of Lord Sheffield, who, in writing about the glassworks of Pennsylvania and New Jersey, said: "Hitherto these manufactures have been carried on by German workmen."

The inhabitants of Germantown were noted for their splendid textile fabrics. Germans were also the pioneers in the manufacture of felt, hats, leather wares, watches, bells, and many other things. As early as 1730 German mechanics in America began to make musical instruments. In the year mentioned **Heinrich Neering** of New York built the first organ for the Trinity community. And in 1775 **Johann Behrent** constructed the first pianoforte in America.

Besides these farmers, craftsmen, artisans and industrials there were also many German merchants, for whom Dr. Rush also expressed appreciation. In his booklet he says: "The genius of the Germans is, however, not confined to agriculture and the mechanical arts. As merchants they are candid and punctual. The Bank of North America bears witness to their fidelity in all pecuniary transactions."

These merchants traded in spices, drygoods, hardwares, agricultural tools, books, musical instruments, clothes and many other things. The larger cities had also German apothecaries and inns, as for instance in Philadelphia "The King of Prussia," "The Black Eagle" and "The Golden Lamb."

Furthermore, there were also a number of German printers, who, like Christoph Saur and Peter Zenger, published newspapers, calendars and books in German as well as in English. Benjamin Franklin states, that of the six printing houses in Pennsylvania four were German or half German, while only two were entirely English. He mentions also, that the Germans imported many books from abroad.

They also had their own ministers and teachers. A pamphlet, printed in 1755 in Pennsylvania, states: "The Germans have schools and meeting houses in almost every township thro' the province, and have more churches and other places of worship in the city of Philadelphia itself than those of all other persuasions together."

In view of all these facts there can be no doubt, that the Germans, living in the colonies, were a very useful and valuable element, well deserving the high esteem, extended to them by all fair-minded people. Concluding his essay about his German fellow-citizens Dr. Rush said:

"Citizens of the United States, learn from the German inhabitants of Pennsylvania, to prize knowledge and industry in agriculture and manufacture, as the basis of domestic happiness and national prosperity.

Legislatures of the United States, learn from the wealth and independence of the German inhabitants of Pennsylvania, to encourage by example and laws the republican virtues of industry and economy. They are the only pillars which can support the present constitution of the United States.

Legislators of Pennsylvania, learn from the history of your German fellow-citizens, that you possess an inexhaustible treasure in the bosom of the State, in their manners and arts. Do not contend against their prejudice in favor of their language. It will be the channel through wich the knowledge and discoveries of the wisest nation in Europe may be conveyed to our country. Invite them to share in the power and offices of government: it will be a bond of union in principle and conduct between them, and those of their enlightened fellow-citizens, who are descended from other nations. Above all, cherish with peculiar tenderness those sects among them who hold war to be unlawful. Relieve them from the oppression of absurd and unnecessary military laws. Protect them as the repositories of truth of the gospel, which has existed in every age of the church, and which must spread over every part of the world. Perhaps those German sects among us (here are meant the Mennonites, Moravians and Tunkers), who refuse to bear arms for the purpose of shedding human blood, may be preserved by divine providence as the centre of a circle, which shall gradually embrace all nations of the earth in a perpetual treaty of friendship and peace."

Promoters of the Cause of Liberty.

Tacitus, the great Roman Historian, writing of the early Germans in his famous book "Germania," declared one of their noblest characteristics to be their independent spirit, lauding their strong love for nature and liberty. Grown up among majestic forests and breathing the pure air of the mountains they regarded towns as prisons and refrained from building them. So great was their love of freedom that it frequently led them to suicide rather than surrender into captivity.

Unconquered by the Romans this spirit survived throughout the many centuries following the famous battle in the Teutoburgian Forests. Many thousands of Germans were moved by it to emigrate to America, in order to escape intellectual or bodily servitude, threatening during the Thirty Years' War. So also during the raids of the French into the Palatinate and other borderlands of the Rhine.

Picture then the dismay of the Germans, who, hoping to find freedom and liberty in America, became aware of the fact that many of the detested institutions of Europe had been transplanted to the New World and had become firmly rooted. Favorites of the British king, after squandering their money in gambling and high living, were entrusted with the government of the colonies and assumed office merely to recoup their lost fortunes. The colonies were overrun, too, by hordes of impoverished aristocrats, cunning adventurers and unscrupulous speculators, all incited by the mad desire to get rich quickly.

By bribing the governors and other officials many of these questionable gentlemen had succeeded in obtaining valuable privileges or securing titles to large tracts of land, where they lived in the luxurious style of lords.

The common people found small protection against the insolence of these drones of society, who looked with disdain upon "the rabble." Immigrants, who could not speak English fluently, were often treated worse than slaves, these insolent officials and aristocrats holding the view, that the English were the cream of creation, and that an imperfect command of their language meant defectiveness. Irritated by their arrogance and oppressions, the people resented their disdain with ill-concealed hate.

The antagonism between the two classes grew to bitter party-strife and revolt during that stormy period, when the crown of England passed from the Catholic King James II. to the Protestant William III. Amidst the upheaval, caused in the colonies by this sudden change, Sir Edmond Andros, Governor-General of the combined colonies of New England, New York and New Jersey, was seized by the people of Boston and together with fifty of his followers sent to England. His representative in New York, Francis Nicholson, a most unpopular official, fled to the fort at the Southern point of Manhattan Island, but he was captured, as the people had been aroused by the alarming rumor, that he intended to burn the city and deliver the colony to the French. The majority of the people being Protestants, they resolved to hold the colonies for the new King William.

To save New York from greater disorder and defend it against an invasion by the French, it became necessary to elect a temporary governor. It was then that the people chose a German, **Jacob Leisler,** a native of Frankfort-on-the-Main, who, upon coming to New York in 1660, had attained great success as a merchant. A man of great energy, high spirits and of noted integrity, he was senior captain of the militia. By marriage he was connected with the Dutch aristocracy of the town. Thus Leisler appeared to be the right person, to save the colony from further unrest and calamity.

However, the people's party had under-estimated the hatred of the Aristocrats. From the moment Leisler assumed charge of affairs, the latter began to denounce him as a demagogue. In connection with the rest of the officials, who had fled to Albany, they started a regular campaign of secret intrigue and open hostility. Flooding the government in London with complaints, they decried Leisler and the members of his council as foreign-born plebeians, mutineers and tyrants, falsely alleging that they had seized their offices only to enrich themselves and to defraud the government of its taxes. At the same time they declined to acknowledge Leisler and his councilors, and incited all colonists to refuse obedience.

To remain silent under such calumniation and provocation was impossible. Leisler commissioned a company of soldiers under command of his son-in-law, Major Jacob Milborne, to go to Albany to compel the aristocrats to acknowledge him and to occupy the fort, as at the Canadian border hostilities by the French and their Indian allies were imminent. Unfortunately the company was not strong enough to capture the fort, the Aristocrats being on their guard and defending Albany successfully, so that Milborne had to withdraw. Soon afterwards, however, the nearby town of Schenectady was surprised by the French and Indians, while the unsuspecting inhabitants were asleep. The whole settlement was burned,

60 people killed and 90 carried away as prisoners. When the news of this assault reached Albany, the frightened aristocrats fled to Massachusetts, leaving the defense of the city to Leisler, who once more proved himself equal to the emergency.

Convinced that the colonies would never be safe unless the French were driven from Canada, and that for an effective resistance against the formidable foe co-operation on the part of all colonies was essential, Leisler invited the governors of all the other colonies to a council at New York. It was the first ever held, and by this act Leisler aroused the colonists to a sense of common interest, which kept on increasing and was destined to culminate in the Continental Congress of 1776.

That memorable council took place on May 1, 1690, attended by delegates from New York, Connecticut, Massachusetts, Plymouth, New Jersey and Maryland. It was resolved, that 855 men, assisted by an auxiliary force of 1600 Mohawk Indians, should attack Canada by land, while at the same time a fleet of 32 vessels should ascend the St. Lawrence River and bombard Quebec. The campaign was undertaken by the colonies at their own cost and responsibility, without the aid of the mother country.

Unfortunately its aims were not realized, as the leaders of the two expeditions, lacking energy, were not victorious in their attacks. Leisler himself, however, gained a success by capturing six French vessels, which had dared to come to the vicinity of New York.

The campaign, undertaken on Leisler's recommendation, burdened the colonies with considerable expense. Its failure was of course used by his enemies to make a scapegoat of him and to undermine his reputation by malicious slander.

This was the situation, when in January, 1691, a vessel from England brought the news, that the home government had appointed a new governor for New York in the person of Colonel Henry Sloughter. It was stated that this official had set out with several vessels and many troops to take charge of the colony.

By misadventure a heavy storm separated his vessel from the fleet and compelled him to a delay of several weeks at the Bermudas. In the meantime the fleet, with Major Ingoldsby the second in command, arrived in the harbor of New York. The aristocrats at once set out to win the favor of the new arrival and to influence him against Leisler. These efforts proved successful when Ingoldsby's demand, to surrender the fort at once, was answered by Leisler with the request for documentary proof of Ingoldsby's authority. As such document was not at hand, Leisler refused to give up the fort. Ingoldsby, feeling himself aggrieved in his honor as an officer, ordered his soldiers to take the fort by force, but was repelled

39

and lost several of his men. Ingoldsby now laid siege to the fort for several weeks; meanwhile Leisler's enemies continued their slanderous activity with renewed vigor.

On March 19 the vessel of Governor Sloughter finally hove into sight. Ingoldsby delivered his report. Amplified by the complaints of the aristocrats, who hurried to pay their respects to the new governor, it so enraged Sloughter that he demanded immediate and unconditional surrender of the fort. Although Leisler immediately complied, he and the members of his council were placed under arrest, and thrown into prison.

Paying no attention to Leisler's side of the story Sloughter next instituted a court martial, appointing several personal enemies of Leisler as judges. These acts sealed the fate of Leisler. Charged with rebellion and high treason, he as well as Milborne were condemned to be executed.

In view of the manifest injustice of this decision Sloughter hesitated to sign the death warrant. But the aristocrats, having invited him to a banquet, procured his signature while he was intoxicated. Even before he could regain his sober senses, the two condemned men were dragged to the place of execution, where, on March 16, 1691, they were hanged and their bodies beheaded.

Thus died Jacob Leisler, the first martyr in the long struggle of the American people for liberty, the first of the men chosen by the people in their efforts to wrest the right of self-government from the hands of their oppressors.

While the aristocrats rejoiced in triumph, their villainous acts aroused bitter resentment in all parts of the colony, and a popular uprising was imminent.

From the tombs of the murdered men arose the spirit of revenge. To perpetuate the memory of its former leader, the people's party now named itself "The Leisler Party," henceforth steadily gaining ground. In the elections of 1699 this party cast 455 votes, while its opponents had only 177; it gained 16 seats out of the 21 in the assembly. Resistance to the insolence and domination of the aristocrats became stronger and stronger and spread to all the other colonies.

* * * *

About that time a German lad, thirteen years of age, arrived in New York. His father, one of those unhappy Palatines who were driven from their homes by the French, had died at sea. But the name of this helpless orphan: **Johann Peter Zenger,** has gone into history and it behooves every lover of American liberty to remember it.

Soon after his arrival Zenger became an apprentice to William Bradford, a printer, who had been allowed by the government to establish a printing office in New York. This permission had of course been granted under great restrictions, as the British government did not look with favor upon the great invention, made by Johannes Gutenberg in Mayence. The crown regarded it as a dangerous means of distributing unwelcome political news, and apt to inform people about incidents and transactions of which it wanted them to remain ignorant. For this reason the few printers who had drifted to the colonies, when attempting to publish newspapers, incurred disfavor and were discouraged at the start. The "Public Occurrences," edited on September 25, 1690, by Benjamin Harris of Boston, were at once stopped. In Virginia and Maryland it was strictly forbidden to set up a printing press. In Philadelphia William Bradford was ordered, in 1692, to close his office. Moving to New York, he succeeded, after many petitions, in getting permission to publish "The New York Gazette." Of course this paper was the organ of the governor's party and promoted his interests and those of the aristocrats only.

Having served as an apprentice in Bradford's office for several years, Zenger later on became Bradford's assistant and partner. In 1733, however, he left the partnership, probably because his political views were in too strong a contrast with those of Bradford, who remained a devoted instrument of the government. Zenger, on the other hand, had become an active member of the people's or Leisler's party.

His first step after his separation from Bradford was to start an independent newspaper, the "New York Weekly Journal." First issued on November 5, 1733, it voiced the sentiments of the people. Among its supporters and contributors were some of the ablest men of the colony, lawyers and judges, who took up all grievances of the public against the government and discussed them in bold and sometimes satirical manner.

To give an idea of the articles that found their way into the columns of the "Journal," we quote the following sentence of one of the contributors, a former judge. "We see men's deeds destroyed, judges arbitrarily displaced, new courts erected without the consent of the legislature, by which it seems to me trials by jury are taken away when a governor pleases; men of known estates denied their votes contrary to the recent practice of the best expositor of any law. Who is there in that province that can call anything his own, or enjoy any liberty longer than those in the administration will condescend to let them, for which reason I left it, as I believe more will."

Such plain speaking had never before been heard in the colonies. No wonder the governor became highly incensed at the "Journal" and directed the Grand Jury to indict Zenger, the publisher, for libel. At the same time he ordered that four numbers of the offending paper be publicly burned by the hangman, "as containing many things derogatory of the dignity of His Majesty's Government, reflecting upon the legislature and tending to raise seditions and tumults in the province." The mayor and the city magistrates were requested to be present at the burning of the papers.

But the Grand Jury failed to see any cause for the accusations against Zenger, nor was the Colonial Assembly willing to concur in a resolution of the council, that the objectionable numbers of the "Journal" be burned by the hangman. The burgomaster and the magistrate also refused to be present at the act and prohibited the hangman, who was subject to their jurisdiction, from executing the mandate of the governor.

Wild with rage, the governor now caused the four issues of the "Journal" to be burned by a negro slave, in the presence of the sheriff and the recorder of New York. Not content with this action he ordered the arrest of Zenger, and had him confined in prison, denying him all writing material. To prevent his release, his bail was fixed at eight hundred pounds, a sum so high at that time, that it was impossible for the printer's friends to raise it. Nevertheless Zenger continued to edit his paper, dictating instructions to his employees through a crack in the prison door.

The Grand Jury again in January, 1735, found that no cause for indicting Zenger existed, whereupon the Attorney-General filed an Information for Seditious Libel against him, and arraigned him for trial before the court he had censured. Zenger's lawyers attacked the constitutionality of the court, but by this objection so enraged the president of that court, that they were at once disbarred for contempt of court and the case adjourned.

As there were no other advocates in New York who dared to defend the printer, his case seemed hopeless. The trial, however, had become more than a personal matter; the cause of all the people being at stake. The friends of Zenger succeeded in summoning to his aid the most famous advocate in the colonies, Andrew Hamilton of Philadelphia. This gentleman presented his arguments so adroitly, and pleaded the cause of his client so eloquently, that the jury could do nothing else but set Zenger free.

Admitting at the outset, that Zenger had published the articles, Hamilton maintained that the question for the jury to decide was not whether or not the articles had been printed, but whether or not the articles which he had printed were a libel. These articles had been described as "false, scandalous, malicious and seditious." Hamilton explained that there was nothing false in these articles, but that they were statements of true facts and that the unreserved expression of opinion, on such true facts, was the undeniable right of every free British citizen. If the paragraphs, published by Zenger, gave nothing but true facts, they could not be condemned as a libel.

In conclusion Hamilton said: "The question before the court, and you, gentlemen of the jury, is not of small nor private concern, it is not the cause of a poor printer, nor of New York alone, which you are trying. No! It may in its consequences affect every Freeman that lives under a British Government on the main of America! It is the best cause, it is the cause of Liberty, and I make no doubt but your upright conduct, this day, will not only entitle you to the love and esteem of your fellow-citizens, but every man who prefers freedom to a life of slavery will bless and honor you as men who have baffled the attempts of tyranny; and by an impartial and uncorrupt verdict have laid a noble foundation for securing to ourselves, our posterity and our neighbors, that, to which nature and the laws of our country have given us a right — the Liberty, both of exposing and opposing arbitrary power by speaking and writing Truth!"

When the jury returned with their verdict of "Not guilty!" the entire population of New York indulged in wild demonstrations in honor of both Hamilton and Zenger, as the heroes of a trial, whereby one of the highest privileges — the **freedom of the press** — became established in America. Encouraged by this success to a realization of its inherent power the people aimed now to free themselves from material oppression by the government and from the greed of English merchants. While the governors always strove to curtail the colonies in those privileges which had been guaranteed to them by their charters, the merchants in London had succeeded, after the French war, in influencing Parliament to pass certain laws, which were in their own favor, but gave not the slightest consideration to the needs and welfare of the colonists. By these laws the latter were forbidden to manufacture any articles that could be procured in England, especially cloth and articles composed of iron. No hats, no paper, no plough-shares, no horse-shoes were allowed to be made in the colonies. Whatever they required of European goods, the colonists were obliged to buy in England, and to have brought over to America in English vessels. Thus the English merchants might set the price to suit themselves, while English ship owners might wax fat on freights. Another law forbade the selling of products, such as tobacco, cotton, hides and furs to any country other than England. This meant that prices offered by the English merchants, although much lower than might have been obtained in international trade, had to be accepted. And worst of all, the colonists were burdened with heavy taxes without the right of representation in Parliament.

No vigorous, self-respecting people would submit to selfish measures of this sort for any length of time. Of men, grown up in the freedom of the American forests and mountains, such servile submission could not be expected, and least of

43

all of these citizens of foreign birth, who had no reason to be loyal to a king because of national ties.

It is therefore not surprising that the Germans in America stood in the front ranks of the patriots who protested against unjust oppression. As early as 1765 many Germans signed a manifesto in which the merchants and traders of Philadelphia threatened to boycott all English goods, in case the government did not repeal the stamp-act. Several years later, in 1772, the Germans joined "The Patriotic Society of the City and County of Philadelphia," to defend those rights and privileges, which had been granted to the province in former times. It is recorded also that they took part in a mass-meeting, to protest against the threatened closing of Boston Harbor on account of the tea episode. This mass-meeting was attended by 8000 persons, and a "Correspondence Committee" was elected for the purpose of consulting with all other colonies about concentrated action for an energetic repulse of English encroachments.

The Germans living in these other colonies also held mass-meetings and adopted resolutions of strong protest. A meeting held on June 16, 1774, in Woodstock, Virginia, with Rev. Peter Muehlenberg as chairman, passed a resolution, bolder in language than any other. The following passages show the spirit pervading it: "Resolved, that we will pay due submission to such acts of government as His Majesty has a right by law to exercise over his subjects, and to such only.

That it is the inherent right of British subjects to be governed and taxed by representatives chosen by themselves only, and that every act of the British Parliament respecting the internal policy of America is a dangerous and unconstitutional invasion of our rights and privileges.

That the enforcement of said acts of Parliament by a military power will necessarily have a tendency to cause a civil war, thereby dissolving that union, which has so long happily subsisted between the mother country and her colonies; and that we will most heartily and unanimously concur with our suffering brethren in Boston and every other part of North America, who are the immediate victims of tyranny, in promoting all proper measures to avert such dreadful calamities, to procure redress of our grievances, and to secure our common liberties."

The spirit of rebellion was also active among the Palatines of the Mohawk Valley, in the province New York. On August 24, 1774, they united in a declaration, never to become slaves, but to defend their liberty at any price.

That these were not empty words, they proved, when the great struggle for independence began.

to grow up with the country, not to abandon it with the first sign of progress.

The discovery of immense deposits of coal and iron in the Ohio regions opened a new field to the iron industry. As the Germans had been a great factor in this industry on the East side of the Alleghanies, so they helped here in its development. **Georg Anschütz**, a native of Strassburg in Elsass, became in 1792 the pioneer of the iron industry at Pittsburgh. **Georg Schoenberger** founded in 1804 the Juniata Forge in Huntington County. **Jacob Meyers** established on State Creek, Kentucky, a smelting work, where he manufactured all kinds of tools, stoves, gun-barrels, cooking-pots, and other things. For several years his workmen suffered from frequent attacks by the Indians, so that half of the men were obliged to be under arms. But as by and by the redskins disappeared, the settlements could develop in peace.

Now the clearings grew to extensive fields. The rude dwellings were replaced by pleasant cottages, separated from each other by gardens and streets. The stockades and block-houses, which in time of danger had served as places of refuge, fell into decay and became dismantled.

Many of such new settlements were founded by Germans or by men of German origin. Columbia, now within the precincts of the city of Cincinnati, was founded in 1788 by Major **Benjamin Steitz,** an officer of the Revolutionary War, and by **Martin Denmann,** a Pennsylvania German. **Israel Ludlow** started together with some Americans in 1795 Dayton. **Ebenezer Zane** or **Zahne** erected in 1796 the first houses of Zanesville. There are in Ohio, Kentucky, Tennessee, Indiana and Illinois many places, whose names indicate their German origin, as for instance Frankfort, Hanover, Potsdam, German-town, Berlin, Freiburg, Wirtemberg, Osnaburg, Oldenburg, Hermann, Spires (Speyer), Betzville, Baumann, New Bremen, Wartburg, New Elsass, and others. Germans also founded Steubenville, commemorating the famous organizer of the American army.

Above all, young and enterprising folks from the East settled here, eager to try, like their fathers, upon new grounds their own abilities. Reinforced by a steady flow of immigrants from Germany, these settlers gave to many towns and cities the same peculiar character, which had been impressed by the older German immigration to many parts of the Eastern States. Highly respected by their fellow-citizens for their thrift, diligence, endurance and sense of order, they helped in peaceful competition to convert the wilderness into those fertile regions, which to-day are counted among the most flourishing in the United States.

Pioneers of the Mississippi Valley and the Far West.

Fully equal to the part played by Germans in the colonizing of the Eastern and Central States was their share in the development of those immense regions stretching from the banks of the Mississippi to the Pacific Ocean. When Louisiana was added to the United States in 1803, the most important problem became that of diminishing the long distance between the settlements in the upper valley of the Ohio River and New Orleans. The natural advantages of that city destinated it to become the emporium of trade for all imports and exports of the entire area surrounding the Mississippi and its tributaries. Communication by rafts and flat boats, which served as the first means of transportation on these waters, was extremely slow. Besides, these clumsy carriers were of use only for one trip down stream, as it was impossible to force them against the strong current of the rivers. In consequence the crew were always compelled to abandon these rafts and boats at the points of their destination and to make their return in canoes.

Even when keel-boats came into use, a round trip between Pittsburgh and New Orleans consumed a whole year! This time was cut in half, when **Martin Baum,** an energetic and prosperous German merchant in Cincinnati, engaged a former skipper on the Rhine, **Heinrich Bechtle,** to build several sailboats, with which Baum now opened the first regular service between Cincinnati and New Orleans.

Several years later, in 1811, another German, **Bernhard Rosefeldt,** constructed in Pittsburgh the first steamboat on the Western rivers. This vessel, named "New Orleans," made her first trip to that city. The captain was **Heinrich Schreve** (Schriewe), a German, from which Shreveport in Louisiana derives it name. For the development of traffic on the Western rivers the activity of this man was of greatest importance, as a steam-saw for cutting "snags," those unrooted trees, which, when entangled in the mud of the rivers are the greatest danger to Western navigation, was his invention. In 1829 Shreve built the snag-boat "Heliopolis," and had charge of the removal of the great Red River Raft, an accumulation of trees, logs and driftwood of every description, firmly imbedded in the channel of the Red River for more than 160 miles. The completion of this tedious and difficult task opened the river to navigation for a distance of 1200 miles.

70

Germans also gave the first impulse to the work of constructing a canal, enabling vessels to go around the falls of the Ohio River at Louisville, which had been another great hindrance to navigation.

With the institution of steam-boats and the simultaneous construction of canals several new ways toward the West were opened. The most frequented route led from New York up the Hudson River to Albany. Here the travellers took Canal boats and went via the Erie Canal to Buffalo, where they boarded steamers, which carried them over the Great Lakes to Michigan, Indiana, Illinois, Wisconsin and Minnesota. Other vessels made regular trips from European harbors and ports at the East coast of North America to New Orleans, where comfortable steamers carried the passengers to the points of their destination in the interior.

To these means of transportation new ones were added by the invention of railroads, which the Americans exploited with the same zeal displayed by them in making nature subservient so as to yield her riches. Enmeshing the country with whole networks of railways, they pushed them far into the uninhabited parts of the continent, in order to provide for the settlers easy ways to new territories with new possibilities.

With this era of steamers and railways began the great American migration, which differs from the migration in ancient Europe in that it was not caused by powerful nations driving weaker ones from their abodes. It consisted of individuals and families, parting voluntarily from the communities in Europe and of the Eastern States to participate in the conquest of the uncultivated western regions of the United States.

The majority of the immigrants from Germany consisted, as before, of farmers, craftsmen and artisans. But with them came also many representatives of the cultured classes, men who, disappointed by the unfortunate political affairs of the fatherland, hoped to find more congenial conditions in America. Many of those immigrants devoted themselves to farming and became the founders of the "Latin Settlements," so called, because their owners, former students of German universities, were able to converse in Latin fluently and took pleasure in keeping alive their learning by a study of the classics in preference to idling and indulging in disputes in the saloons.

Large numbers of these "Latin Farmers" settled in the Mississippi Valley. Opposite St. Louis they founded Belleville, a prosperous little city, which became the birth place of many men of prominence.

Immigration into the Mississippi Valley increased from year to year. Its magnitude can be judged by the fact, that during January, February and March of 1842 St. Louis saw the arrival of 529 steamers with 30,384 passengers. St. Louis grew to be a city of 40,000 people. That among them were many Germans, is indicated by the fact, that they maintained two daily papers in the German language.

Attracted by enthusiastic descriptions, whole expeditions of emigrants set out from Germany, to establish new settlements in these new regions. One of these undertakings was that of the Giessener Emigration Company, started by **Paul Follenius,** a lawyer, and **Friedrich Münch,** a minister of Giessen, a city in Hessen. Several hundred strong, the members of this party started in 1834 from Bremen for Missouri. But here they separated, as many preferred to proceed independently.

A similar undertaking was that of the Mainzer Adelsverein, who acquired in 1842 large tracts of land in Texas, northeast of San Antonio. Here several German settlements were started, among them New Braunfels and Fredericksburg. But soon afterwards the company dissolved, when in 1848 Germany was upset by revolutionary movements. The settlers, left to their own resources, struggled against the greatest difficulties through many years, but, by their energy and thrift, succeeded in time to make their colonies the most flourishing of all Texas. —

Among the regions, most favored by the Germans for their fertility and beautiful sceneries, were the Upper Mississippi Valley and the countries lying west and south of Lake Michigan and Lake Superior. New settlements, towns and cities sprang up here like mushrooms. Alton, Quincy, Keokuk, Burlington, Davenport, Dubuque, La Crosse, Winona, Red Wing, St. Paul, Minneapolis, Chicago, Milwaukee, Duluth and other places became brisk with German life. And at the same time starting points for parties of enterprising Germans, who established new settlements at the tributaries of the Mississippi as well as at the borders of the countless lakes, glimmering like blue eyes among the forests and prairies of Wisconsin, Minnesota, Dakota, Nebraska and Iowa. As in the region south of the Great Lakes so here many settlements indicate by their names the German origin. In Iowa we find, for instance, Guttenberg, Minden and New Vienna; in Wisconsin Germantown, New Koeln, New Holstein and Town Schleswig; in Missouri Westphalia, Hermann, New Hamburg, Altenburg, Wittenberg, Carola, Dammueller, and Frohne. In Minnesota a number of enterprising Germans from Chicago established in 1856 New Ulm, a settlement which grew within six years to a lively town of 1500 people, but in 1862 suffered a sudden set-back, when large bands of Sioux Indians, embittered by the countless impositions of dishonest Indian agents, went on the war path and in mad desire for revenge swooped upon the settlements. New Ulm, being farthest west, was attacked on August 19, 1862. Not prepared for the sudden assault, the inhabitants retreated toward the center of the town, where hastily a large square was formed of boxes, barrels, wagons, ploughs and all kinds of materials, the women and children huddling together within this barricade. After severe fighting, which lasted through the entire day, the enemies were repelled. But on August 23d they returned in far larger numbers, resolved to finish the town.

Their advance upon the sloping prairie in the bright sunlight was a most picturesque and exciting spectacle. When within about one mile of the Germans, who awaited the attack outside of the town, the savage warriors, all on horseback and bedecked with gay colors and fluttering feathers, began to expand like a fan. Then, uttering terrific yells, they came down like the wind. Again the settlers were compelled to fall back into the town, which the Indians promptly commenced to set afire. The wind, coming from the lower part of the place, fanned the flames and permitted the Sioux to advance behind the smoke. The conflagration became general and brought the defenders of New Ulm into a most critical situation, as the space, held by them, grew smaller and smaller. Finally they were concentrated upon the barricaded square in the center of the town. They defended this last position so gallantly during the rest of the day, during the night and the following morning, that at noon the enemies, despairing of success, retreated. 178 dwellings had gone up in flames, and many men, women and children were killed or wounded. As other attacks were likely, the survivors left the destroyed town and retreated to points in the neighborhood that could be more easily defended. Here they remained until order was re-established. During this revolt of the Sioux 644 settlers and 93 soldiers lost their lives, while the material damage amounted to more than 2,000,000 dollars. Later on many of the inhabitants of New Ulm returned. And as the government reimbursed the settlers for their losses, the town soon regained its former bright appearance.

* * * *

Back in 1803, when Louisiana became a part of the United States, nothing was known about the immense territories west of the Mississippi. No boat had plied yet upon the mysterious rivers rushing forth from the endless prairies, which no white man had ever traversed. Accordingly, on the maps, the region between the Mississippi and the Pacific Ocean was a blank spot bearing the ominous inscription: "The Great American Desert; unexplored."

But American energy would not tolerate such conditions. Soon after the Louisiana purchase had become perfect, the captains Lewis and Clarke were sent on their memorable exploring expedition, which led them up the Missouri River and through the passes of the Rocky Mountains to the mouth of the Columbia River, whose harbour had been mentioned by early navigators. The feasibility of an overland route having thus been demonstrated, an enterprising German merchant, **Johann Jacob Astor,** was the first to follow it.

Born 1763 in Waldorf, a little village in Baden, Germany, he came to New York in 1784. At once he engaged in the fur trade, his attention having been called to its vast possibilities by a fellow-countryman. Entering this occupation with unremitting vigor and keen judgment he rose, in a comparatively very short time, to be one of the most renowned merchants of America. During the first years his enterprise called quite often for his presence among the Indian tribes, with whom he established trading relations. In company of trappers and voyageurs he traversed the forests of New York, Michigan and Lower Canada. In a birch canoe with a couple of redskins he shot the dangerous rapids of Sault Sainte Marie. He camped with the Iroquois of the Mohawk Valley and with the Chippèwahs of Lake Superior. But wherever he went he dealt with the Indians in a spirit of fairness and humanity. In a dozen years Astor had diverted some of the most profitable markets from his competitors, and was head of the American Fur Company, which had branches in Albany, Buffalo, Pittsburgh and Detroit. The furs, collected at these places, were shipped to London, the vessels returning with English goods. It was not long before Astor was able to buy ships of his own, and before the end of the century he had, to quote his own expression, "a million dollars afloat," invested in a fleet of a dozen vessels. Astor was the first American to conceive the idea of regularly circumnavigating the globe, sending vessels with American furs to England, thence carrying British goods to China, and return to New York with tea, silk and other Oriental ware. For about twenty-five years his ships sailed round the world, some going eastward and some westward, each occupying two years, more or less.

With the ascertaining of the overland route to the Pacific Astor conceived the idea of organizing the fur trade from the Great Lakes to the Pacific Ocean, by establishing a line of trading stations which should stretch from the Great Lakes along the Missouri River and across the Rocky Mountains to the mouth of the Columbia. The end station was to be located at the latter point and was to be provided from New York by vessels loaded with wares suited to the Indian traffic. Then the same vessels were to carry the furs, collected at that station, to China, where a large demand for furs had arisen. There the vessels were to be freighted with tea for England, and finally they were to return with British manufactures to New York.

Preparations for the realization of this great plan were made on a most liberal scale, and nothing was left to chance. While an expedition of 60 trappers, agents, guides and interpreters went from St. Louis overland, following the route of Lewis and Clarke, the ship "Tonquin," with an equipment of everything a new-fledged colony could require, sailed from New York around Cape Horn to the mouth of the Columbia, arriving there in March, 1811, nine months ahead of the land expedition. A site for a trading station was chosen ten miles up the river, and the erecting of comfortable dwellings and ware houses began at once. In honor of its projector the settlement was called Astoria. When in January 1812 the men of the overland party arrived utterly destitute, they found relief within its walls.

Unfortunately the history of this great undertaking was brief. While the "Tonquin" was on a trading expedition, she was approached by large numbers of Indians, offering furs, and apparently unarmed. In violation of Astor's instructions that Indians were to be allowed on shipboard only a few at a time, they were suffered to clamber up the sides of the ship and to come on deck. Drawing knives, concealed in the bundles of fur, which they pretended to sell, the redskins fell upon the whites before the latter had time to prepare for an attack and massacred them. Only four of the crew escaped the slaughtering and barricaded themselves in the cabin. They even succeeded in ridding the ship of the invaders by opening a brisk fire from their rifles. But when on the next morning the enemies appeared again in overwhelming masses and swarmed on deck with yells of triumph, the sailors exploded the powder magazine, killing themselves and hundreds of their foes.

To the loss of the "Tonquin" came another mishap, much more serious. During the war, which broke out in the same year between the United States and England, the government was unable to defend Astoria. Finding themselves cut off from help and threatened with capture by a British gun-boat, Astor's agents sold the property to the Hudson Bay Company, which took possession of the station and held it till 1846, when England was compelled to abandon all claims on the region of the Columbia River.

While Astor's plan ended in failure, it stands nevertheless among the great commercial undertakings as a shining monument of German American enterprise, the more, as it found a historian in Astor's famous friend Washington Irving, whose classic work "Astoria, or Anecdotes of an Enterprise Beyond the Rocky Mountains" was read in all civilized countries of the world with great interest.

*   *   *   *

As Astor is known as the first to initiate a commerce with the farthest Northwest, so another German is the most prominent of the pioneers of California: **Johann August Sutter.**

Born in February 1803 in Kandern, Baden, he visited a military school in Switzerland and, later on, became a colonel of a batallion of infantry. In 1834 his adventurous spirit brought him to St. Louis, then the center of the western fur trade. From here in every spring numerous caravans of traders went forth to purchase the pelts, the Indians and trappers had collected in wintertime. Other caravans went from St. Louis over the so-called Santa Fe Trail to the far Southwest, to trade with the inhabitants of Texas, New Mexico, Arizona and California. One of the most successful of these merchants was A. Speier, whose expeditions went as far as Chihuahua. As a member of such caravans Sutter made several trips to Santa Fe. In 1838 he went with a number of trappers to Oregon, Vancouver Island and Hawaii. At Honolulu he bought a vessel and undertook a trading expedition to Alaska. Two years later Sutter obtained from the Mexican Government the titles for two landgrants, comprising together 141,000 acres at the Sacramento River in California. Here he established a settlement, which he named New Helvetia. For its protection he built Fort Sutter and surrounded it with high adobe-walls, through whose embrasures forty guns pointed in every direction. The garrison was composed of Americans, Europeans and Indians. In view of Sutter's former training it can not surprise, that he maintained a sort of military discipline, and that every evening the garrison was drilled by an officer, generally a German, marching to the music of fife and drum.

In recognition of his valuable services Sutter was made a governor of these most northern possessions of Mexico. He lived here, however, rather independently, raising with Indian laborers enormous quantities of wheat and large herds of cattle. The number of men employed by him ran from 100 to 500, the latter at harvest time. Among them were blacksmiths, carpenters, tanners, gun-smiths, farmers, vaqueros, gardeners, weavers, hunters, sawers, sheep-herders, trappers, millwrights and distillers. In a word, Sutter started every business and enterprise conceivable. The prospects for the future of the colony were unparallelled, and Sutter was regarded as the richest man in California, when suddenly, by one of the queerest caprices of fate, came frustration and ruin.

On January 19, 1848, soon after California had been annexed by the United States, James W. Marshall, a carpenter in Sutter's service, while building a saw-mill, discovered in the millrace many flakes and kernels of yellow metal. All at once it flashed upon him, that these shining particles might be gold. Gathering a handful, he rode in hot haste to the fort, to inform his employer of his find. When chemical tests proved the truth of Marshall's assumption, Sutter, fearing that the news would upset all conditions of his colony, made efforts.

76

to keep the discovery a secret. But in vain. It leaked out and was soon known in the fort and at the mill. And now the cry "Gold! Gold!" was borne on the wings of the wind to the sea-coast, and from the sea-coast to the four quarters of the globe.

What Sutter had apprehended became true. Almost all his men deserted him. The whole population of New Helvetia, of San Francisco, of Monterey, of California was caught with the infection and started to the gold fields, which soon were disclosed in many districts. Public buildings in the towns and cities became deserted, as the officials abandoned their posts. Newspapers suspended their issues indefinitely, as the editors vanished without asking furlough. Vessels were unable to depart, as their crews deserted. Workshops, stores, dwellings, and even fields of ripe grain, wines and families were left to take care of themselves. Even churches had to be closed, as their ministers also succumbed to the lure of the yellow metal. And when reports of the discovery of gold reached the Atlantic States, thousands and thousands of men left their homes, to seek their fortunes among the gulches of the wild Sierra.

Whole armies of adventurers and desperate characters, all craving for gold, swarmed over Sutter's property, trampling down his crops, killing his cattle and turning everything upside down. Without power to drive the intruders away, Sutter saw his property ruined. All remonstrations remained unheeded. Even his titles to his estates were disputed, as they had been acquired from the Mexican government, but not indorsed by the United States. All appeals for justice were in vain. Never regaining possession of his property, he would have died in poverty had not the State of California voted to him in 1865 a pension of 3000 dollars annually for seven years, on account of state taxes which Sutter had paid on the land when it was no longer his property. When Sutter died in 1888, America lost one of her most remarkable men, whose memory will survive in the history of California for all time to come.

More favored by fate was another German pioneer, who arrived in California in 1841: **Karl Maria Weber.** For some time he was in Sutter's service, but later on became a great cattle-raiser of his own. Leading an adventurous life, he was, like Sutter, one of the earliest promoters of American against Mexican interests. For this reason he was several times condemned to be shot by the Gringos. After the discovery of gold Weber founded the "Stockton Mining Company" and laid out a city, Stockton, which received her name in honor of Commodore Stockton, who aided in getting the concessions for the colony. Weber made not only the plans for this city, but supplied her also with macadamized streets, natural gas, electricity and other modern improvements. Before his death

77

he donated also all real estate needed for the erection of public buildings and parks.

Another remarkable German pioneer of the Far West was **August Laufkoetter,** who with a band of 26 Delaware Indians made trading expeditions to Arizona. Later on he was among the first settlers of Sacramento, California.

In Texas and Arizona **Herman von Ehrenberg,** a topographical engineer, made history. He was one of the 600 men, who in 1835 drove 2000 Mexicans from San Antonio and forced the fort Alamo to surrender. He had also part in the battle at San Jacinto on April 21, 1836, in which the independence of Texas was secured. Later on Ehrenberg was a member of the commission to establish the frontier between Arizona and Mexico. Afterwards he organized the Sonora Exploring and Mining Company, and also bcame a great landholder. Ehrenberg, a city on the lower Colorado River in Arizona, was named after this enterprising German.

To this brief list of German pioneers of the Far West many other names might be added. Wherever we investigate the history of our Western States and communities, we discover German names, made known by their bearers in some direction.

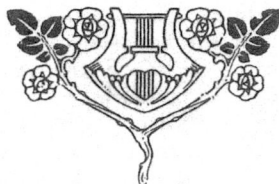

The Men of 1848.

The first half of the nineteenth century witnessed the arrival on American shores of a vast number of German immigrants, who gained a most significant place in American history: "the Men of 1848."

Their peculiar name needs explanation. As is commonly known, all political conditions of central Europe had at the beginning of the nineteenth century been overthrown by Napoleon Buonaparte, that great adventurer, who aimed at the erection of a Cæsarean Empire, the like of which the world had not seen before. This dream was defeated in the great battle at Leipzig by the inhabitants of the kingdoms and principalities of Germany and those of Austria. Having taken such a heroic part in this gigantic struggle for liberation, the people had hoped for the establishment of constitutional governments, in which they might have part. But this justified expectation was sadly deceived. The rulers, forgetful that the people had saved their thrones, denied it such right, and opened instead a long period of reaction, which manifested its triumph in dark acts of oppression and tyranny. Dissatisfied by the ingratitude of the sovereigns, many patriots, detesting violence, turned their backs on the land of their birth, hoping to find in America new fields for their abilities. Others, unwilling to submit to the petty tyranny of the rulers, resolved to resist and became leaders in a bitter struggle for liberty, which, dragging along for many years, culminated in the revolutionary outbreaks of the year 1848. The symbols of that sanguinary year were chosen to denote all those Germans and Austrians, who took part in the long struggle, though their participation dated back to earlier years. Among those men were thousands who had reached the highest pinnacle of intellectual development, men with ideal inspirations, who became in America successful promoters of the ethical, moral and material welfare of the people, and gained also widespread influence in the direction of affairs in our federation of States.

Among the earlier arrivals, who came between 1820 to 1848, were **Karl Follen, Karl Beck, Franz Lieber, Joseph Grund, Johann August Roebling, Georg Seidensticker** and **Max Oertel,** every one an apostle of science, art and home culture.

Among the men, who came in 1848 and the years following,

were Karl Schurz, Franz Sigel, Peter Osterhaus, Friedrich Hecker, Gustav Körner, Gustav von Struve, Karl Heinzen, Hans Kudlich, August Willich, Konrad Krez, Max Weber, Karl Eberhard Salomo, Julius Stahel, Max Weber, Hermann Raster, Johann Bernhard Stallo, Friedrich Kapp, Lorenz Brentano, Friedrich Hassaureck, Oswald Ottendorfer, Caspar Butz, Theodor Kirchhoff, Karl Douai and many thousand others. In all, Germany lost during the so-called "Reaktionszeit" more than one and a half million of her best citizens.

Germany's loss meant for the United States an invaluable gain, as so many hundred thousands of highly cultured men and women came into this country. While the former German immigration had consisted essentially of farmers, workmen and traders, now scholars and students of every branch of science, artists, writers, journalists, lawyers, ministers, teachers and foresters came in numbers. The enormous amount of knowledge, idealism and activity, embodied in these political exiles, made them the most valuable immigrants America ever received. As they accepted positions as teachers and professors at the schools and universities, or filled public offices, or founded all sorts of newspapers and periodicals, learned societies and social clubs, these men inspired the hitherto dull social life of America, that it gained a much freer and more progressive character.

By their able leadership the older German element in the United States improved also greatly. Formerly without close connection and compared with an army of able soldiers but without officers, it now began to form under the leadership of the men of 1848 a community, whose prime efforts were directed toward the welfare of their adopted country and to keep unsullied the fountains of liberty and the rights of men. That among the exiles of 1848 were characters of the same calibre as Franklin and Washington, though her revolution at home had been unsuccessful, will be clearly revealed by the shining examples of which the coming chapters will relate.

Distinguished Germans in American Politics.

While it is true that comparatively few men of German birth are found holding political office and that representation of the German element in the halls of the legislatures and in administrative places is in no way commensurate with their numerical strength, it must not be assumed that their influence in American politics is or was negligible. Here as elsewhere we find the Germans disposed to deal with public affairs as statesmen rather than as politicians. Precisely this quality, however, gave their views an importance which exerted a considerable and wholesome influence on American politics, oftimes sufficient to render them the decisive factor on great issues. Thus, for instance, on the question of slavery, first raised, as shown in a previous chapter, by the inhabitants of Germantown. They steadfastly advocated its abolition through all the 18th and the 19th century, standing their ground until the issue was consummated in accordance with their views.

Due to their verdict also were the prevailing of common sense and true statesmanship in the political battles waged for Sound Money, Civil Service, Party Reform, Conservation, Temperance and Personal Liberty.

In the discussion of all these questions the German Americans were invariably guided by men of sound judgment and keen intellect. Pastorius and Leisler were followed by Zenger, Saur and the Muehlenbergs, the latter family represented by several eminent members, who distinguished themselves in public and political life. **Peter Mühlenberg** was a member of Congress during three sessions. His brother, **Frederick August Mühlenberg**, was not only member and speaker of the Pennsylvania State Legislature, but also a member of the First, the Second, the Third and Fourth session of Congress. Manifest proof of the excellency of his character was the fact, that he, a citizen of foreign origin, was elected as the very first Speaker of the House of Representatives, and that he was re-elected to the same position during the third session. His son, **Henry August Mühlenberg**, was one of the representatives of Pennsylvania for a period of nine years.

The most remarkable German leaders of the 19th century were **Franz Lieber and Carl Schurz**. Lieber, born on March 10, 1800, in Berlin, received his training in science at the Universities of his native city and of Jena and in close intercourse with some of the most noted men of his time, especially Ludwig Jahn, the famous promoter of physical exercise. Through him Lieber became imbued with the deep love for liberty, which distinguished those noble patriots, who in the years 1813 to 1815 threw off the yoke of Napoleon. Unfortunately the reactionary men, then at the helm of government in his native country, regarded all persons with liberal sentiments as enemies of the state. So it came to pass that Jahn and Lieber were placed several times under arrest. Heavy of heart, Lieber emigrated to America, arriving here in 1827.

Before he found permanent employment, his struggles were very hard. In 1828 he began with editing the "Encyclopædia Americana," an adaptation of the famous "Brockhaus Conversations Lexikon," but containing many original articles, written by Lieber on political science and subjects. This work was first published in Philadelphia, later on as the "American Encyclopædia" by Appleton in New York.

In 1835 Lieber was appointed professor of history and political economy at South Carolina College, Columbia, S. C. This position became untenable, when the question of slavery grew acute, and Lieber, whose whole soul longed for liberty, became one of the earnest advocates of the abolishment of human bondage.

In 1857 Lieber accepted a call to Columbia College, New York City. This was the first recognition by a Northern college of History and Politics as properly co-ordinated subjects. Lieber spent nearly forty years at imparting a knowledge of this most vital branch to the youth of the republic.

During this time he wrote three monumental works, whereby he founded his fame as one of the greatest publicists of the world. In his "Manual of Political Ethics," published in 1837, he gave the first great original treatise on political science in America. Its subjects include the ethical nature of man, public opinion, parties, factions, opposition, love of truth, perseverance, the duty of representatives, judges, lawyers, office holders, and the pardoning power. The keynote of this remarkable work is Lieber's favorite motto: **"No right without its duties; no duty without its rights."**

Two years later this great work was followed by another important contribution to political science, "The Legal and Political Hermeneutics." Its value was recognized in the "Nation" as follows: "Many of the topics discussed in this book were at Lieber's time new, doubtful, and difficult. Of the conclusions arrived at by Lieber and first expressed by him, writers of the present day often speak as familiar political truths, without, perhaps, any conception on their part of the source whence they were derived."

In 1853 appeared Lieber's greatest and best known work:

"Civil Liberty and Self-Government." Another great work on the "Origin and the National Elements of the Constitution of the United States," which promised to be Lieber's best, unfortunately remained a fragment.

During the later years of his life Lieber became deeply interested in the subject of international law. He was the first to propose the idea of professional jurists of all nations coming together for the purpose of working harmoniously together, and seeking to establish a common understanding, and thus serving as an organ for the legal consciousness of the civilized world. From this impulse proceeded Rolin-Jacquemyn's circular letter, to found a permanent academy of international law, the "Institut de Droit International," which was started in Ghent in 1873, only one year after Lieber's death, which occurred on October 2, 1872.

While Lieber's heart was devoted to the welfare of his adopted country, he never descended to the level of the partisan. The motto of his study and life was: **"Dear is my Country; dearer still is Liberty; dearest of all is Truth!"**

Inspired by the same idealism was **Carl Schurz,** the greatest of all Germans, who made America their home. Born on March 2, 1829, in Liblar, near Cologne, Schurz, as a student at the University of Bonn, also became so deeply involved in the revolutionary movement of 1848, that he was compelled to flee. After a stay of several years in England and France he arrived in 1852 in Philadelphia. Here he resided for three years. Later on he went to Wisconsin, where he practiced law. At this time the great struggle between the North and the South was brewing and it became evident that the old cause of human freedom was to be fought for on the soil of the new world.

Like Pastorius and the inhabitants of Germantown had been opposed to slavery, so almost all Germans in the United States favored abolition. Schurz became at once their most eloquent spokesman and most potent leader.

"Before the Lincoln presidential campaign," so Andrew D. White states in his autobiography, "slavery was always discussed either from a constitutional or philanthropical point of view, orators seeking to show either that it was at variance with the fundamental principles of our government or an offensive against humanity. But Schurz discussed it in a new way and mainly from the philosophic point of view, showing not merely its hostility to the American ideas of liberty and the wrong it did to the slaves, but, more especially, the injury it wrought upon the country at large, and, above all, upon the Slave States themselves. In treating this and all other public questions he was philosophic, eloquent and evidently sincere."

While taking an active part in the campaign of the Republican party against the extension of slavery, Schurz attained an influence in the councils of the party and with the voters, especially the Germans, that made his rôle in the struggle of 1860 extremely important, and, in the reckoning of shrewd observers, wellnigh decisive. Lincoln, after his election, acknowledged the great services of Schurz by appointing him U. S. Minister to Spain. But his stay at this post was only of short duration. As soon as the Civil War broke out, Schurz resigned in order to enter the Union Army. His part in the dreadful struggle is outlined in another chapter.

On conclusion of the war President Johnson commissioned Schurz to make a tour through the Southern States, to investigate their conditions. His report was full of valuable suggestions and was the basis of the reconstruction policy adopted by Congress, with the difference, however, that Schurz steadily pressed the enactment of general amnesty and of impartial conditional suffrage.

In the Presidential campaign of 1868 Schurz was again one of the most effective speakers of the Republican party, and in the following year was chosen United States Senator from Missouri. The Senate was the ground, where his great gifts and extraordinary eloquence came to full development. "Schurz's greatness as an orator," so said the N. Y. Evening Post in an editorial of May 14, 1906, 'lay in this, that he not only spoke as a rational man to rational men, but as a man of heart and conscience, who judges every man by himself and feels that his best hold is in appealing to the better nature of his hearers. Unlike many of his most distinguished colleagues, he never resorted to inflated or bombastic rhetoric and never stooped to any of the well-worn artifices with which demagogues from time immemorial have been wont to tickle the ears of the mob. What he said of Sumner in his unsurpassed eulogy of the Massachusetts Senator, that 'he stands as the most pronounced idealist among the public men of America,' might with equal truth be said of himself."

That Schurz was among the American Statesmen an idealist of the noblest type, who believed in the great mission of the United States, and himself strove at the highest goal, is indicated by a significant remark, made by him one day: **"Our ideals resemble the stars, which illuminate the night. No one will ever be able to touch them. But the men who, like the sailors on the ocean, take them for guides, will undoubtedly reach their goal."**

And another motto of Schurz may find a place here, as it is the key for his attitude in all political questions: **"My Country! When right keep it right; when wrong, set it right!"**

In 1877 President Hayes selected Schurz for Secretary of the Interior. His administration of this office was marked by energy, integrity, and a determination to enforce the laws.

CARL SCHURZ

At the same time he introduced many reforms, the great importance of which was acknowledged and appreciated only in later years. So for instance he was the first official, who called the attention of the preservation of our forests and other natural resources, which were ransacked by rapacious corporations without the slightest regard of the future.

Further, Schurz applied in his department, immediately after his appointment, the methods of civil service reform. The many evils, connected with the spoils system, inaugurated under President Jackson, had under President Grant grown to unheard-of proportions. Embezzlement, graft, bribery and all other forms of corruption went hand in hand with incapability and neglect, and threatened to demoralize the whole administration. Public scandals, in which high officials were involved, became daily occurrences. The taint of dishonesty affecting official life caused many able citizens, especially the German Americans, to look upon politics as something to be shunned.

Schurz at once made good behavior, honesty and efficiency the first condition for all appointments, removals and promotions in his department. A board of inquiry, composed of three clerks of the highest class, was designated to investigate and determine all cases in regard to these questions.

This strict application of the principles of the merit system, inaugurated by Schurz for the first time in the history of any department of the United States Government, has since become the criterion of most of the succeeding administrations. For many years Schurz was a member and president of the National Civil Service Reform Association, and in this capacity, by fighting the spoils system with all his determination, intelligence and patience, he rendered, perhaps, the greatest service to this country.

With equal energy he devoted his efforts to the exposure of the grave perils involved in paper money, the "silver craze," and all other wild financial schemes, by which the basic principles of sound currency during the period from 1860 to 1896 were threatened.

During his political life Schurz firmly maintained a position of independence of judgment and of action, and held himself wholly free to follow the dictates of his conscience and to pursue what he believed, on mature reflection, to be the best policy for the public good. Of course this independence would have been of little avail had it not been accompanied, on the one hand, by generally sound and intelligent judgment in the formation of his opinions, and, on the other, by the very great powers of persuading and convincing the minds of men. Both these Schurz had in an extraordinary degree, and he exercised them with an energy, a patient persistence, with an amount and kind of skill and penetration and a fervor of advocacy that, on the whole, have not been surpassed in the history of the United States in the latter half of the nineteenth century, momentous as that period was and rich as was its product of able men. In the six volumes of his speeches, correspondence and political papers, selected and edited after his death by the Carl Schurz Memorial Committee, he appears as the highest personification of true Americanism, as a shining light, which served many of his contemporaries as a safe and reliable guiding star. —

Other distinguished German leaders of the 19th century were **Friedrich Münch, Gustav Körner,** General **J. A. Wagener, Gustav Schleicher, Michael Hahn, Johann Bernhard Stallo, Samuel Pennypacker** and many others, who as members of Congress, governors, mayors, or in other high positions worked faithfully for the welfare of our United States.

One of the most remarkable figures in Congress was at the end of the 19th and at the beginning of the 20th century **Richard Bartholdt** from Missouri, who as representative of the Tenth Missouri District served for 22 years. During this long period he was one of the most ardent defenders of personal liberty.

, The attitude of Bartholdt and of the whole German element on this question, which comprises the so-called Temperance Question and Sunday Observance, has been defined in a clearcut manner many times. The Germans believe, that the Prohibitionists do not keep the ideas of temperance (moderation) and prohibition (disallowance) apart. Temperance is — so the Germans explain — a virtue, which should be acquired by self-control. It is practiced and recommended by the Germans just as strongly as by all other reasonable men. Prohibition, on the other hand, is regarded as a restriction in contravention of the right of personal liberty guaranteed to every citizen of the Republic by its Constitution. This restriction is insisted on by certain elements, who have no understanding nor feeling for true liberty, liberal thoughts and the cheerful enjoyment of life by others. It interferes with the customs and necessities of many million inhabitants of the United States, who have the same right on American soil as those holding Puritan views.

In regard to the Sunday question the German American Alliance expressed in 1903 the following views: "Sunday should be interpreted as a day of rest and recreation. Man was not made for the Sabbath, but the Sabbath for man. The individual should be given perfect liberty to spend the day as he wishes. The fanatic would suppress all public life on Sunday, including traffic, the selling of newspapers and the necessities of life. The question of Sunday observance as a day of prayer and repentance is a religious one, and the state must remain apart from the church in consonance with the principles laid down in the Constitution."

Bartholdt's activity during the 22 years of his service in Congress was furthermore devoted to the improvement of the immigration laws and to the interests of international peace. Having become acquainted in 1899 in Christiania, Norway, with the Interparliamentary Union he organized in Congress an American group of this union, was elected her president and held this position till 1915, when he returned

RICHARD BARTHOLDT.

to private life. It was through his influence that the union held in 1904 its annual meeting in St. Louis, which was attended by 156 delegates from European countries and several hundred delegates of American republics. Here Bartholdt was elected president of the Union for the same year. It was by his efforts, that the Second Peace Conference at The Hague in 1907 came to pass.

The last great speech of Bartholdt in Congress he delivered

on February 19, 1915. It was devoted to the defense of the American citizens of German descent, who have been made the objects of gross insults by many American newspapers since the outbreak of the European war for their sympathies with the Fatherland. As Bartholdt's speech treated a subject of vital interest to the population of the United States, the most important parts may find here a place.

"The United States has a composite population. Not England alone, but all Europe is its mother, and contributions to the blood which now circulates through the Nation's veins have been made by practically all countries, the largest share next to Great Britain having been contributed by Germany or the States now constituting the German Empire. American statesmen recognized early in our history that ours was not a ready made nation, but a "nation to be" whose character was to be shaped by the impress made upon it by the various elements constituting its growing population. It was also recognized that Saul could not at once turn into Paul, that the newcomer could not change his traits overnight. It is probably true that the Anglo-Saxon is less free from racial or national prejudices than the cosmopolitan German — a strange phenomenon, for they come from the same cradle — yet such was the tolerance of our older statesmen that they never regarded the love of the immigrants for the old country as in any wise irreconcilable with his allegiance to the new. And why? Because reverence for the mother never detracts from love for the bride, and, furthermore, because that reverence is a natural impulse which can no more be regulated or controlled than can the throbs of the human heart. We can educate an immigrant in our way of thinking, induce him to adopt our customs and make a good American citizen of him, but we cannot change his heart to the extent of eradicating his regard for his native land. Along with freedom of thought and conscience we must grant him the liberty of placing his sympathies and affections where he pleases. It is a natural right which no law can limit and no government can deny him as long as our own country is not involved. American statesmanship had the choice of either closing the gates of the country or of taking its chances with the constant human influx. It chose the latter course, and history does not record a single instance to prove that policy to have been a mistake. While the people of the United States have been gathered from all nooks and corners of the globe, while many of them still differ in habits, customs, and language, and while on occasions the sympathies of the first, second, and even third generations still go out to the land of their ancestors, no serious problem has thereby been created. Our adopted citizens and their native descendants have stood the test of loyalty in every crisis in the country's history, and thus irrefutable proof has been adduced that memories of the Fatherland conjured up by impulses of the heart do not and will not detract from the allegiance due to the adopted country.

"Because of their sympathies with the Fatherland, the Americans of German descent have been openly accused of divided allegiance and downright disloyalty. They know this wanton insult to emanate from English and French press agents, and consequently treat it with the contempt it deserves. But what they resent is that, in the face of our own history, the American press should have opened its columns to such calumnies. Germans have fought and bled on the battlefield of four American wars and furnished a larger proportion to the fighting strength of our country than any other of the so-called foreign elements. In the Revolutionary War, with Baron Steuben they espoused the cause of the Colonies, and the implicit confidence which the Father of our Country placed in their loyalty is a matter of history. In 1861, when many of the English, with instinctive aversion to American naturalization, took out British protection papers, the Germans — that is, nearly 200,000 of them — rallied around the flag of Abraham Lincoln to save the Union. They displayed the same valor in the War of 1812 and in the Spanish-American War, and their loyalty to the flag in times of war is equaled only by their loyalty to American ideals in times of peace. I should have much preferred if just at this time these historical truths had been uttered by other than a German-American tongue; but while our pro-English press is ignoring them, Americans of German blood should at least have expected immunity from libels and insults. Yet such insults are heaped upon that element by newspapers permitting agents of the allies to use their space for that purpose. We can best judge the future by the past, and the lessons of the past justify me in proclaiming it as an irrefutable fact that if unfortunately the United States should ever again be embroiled in war, which the Heavens forbid, the Germans of this country would again as loyally rally around the Stars and Stripes as they did against our enemies in every crisis of the past. Let me again assert in most positive terms what I said on the floor the other day, that the Germans are for America against England, for America against Germany, for America against the world! They will never waver for one second in their allegiance to the land of their choice and adoption.

These few words will suffice, I trust, to lay bare the charge above referred to in its whole naked infamy. But let me proceed with my argument. If sympathy for Germany is an evidence of disloyalty, as is claimed by our traducers, you will agree that sympathy for the allies is exactly the same thing; and if that be true, we would be confronted with the monstrous fact, that the whole American press printed in English, with but few exceptions, is disloyal to the United States.

It is absurd, of course, but I make this deduction merely to show that I am not a less patriotic American by sympathizing with the Fatherland and its ally than I would be if my sympathies were for England and her allies; and certainly no true American will claim that to side with England and to oppose Germany is a prerequisite of loyal American citizenship, for that would mean both truckling to a former enemy and the betrayal of a traditional friend, of course absolutely unjustifiable by any standard of American loyalty.

There is no question, but what at the present time the Germans of this country are stirred as they were never stirred before. Their state of mind manifests itself in great mass meetings and in hundreds of thousands of petitions addressed to Congress in favor of an embargo on arms. It would not be quite correct, however, to ascribe the prevailing excitement solely to sympathy for Germany. In reality it is as much, if not more, injured pride and an outraged sense of justice which have caused their indignation to rise because of the outrageous prevarications of truth and the cruel misrepresentations of Germany, her people, and institutions contained in the manufactured news from England and reprinted in the American newspapers. Proud of their American citizenship, they have in a political sense absolutely nothing in common with Germany or its government, but their more or less accurate knowledge of conditions in that country taught them that the alleged news we were getting was a brutal attempt at defamation to poison the American mind against Germany. The war was started with a monstrous lie, and in order to support it a thousand other lies had to be told. The Germans were denounced as Huns and barbarians, as ravishers and plunderers, and as perpetrators of the worst imaginable atrocities. The Emperor was described as an Attila, who one day had had 110 Socialist deputies executed; the Crown Prince as a thief, and so forth. You might say that it is natural for enemies to revile each other, but I must answer that, so far as Germany is concerned, she herself, though obliged to fight the lie as one of the worst of her many enemies, has not yet stooped to a departure from the truth either in her own newspapers or in the messages she has sent out to the world.*) And permit me to add parenthetically that to the neutral world the present struggle has an enhanced significance in that it is also a warfare

---

*)This fact has been acknowledged by several American papers. We quote here the following remarks of the New York American:
"We are bound to say one thing about the German press. The serious and dignified tone in which the German newspapers have invariably discussed the progress and the problems of the war is an example which the American press might follow with benefit to itself and to the public.
We do no see in any German newspaper opprobrious epithets applied to the American people. We do not see any cartoons ridiculing

of falsehood against truth. If the international lie should succeed, I believe the world would eventually suffocate in its slime.

The Germans of this country could understand why England to secure recruits should want to incite her own people by these falsehoods, but they could not understand nor will they forgive the American newspapers for reprinting them in our country. To do so was a most serious and unpardonable reflection on the German element of this country. As an integral part of the American people, whose characteristics and virtues are reflected as much in the composite character of this Nation as are those of the citizens of English descent, they believed themselves to be entitled to some consideration at the hands of the press of their own country. Such consideration was denied them, however, and with utter disregard of their feelings they were rudely informed that their brothers on the other side of the ocean are barbarians, ghouls, and vandals, and that is not all. (From the first day of the war) up to the present whatever the allies did was right, while every act of the Germans was all wrong, even if it was an exactly similar thing; for instance, the dropping of explosives from aeroplanes. The alleged violation of Belgian neutrality was harped upon with sickening persistence even after it had been ascertained that the neutrality treaty had expired in 1872, and that, if it had still been in force, the Belgian Government had itself thrown it overboard by its secret agreement with England regarding the landing of English troops on Belgian soil. On the other hand, not a word is said about the violation of Chinese neutrality by Japanese and English troops, although this matter is of infinitely greater consequence to American interests than the affairs of Belgium can possibly be. The present international status of China is due to the skill of American statesmanship, it being an achievement of John Hay, made possible by the support of Germany alone. The integrity of China, already violated by England and her ally, should (be restored and maintained at all hazards, but we look in vain for any appeals in the press in favor of the conservation of American interests in that quarter. It might embarrass England, you know, if just now the press insisted on our own rights. As to Belgian atrocities, five American newspaper men

---

or picturing the President of the United States as a ruffian and murderer.

In fact, we have not seen in any German newspaper a single word or a single picture which was intended to express hatred or contempt or bitterness against America.

In the face of the bitter and ugly and vulgar and unmanly billingsgate, abuse and pictorial ridicule and hatred heaped by so many of our newspapers upon the German people and the German government, we are bound to say, in common fairness, that the dignity and self-control of the German press are highly to its credit."

of the highest standing affirmed under oath that there was no such thing, yet these alleged atrocities are presented to American readers in glaring headlines, while the authentic refutation of the stories is published in small type on the sixteenth or seventeenth page. We may be foolish, but we are not blind to such notorious evidences of partiality. The Americans of German blood are a unit in bitterly resenting not only these unneutral efforts to poison the fountainheads of American public opinion against Germany but also the palpably unneutral "most-favored-nation" treatment systematically accorded to Great Britain. (Touching the last-named fact, it seems to them as if we were using kid gloves against England and the mailed fist against Germany, as if, indeed, everything was being avoided, even to the disregard of American interests, that might embarrass the former country in her effort to crush Germany.

The bill of complaints is too long to recite here in full, but let me merely ask: Have we protested against American citizens having been dragged from neutral steamers and thrown into English prisons simply because those men, Americans to the manner born, happened to bear German names? No. Have we protested against England's inhuman policy to starve to death the noncombatant population of Germany, by stopping, in open violation of international law, all food supplies, even if carried from a neutral country and in neutral bottoms? No. Have we protested against England declaring the whole North Sea as a war zone? No; but when Germany did the same thing in practically the same language we immediately dispatched a stiff note to Berlin, while the milder one was directed to England, though it would seem that the latter country was the chief offender in allowing the use of false flags. However, whatever the administration does in foreign affairs, as Americans it will be our duty to uphold it.

After this explanation can you understand, Mr. Chairman and gentlemen of the House, why the German mind in this country is agitated, and can you blame that element if their feelings are ruffled? When, moreover, it dawned upon them that all our arms factories were running night and day to supply the allies with weapons for use against their brothers and kinsmen, nothing could convince them that the United States was not actually a silent partner of the allies. Then it was that they demanded, and they are still demanding an embargo on arms to enforce honest neutrality, the kind of neutrality which the President proclaimed when he said: "We should be neutral in fact as well as in name, and should put a curb on every transaction which might be construed as giving a preference to one party to the struggle above another." This shameful traffic in arms, they argue, gives the lie to our prayers for peace, because it tends to prolong the war, and its permission by international law, they believe, imposes no obligation on our citizens to carry it on, no more on us than on the other neutral countries which have all stopped it upon the demand of England herself. I should like to discuss this important question at length, if my time permitted, but let me say just one more word. Whether the President would use the authority or not, there ought to be a law on our statute books which confers such authority upon him in order that he might enforce his demands for a free and open sea and unrestricted commerce in noncontraband goods. In our present demands against England our only alternative is either to give in or declare war. (The threat of an embargo on arms, however, would quickly bring the "Mistress of the Seas" to terms and without war. Hence the legislation demanded by what the pro-English press is pleased to call German mass meetings, will be a preventive of, rather than a provocation to war with England, and thus falls to the ground another of the silly charges preferred by the press bureau of the allies against me and the several millions of American citizens who think as I do on this subject.

Continuing as an interpreter of the feelings of these millions, all good American citizens, permit me to say that the hostility of the Anglo-American press against Germany and the Germans has forced many to a conclusion which, if correct, would be the most painful disappointment of my life. ∠They believe this attitude to be less pro-English than anti-German, and, indeed, regard it as the outgrowth of racial prejudice against the Germans even of this country, and as a revival of the old Know-nothing spirit which aimed at a sort of guardianship by those of English descent over this country, to the exclusion of all other elements, the latter to be classed simply as "foreigners," and degraded to the rank of second-class citizens. How could such a conclusion be reached? Well, they ask whether the history of the American Germans has not been an honorable one. They fought for independence, opposed slavery, and loyally gave their bodies and lives that the Union might live; they were almost a unit for sound money, and are imbued with the true American spirit of freedom to such an extent that they love liberty better than whatever good might come from its restriction. As a rule, they modestly refrained from seeking political preferment, but filled America's life with music and song and innocent social pleasures. They are peaceful and law-abiding citizens, who by industry and thrift have made the best of the opportunities which the country of their choice generously offered them, and thus they have contributed their honest share to the growth, the development, and the grandeur of the Republic. If such a record of good citizenship is not sufficient, it is argued, to insure the German element immunity from libels and insults, what else can account for it but racial aversion, the innate prejudice of the | Anglo-Saxon against everything foreign?

94

There should never be a division in the United States upon racial or national lines. Under the American sun, in their capacity as citizens, the Teuton and the Slav, the Irishman and the Englishman, the German and the Frenchman extend to each other the hand of brotherhood as equals, and the great flag covers them all. Ancient prejudices have melted away under the sun of freedom until, no longer English, Irish, German, Scandinavian, we are, one and all, heart and soul, Americans!

In conclusion let me reiterate the steadfast devotion of all citizens of German blood to American ideals and the flag. Impatient of injustice though they be, their hearts are true to the core. They feel themselves as one with every other citizen of the Republic, and they will share the fate of their adopted country and of their children's fatherland. Whatever their secondary sympathies may be, they are with all other true Americans for America first, last, and all the time. They are for a united Nation, and shall ever uphold the ideal of national unity and dignity with that loyalty which has characterized their whole history on American soil."

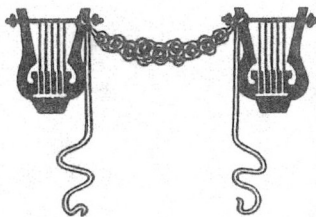

The German Americans during the Wars of the 19th Century.

Splendid as had been the proofs of loyalty to their adopted country shown by the Germans during the War for Independence, equally impressive evidence is found in the staunch support invariably extended by them to this country in the wars in which the United States was involved during the 19th Century.

When the British in 1812 had captured the city of Washington and burned the Capitol, the Executive Mansion, the Treasury, the State and War Department as well as many other buildings, they also set out to take Baltimore. It was then, in the defense of the city, that two Americans of German origin took the most prominent part. The commander of the militia was General **Johann Stricker,** born at Frederick, Maryland, in 1759.

The enemy having landed at North Point, he led his men against him in a running skirmish, in which General Ross, the British commander, was killed.

Fort McHenry, protecting the harbor of Baltimore, was gallantly defended by Major **George Armistead,** the son of **Johann Armstadt,** a Hessian, living in New Market, Va. It was in the morning of September 12, 1814, when the British fleet, consisting of sixteen frigates, opened a terrific bombardment on the fort, which was held by a garrison of one thousand men. The cannonade lasted for 36 hours. It was on the waning of that memorable night of the 12th to the 13th, that Francis S. Key, while detained on board of a British ship, watched during the long hours, anxiously asking:

"Oh say can you see, by the dawn's early light,
What so proudly we hail'd at the twilight's last gleaming."

That the star spangled banner still waved, was due to the bravery of the noble defender of Fort McHenry and his men. They answered the terrific fire of the enemy so effectually, that on the morning of the 14th the fleet withdrew, without having attained any success.

* * * *

In the war with Mexico, during the years 1846 and 1847, many Germans also served with great distinction. Among them were numerous officers, who had been active in the old Fatherland and, later on, during the Civil War and the Indian

Wars, came to great renown; as for instance August Mohr, von Gilsea, August V. Kautz, Samuel Peter Heinzelmann and others.

The most dashing soldier of German origin in the Mexican War was, however, Johann Anton Quitman, the son of Friedrich Anton Quitman, a Lutheran minister at Rhinebeck-on-the-Hudson. Born in 1798, Quitman had emigrated to the Southwest, where he took part in the struggles of Texas, striving to separate herself from Mexico.

When in 1846 the war with Mexico broke out, Quitman was made a Brigadier-General. With greatest distinction he fought at Monterey, and it was he, who at the head of his soldiers reached as the first the market place of the hotly defended city. He also raised the victorious American flag on the tower of a church.

During spring of 1847 Quitman was in command of the land batteries, which in conjunction with the American fleet bombarded Vera Cruz and compelled this strongly fortified city to surrender.

Also he distinguished himself at Cerro Jordo, after which engagement he was brevetted Major-General, and was voted a sword of honor by Congress for gallantry. On September 13th he stormed with his men the old fortress of the Montezumas, Chapultepec, which the Mexicans believed to be impregnable. On the following day he opened the bombardment of the City of Mexico, effecting an entrance on the 15th.

In appreciation of his gallant service General Scott appointed Quitman governor of the city, which position he held till order was established. Several years later he was elected governor of Mississippi. Elected to Congress by large majorities, he served from 1855 to 1858, the year of his death.

*   *   *   *

Historians, who studied the part taken by the Germans in our Revolutionary War, have not hesitated to declare that the independence of the United States would probably not have been attained without the patriotic support of that element.

There is also good reason to doubt, whether without its loyal aid the preservation of our national unity would have been possible.

That the Germans were opposed to all forms of oppression and that in their agitation against slavery they overshadowed all foreign-born citizens, has been shown in former chapters. Consistent with such sentiment the overwhelming majority of the Germans gave aid to the North, convinced that the future of the whole country depended on the preservation of the Union. And so thousands and thousands of Germans combined, firmly resolved that slavery must be abolished and that not one of them would permit a single star to be ruthlessly torn from the blue field of the nation's glorious banner.

How many Germans and German Americans hurried to the arms, in order that the stars and stripes might continue to wave intact

"O'er the land of the free and the home of the brave"

cannot be told with absolute correctness, as during the bitter conflict between the North and the South no statistics about the nationality or extraction of the soldiers were kept. Not before 1869 was any attempt made to answer proximately this interesting question. From investigations, made by Dr. B. A. Gould, it appears, that of the 2,018,200 white soldiers who fought for the Union, 45,508 were English, 144,221 Irish and 176,817 Germans. William Kaufmann, author of the valuable work, entitled: "Die Deutschen im amerikanischen Bürgerkriege," believes, however, that the volunteers born in Germany, numbered roundly not less than 216,000. It appears thus that the contingent, furnished to the armies of the North by the Germans, was far greater than that of any other nationality. To the above number must be added many hundred thousand men of German origin included in those 1,523,207 soldiers who registered as "native Americans."

How considerable must have been the quota of Germans among these men, may be judged from the number of members contributed to the Northern armies by the well-known family Pennypacker, descendents of **Heinrich Pannebäcker,** a German who immigrated in 1699 and settled on the Shippack Creek in Eastern Pennsylvania. This family was represented by 2 major-generals, 1 lieutenant-general, 1 colonel, 2 physicians, 2 captains, 1 lieutenant, 5 sergeants, 8 corporals, 1 musician and 65 common soldiers; in all 88 men.

The great value of the contingent of the Germans, born abroad, was increased by the fact, that large numbers of them, especially the officers, of whom there were more than 5000, had received practical training in the military academies and in the armies of their fatherland. The participation of so many efficient officers and soldiers was of immeasurable importance to the North, for at the outbreak of the war the Confederates had far the greater number of officers who had received their training at West Point.

Like in all former wars so the Germans inspiringly demonstrated their loyalty in many ways. As early as January 9, 1861, **Karl Leopold Mathies,** who later on became a general, offered to the Union a company of soldiers, the whole equipment of which he paid from his own purse. Equally generous was **Dr. Karl Beck,** professor at Harvard, when his request for his own enlistment had been refused in view of his age, which was 60 years.

And when President Lincoln, on April 15, issued his first call for volunteers, the Germans responded in masses. Not more than three days thereafter 1200 Germans in Cincinnati stood ready to march. It was the "Ninth Regiment of Ohio," which for its gallant service won distinction and fame. In addition the Germans of Ohio formed the regiments No. 11, 28, 37, 47, 58, 67, 74, 106, 107, 108 and 165. Also the third regiment of cavalry and three batteries.

In New York the Germans were not less enthusiastic. The Turners formed the regiment "United Turner Rifles," whose entire outfit was donated by German citizens. Other German regiments were the Steuben Regiment; the 1st German Rifles; the 1st Astor Regiment; the 5th German Rifles; the Fremont Regiment; the Sigel Rifles; the 54th Regiment of Schwarze Jaeger; the 86th Regiment or Steuben Rangers; furthermore the Dickels Mounted Rifles; the 4th New York Cavalry; and Blenker's Battery.

The Germans of Pennsylvania formed the regiments 74 and 75, besides furnishing strong contingents to numerous other regiments. In Indiana the 36th regiment was entirely German; in Illinois the 24th and the 82nd. The 43rd regiment consisted entirely of the sons of "Latin Farmers" of Belleville. The Germans of Wisconsin were represented by the 9th and 26th regiment of that state; the Germans of Missouri in the 1st, 2nd, 3rd, 4th, 5th, 12th, 15th, 17th, 39th, 40th and 41st regiment.

This splendid response aroused in all Northern states boundless enthusiasm. Augustus Choate Hamlin, Lieutenant-Colonel and historian of the 11th army-corps, writes in his remarkable work "The battle of Chancellorsville": "The country rejoiced with great joy when it became known that the entire German population of the North rallied without hesitation to the support of the endangered Republic. The support was magnificent, and deserving the highest gratitude of the country. It is also remarkable that all of the revolutionists then in this country, and who had followed Kossuth, Garibaldi, Sigel and Hecker, should offer their services to the United States. It was, indeed, a grand sight, when the entire mass of German-speaking and German-born people rose as a man and stood firmly by the flag of the Republic. What would have been the fate of Missouri, Illinois and Indiana, at the commencement of the war, had it not been for the patriotic efforts of Sigel, Osterhaus, Schurz and Hecker, and their resolute German followers? Has the country yet recognized the importance and the full weight of these facts? Missouri certinly would have drifted away with the Southern tide, had it not been for the influence and resistance of these gallant men. The Germans were the first to take up arms and attempt to save the state. The first three loyal regiments raised in St. Louis were Germans almost

DEPARTURE FOR THE WAR. 1861.
(After a Painting by Thomas Nast).

to a man, and when the Home Guards of Missouri were first formed, none but Germans joined them. This movement on the part of the Germans was of vast aid to the Northern cause, and contributed greatly to its final success, and its influence and its value cannot be estimated with the gold of the nation."

Of the officers of German birth or origin many attained the highest military honors and degrees. Inseparably connected with the history of this great war are the names of the Major-Generals Peter Osterhaus, Karl Schurz, Franz Sigel, Julius Stahel, Samuel Peter Heinzelmann, August Kautz, G. Pennypacker, Friedrich Salomon, and Gottfried Weitzel. Also the names of the Generals Ammen, Louis Blenker, Louis von Blessing, Heinrich von Bohlen, Adolf Buschbeck, Adolf Hassendeubel, Friedrich Hecker, J. H. Heinzelmann, Knobelsdorff, Johann A. Koltes, William C. Küffner, Konrad Krez, Karl Leopold Mathies, August Mohr, Julius Raith, Prince Felix Salm-Salm, Karl Eberhard Salomon, Georg von Schack, Alexander von Schimmelpfennig, Alban Schöpf, Alexander von Schrader, Schriver, Schiras, Adolf von Steinwehr, Louis Wagner, Hugo Wangelin, Max Weber, August Willich, Isaak Wister and others.

The limited size of this volume forbids a recital of all gallant services performed by these Germans during the Civil War. We can mention only a few. First of all it should be remembered, that on April 18, 1861, three days after the fall of Fort Sumter, when the whole administration was in consternation, 530 Pennsylvania Germans rallied round the flag and entered Washington, to shield the capital from a threatening assault of the Secessionists. This resolute step and the fact, that the German Turners of Baltimore declared for the Union, kept Washington and the wavering State of Maryland from the hands of the Confederates.

The State of Missouri, the most important of all the uncertain border states, was also saved for the Union by German volunteers. The situation here was most critical, as in the city of St. Louis was located the great United States Arsenal of the West, containing the arms and amunition for at least 40,000 to 50,000 soldiers. Floyd of Virginia, while Secretary of War preceding Lincoln's administration, had stocked this arsenal to its utmost capacity in the expectation that it would certainly fall into the hands of the South. His hope in this respect was strengthened, when Governor Jackson of Missouri manifested the stand he would take in his reply to President Lincoln's requisition for Missouri's quota of the first call for troops with the defying words: "Your requisition, in my judgment, is illegal, unconstitutional, and revolutionary in its object; inhuman and diabolic, and cannot be complied with."

It was during this time, when the magnitude of the danger threatening the country was barely realized, that the German

Turners of St. Louis passed a resolution by which the Turn-Verein was dissolved, and in its stead a military organization formed to guard the Union and to sacrifice life and property, if necessary, to keep the county of St. Louis loyal to the administration in case the State of Missouri should decide to secede.

When it became known, that the Secessionists planned an assault on the arsenal, the Germans of St. Louis quickly formed four companies of volunteers under the command of their leaders Blair, Lyon, Sigel, Osterhaus, Schaefer and Schuettner. Then they took possession of the arsenal, and also captured on May 10, 1861, one thousand Secessionists, who had assembled at Camp Jackson near the southern part of the city, to seize the arsenal.

Among the higher German officers the most prominent were Osterhaus, Sigel and Schurz, conspicuous types all three of those champions of liberty, who upon the failure of the German revolution of 1848 came to America as political exiles.

Peter Osterhaus had become a citizen of Belleville, Ill. When the situation became critical in Missouri, he had an active part in organizing the German volunteers of St. Louis and in the capture of the arsenal and Camp Jackson. He was valiantly engaged in the battles at Wilsons Creek and Pea Ridge as well as in the campaign against Vicksburg. During the terrific struggle at Chatanooga in November 1863 he commanded the first division of General Grant's army corps and won glory in the famous "Battle among the Clouds" on Lookout Mountain. After fighting for hours, his troops ascended step by step the steep and rough mountain side, through deep gutters and ravines, over great rocks and fallen trees, until, reaching the earth-works of the enemy on top of the mountain, they carried his positions one and all.

Subsequently Osterhaus was with his troops in the daring assault on Missionary Ridge. Here he defeated the southern wing of the enemy, making many thousands of prisoners. As commander of a strong division Osterhaus participated also in Sherman's famous "March through Georgia." Later on he was chief of staff to General Canby during the Mobile campaign and at the surrender of General Kirby Smith's army.

Franz Sigel, who in 1848 had been general of a revolutionary army in Baden, was at the outbreak of the Civil War a citizen of St. Louis. During the occupation of the arsenal and the capture of Camp Jackson he was one of the leaders. These feats accomplished, he fought as commander of several regiments and batteries in Missouri and gained on March 6, 1862, with General Curtis against overwhelming forces the glorious victory at Pea Ridge, Arkansas. The battle lasted for three days. The decision came, when Sigel ordered his regiments to fall back behind the lines of artillery. as if preparing for retreat, while the artillery fired only blank shots, as if short of ammunition. Deceived by the ruse, the Confederates, sure of victory, advanced in close formation. But at once Sigel's regiments re-entered their positions between the batteries and, supported by the heavy guns, opened a rapid fire on the enemies, who thus surprised, were thrown into confusion. At this moment Sigel's cavalry dashed amidst their lines, slashing down all who had been spared by the bullets.

MONUMENT TO FRANZ SIGEL IN NEW YORK.
(Modelled by Karl Bitter).

Promoted to the rank of major-general, Sigel afterwards was ordered to Virginia. At Bull Run he commanded the right wing of Pope's 1st army corps and won on August 29 a decided advantage over Jackson. This success, though, was fruitless, as on the following day Pope's regiments were defeated by the enemy's forces, vastly superior in number. Sigel covered the retreat in masterly fashion, preventing a general rout.

103

After this battle Sigel commanded several army-corps in Pennsylvania, suffered at New Market a defeat by overwhelming forces, but made good again by repelling obstinate attacks on Harper's Ferry and the Maryland Heights.

Like all other German officers Sigel was greatly hampered by the petty jealousy and disdain of the American comrades in arms. Especially reprehensible in this regard was the conduct of those who were graduates of West Point. Of this circumstance Lieutenant-Colonel Hamlin, the historian of the 11th army-corps, in one of his works records a bitter complaint. Sigel felt himself in his operations so much hindered by such jealous men, that he resigned in May 1865 and returned to private life.

Similar were the experiences of **Carl Schurz,** who had been appointed brigadier-general in the army of the Potomac, which, however, in consequence of a continual change of commander-in-chief, one unfit man following on the heels of another, went from defeat to defeat. The most serious were those at Bull Run, Fredericksburg and Chancellorsville. At Chancellorsville the division of Schurz, together with those of Adolf von Steinwehr and General Devens, formed the 11th corps, which under command of General Howard, held the right wing of General Hooker's army. In the morning of May 2, 1863, Schurz, Steinwehr and other German officers discovered that the enemy, feigning a retreat, was preparing to turn the right wing of the Federal army. Without loss of time Schurz and Steinwehr informed headquarters of these suspicious movements, urgently requesting leave to take timely counter-action. But Hooker, believing that the enemy was in full retreat, did nothing to protect the threatened wing. Schurz now on his own responsibility ordered his regiments to take up positions fronting toward the West, from where he anticipated an attack. It came at 5 o'clock in the afternoon, when suddenly 18,000 Confederates, commanded by the able General Stonewall Jackson, burst from the forests and overran the division of General Devens. It was swept away in wild disorder, threatening to carry with it the German regiments. These, however, only 3000 strong, made the most strenuous efforts to stem the assault. It was pending these efforts that Colonel **Friedrich Hecker,** one of the men of 1848, was wounded seriously as he led his troops to a charge, carrying the flag of his 82d Illinois Regiment in hand. The situation became still more critical when the enemies appeared also in the rear. compelling the Germans to withdraw to better positions. But here their resistance was so obstinate, that the further advance of the Confederates came to a standstill.

Among the officers. who fought here like heroes, were Colonel **Buschbeck,** and Captain **Hubert Dilger,** whose battery

104

was most effectual in blocking Stonewall Jackson, who forfeited his own life for his victory.

The German regiments of Schurz and von Steinwehr held also in the battle at Gettysburg the most exposed positions, namely on the famous Cemetery Ridge, the strategic importance of which Steinwehr had first recognized. The battle, the bloodiest of the whole war, lasted for three days and culminated on July 3, 1863 in a grand assault by the Confederates.

The prelude to this attack was a bombardment from 145 heavy guns, which blazed forth like so many volcanoes. The air seemed full of missiles from every direction, their explosions enveloping Cemetery Ridge in clouds of smoke and poisonous gases. The terrific fire, answered by 100 guns, lasted for two long hours. Then suddenly emerged from the forests 15,000 Confederates, rank upon rank in gray, with shining bayonets, a never-to-be-forgotten sight. Approaching in double-quick pace, they reached in spite of the volleys of the Union soldiers the positions of the latter, and now a desperate struggle ensued man against man, during which the mutilated bodies of human beings and horses towered to heaps and hills. But the furious onslaught shattered on the heroic resistance of the defenders of Cemetery Ridge. The Confederates were thrown back with fearful loss in utter dissolution and compelled to retreat to Virginia, having lost more than 30,000 killed, wounded and prisoners. The loss of the Federals amounted to 23,000.

Schurz, Osterhaus and Steinwehr participated also in Sherman's march to Georgia and fought with distinction in the battles at Tunnel Hill, Buzzards Roost, Dalton, Resaca, Marietta and Atlanta.

Many were the skirmishes and engagements of minor importance in which it fell to the lot of the German soldiers to bear the brunt of battle. In what esteem their bravery was held by friend and foe, may appear from the following two episodes. When on June 7, 1862, the soldiers of General James Shield during the campaign in the Luray Valley complained of the hardships they had to endure, he answered, "The Germans are not half as well off as you are, but they hang on the enemy without respite." And General Lee, the commander-in-chief of the Confederate army, is reported, on best authority, to have exclaimed: "Take only these Dutch out of the Union army, and we will whip the Yankees easily."

A testimonial of great weight is also the splendid work on "The Battle of Chancellorsville" by Augustus Choate Hamlin, lieutenant-colonel and medical inspector of the U. S. army.

Of the major-generals and generals, born in Germany, several fell. The brilliant career of **Heinrich von Bohlen** ended on August 22, 1862, in the battle at Rappahannock

River, while leading his troops to attack. **Adolf Engelmann** and **Julius Raith** were killed in April 1862 at Shiloh; **Johann Koltes** died on August 30, 1862, in the battle at Bull Run. **Franz Hassendeubel** was mortally wounded during the siege of Vicksburg and died July 16, 1863. **Hugo Wangelin** lost at Ringgold his left arm, but after his recovery reported again to service and did valuable work in Georgia and Missouri. **Max Weber** was wounded in the battle at Antitam so seriously, that he had to quit service. The number of colonels, majors and other officers of German origin, who died on the battle-field, runs up to several hundred, that of the soldiers to many thousands. Almost all German regiments suffered terrific losses. The Sigel Rifles, forming the 52d regiment of New York, returned in October 1864 under command of Major Retzius with only 5 officers and 35 men. Brought up once more to its original strength of 2800 men, it came back at the end of the war only 200 strong. Of the 1200 United Turner Rifles only 462 returned; of the 1046 men of the De-Kalb regiment only 180.

So the history of the Civil War exhibits abundant evidence, that the German-Americans offered readily blood and life for the preservation of the Union.

* * * *

Many officers of German stock fought also with great distinction in the numerous Indian wars. The best known is General **George A. Custer,** whose ancestor, a Hessian soldier, was paroled in 1778 after Burgoyne's surrender at Saratoga. His name, Kuester, hard to pronounce for English tongues, was, like so many others, changed to a form of easier pronunciation. Custer was a graduate of West Point. As a commander of cavalry divisions he fought in many battles of the Civil War, and was appointed brigadier-general for gallantry. With great distinction he served in several campaigns against the Indians. But on June 26, 1876, when he with 250 men dashed into overwhelming masses of Sioux Indians, he became surrounded. In the desperate battle Custer as well as his brother, First Lieutenant **Thomas Custer,** and all soldiers were massacred to the last man. The fight is known as the Custer-massacre at the Little Big Horn River, Montana.

* * * *

Of German origin too, was Admiral **Winfield Scott Schley,** the hero of the great naval battle at Santiago de Cuba.

The first American ancestor of the Schleys was **Johann Thomas Schley,** a German schoolmaster, who in 1745 erected the first house in Frederick, Maryland. Many of his descendents became prominent in public life; but none of them rose to such fame as our admiral, who was born near Frederick October 9, 1839. A graduate of the U. S. Naval Academy at Annapolis, he took part in many engagements during the Civil War. In 1871 he participated also in the attack on the forts at the Salu River in Corea.

In 1884 he commanded a relief-expedition, sent out to find the Arctic explorer A. W. Greely, whose whereabouts were unknown. Schley succeeded in discovering him and six other survivors at Cape Sabine. All were in the very last stage of starvation. But by utmost care it was possible to keep the explorers alive and bring them back to the United States.

During the Spanish-American War of 1898, when Spain sent out a fleet of four cruisers and three destroyers, Schley was placed in command of the "Flying Squadron," which was dispatched to ward the hostile fleet off the coast of the United States and to prevent the same from reaching Havana along the north coast of Cuba. Admiral Sampson at the same time received orders, to close with a strong fleet the Channel of Yucatan. Deficiency in coal had compelled the Spanish fleet to seek refuge in the harbor of Santiago de Cuba. Here it remained, till forced by a strong American land army to leave this retreat. The sally occurred on July 3, at a time, when Schley happened to be in immediate command of his "Flying Squadron" as well as of the fleet of Sampson, who with one of his vessels was absent. The Spanish cruisers, followed by the destroyers, left the harbor in full speed, to make good their escape. But the American vessels kept close at their heels, opening at the same time a bombardment with their heavy guns. One after another the Spanish cruisers, hit by shells, caught fire and were run ashore by their crews, only to become total wrecks. 2000 of the crews, among them Admiral Cervera, were made prisoners. The news of the great victory reached the United States on the morning of the Fourth of July.

Never before, perhaps, was the great national holiday celebrated with such overwhelming enthusiasm.

Leaders in Agriculture, Industry and Commerce.

Great as were the services rendered to this country by German Americans in times of war and in political progress, these cannot be compared with the mighty impulse given to American culture. Everywhere about us in the United States can be found lasting evidence of the development wrought by their hands.

Viewing the hundreds of thousands who with their fellow citizens of native or alien birth marched into the virgin wilderness of the New World, we see them transforming the former abodes of beasts and Indians into fruitful lands and pleasant homesteads. Numerous States, especially Pennsylvania, New York, New Jersey, Maryland, the Virginias, Ohio, Indiana, Illinois, Michigan, Wisconsin, Minnesota, the Dakotas, Iowa, Nebraska, Missouri, Kansas, California, Oregon and Washington owe their prosperity essentially to the Germans. As agriculturists they won the admiration of all their neighbors. The comparative meagreness of the soil of their fatherland taught them to take care of their farms in a wise and economical way. They never fell into the habit of abusing the soil, which, as shown by many examples, in the New England States and in other parts of the country, results eventually in soil-exhaustion and the abandonment of farms. Whoever visits the beautiful counties of Pennsylvania, settled by the so-called Pennsylvania Dutch, must agree that farms in better condition than those which exist there cannot be found. And these farms are still inhabited by the descendants of the early German settlers, who attained prosperity by diligence and rational management.

The great importance of the Germans in American agriculture is best seen by the census of 1900, showing that in this year 525,250 farms, or 10.6 per cent. of all farms in the United States were in German hands and that 41.3 per cent. of the whole farming population were Germans. These numbers include, however, not the farms owned by Americans of German stock.

Among the German farms of the Western and Northwestern states many embrace enormous stretches of land. To fence for instance the wheat fields owned by **Johann P. Vollmer** in Idaho, 250 miles of wire are required. Similar big farms are owned by **A. L. Stuntz** in Idaho; **S. A. Knapp** in Iowa; **John Dern** in Nebraska, and others.

108

German influence on development in American agriculture during the 18th century has been sketched briefly in a former chapter. To the Germans is attributed by Rush the distinction of being the first to use artificial fertilizer.

Johann Schwerdkopf was the first who grew strawberries by the acres on Long Island and provided with these luxurious fruits the markets of New York. Other Germans, as **Thomas Echelburger** in York, Pa.; the **Rappists** of Harmony, **Indiana; Martin Baum** in Cincinnati; **George Husmann, Michael Pöschel, Hermann Burkhardt** in Missouri and many others followed the example of the settlers of Germantown and began to cultivate grapes in different parts of the United States.

The Germans were instrumental also in establishing the culture of vine, oranges, lemons, apricots, pears, apples, prunes, cherries, figs, and many other fruits in California and elsewhere. They also introduced the sugar-beet, the culture of which has in recent years grown in many states to immense proportions.

For the scientific development of agriculture the works of **Eugene Woldemar Hilgard** became of greatest importance. This man was born in 1833 in the Palatinate, but was brought by his father at an early age to Belleville, Illinois, the center of the "Latin Settlements." Later on Hilgard studied in Germany, then became a professor of geology and agricultural chemistry at the University of California and director of the State Agricultural Station. In this position he devoted his efforts to the utilization of the arid deserts of California and Arizona, and succeeded in transforming many of them into fertile regions. Of his literary works his book on "Soils," published in 1906, is one of greatest value among writings on this subject.

A similar position as that of Hilgard was held for many years by **Charles A. Goessmann,** a native of Naumburg, Germany. He has been director of the Massachusetts Agricultural Experiment Station and professor of chemistry in the Massachusetts Agricultural State College. **George Ellwanger,** a native of Würtemberg, founded in 1839 in Rochester, N. Y., a nursery in fruit- and ornamental trees, which in time became the most famous in America and a model-institution for others.

Forestry was also taken up by the Germans. **George H. Wirt, Samuel Pennypacker, John Frederick Hartranft** and **Carl Schurz** called the attention of the American nation to the heavy sin, committed by the thoughtless or covetous destruction of the forest, of which many had disappeared entirely. At first, people would laugh about the "German idealists," but soon enough became aware, that they were right. The reports Schurz had made to Congress on this subject were remembered, and when at the same time Baron von Steuben, a Prussian high-forester and a relative of Major-General von

Steuben, visited the United States and called attention to the rapid decline of her forests, public interest on the question was aroused. On suggestion of **Bernhard E. Fernow,** a practical forester, in 1882 an American Forestry Congress was called to meet in Cincinnati, resulting in the organization of the American Forestry Association. Through the agitation of this society the Department of Agriculture as well as numerous states and universities were induced to establish schools of forestry, which promise to become a real blessing to our country.

The custom of the Germans, to beautify their homesteads with trees and flowers, led to horticulture, which is still a specialty with the German Americans. Many of the most beautiful parks and cemeteries of the United States were planned by German landscape gardeners. Of these one of the most successful was **Adolf Strauch,** a native of Silesia. His training he received from the famous landscape gardener of the Imperial parks at Schoenbrunn and Laxenburg, near Vienna. While visiting America in 1854, he was induced to design the plans for several private parks near Cincinnati. His greatest work was the Spring Grove Cemetery of the same city, an artistic combination of park and burial ground. A complete artistic success when finished, Spring Grove Cemetery served as model for many other cemeteries, among them Woodlawn, New York; Crown Hill, Indianapolis; and others in Chicago, Nashville, Detroit, Cleveland, Buffalo, Hartford, etc. In laying out the world-known Central Park of New York in 1859, Germans performed by far the largest share.

In the manufacturing of food products the German Americans have long been in the lead. The **American Cereal-** or **Quaker Oats Company** in Akron, Ohio, was organized by **Ferdinand Schumacher,** a Hanoveranian. The **Havemeyers** in New York and the **Spreckels** in San Francisco made themselves the chief factors in the American sugar industry. The first became the sugar-kings of the East and organized the **American Sugar Refining Company,** better known as the Sugar Trust, who commanded in 1900 a capital of more than $150,000,000 and occupied in its twenty refineries and many offices more than 20,000 people, while other 10,000 were kept busy in the barrel-factories, in shipping and other work.

The Spreckels monopolized the whole sugar production west of the Mississippi. When Claus Spreckels, the founder of the Company, died in 1908, he left a fortune of more than 60 million dollars.

The **H. J. Heinz Company** in Pittsburg, founded by **Heinrich J. Heinz,** a Pennsylvania German, is known throughout the United States for their "57 varieties" of preserved fruits and vegetables. Its plants cover an area of more than 160 city lots; in addition branches are maintained in other states as well as in Canada and Spain. The products of more than 30,000 acres flow into the different factories, which keep 4000 persons permanently busy, while at the time of gathering in the crops about 40,000 people are employed. A rival firm in the preserving and pickling business is that of the **Lutz & Schramm Company,** also in Pittsburgh. Other well-known pickling establishments are the **J. O. Schimmel Preserving Company** of Jersey City, and the **Bosman & Lohman Company** at Norfolk, Va.

The most prominent firms in the production of bakers' and confectioners' supplies are also of German origin. **William Ziegler,** a Pennsylvania German, was the founder of the **Royal Baking Powder Company** in Chicago. **John Valentine Hecker,** member of the German firm **Hecker Brothers,** manufacturers of the Heckers' self-raising flour, effected a consolidation of the flour-mills of New York, called the **Hecker-Jones-Jewell Milling Company,** of which Hecker became president.

Karl and **Maximilian Fleischmann** organized the **Fleischmann Company,** which is the most prominent concern among producers of yeast.

In the coffee trade **Hermann Sielcken** made the importing firm of **Crossman & Sielcken** in New York one of the leading in America.

In the production of beverages German Americans take the lead, — especially in the brewing industry, which grew to astonishing proportions through their energy. Beer had been brewed in America by the Dutch and English during the seventeenth and eighteenth centuries. In 1810 the whole output amounted to 182,000 barrels. This quantity increased to 740,000 barrels in 1850. The brewers, up to that time exclusively Anglo-Americans, produced a heavy, very intoxicating beer similar to the English ale. In the place of this the Germans introduced the lagerbeer, which contains much less alcohol and for this reason is more suited to the American climate. In time it displaced the ale almost entirely, incidentally it helped greatly to lessen the consumption of whiskey and other liquors, in which the people of America were wont to indulge heavily in former times. And so the claim, that the introduction of the lagerbeer had beneficial effect upon the population in behalf of temperance, is, to some extent, justified.

To what enormous proportions the brewing industry has been developed by the Germans is seen from the fact that at present the output of beer amounts to more than 66 million barrels per year. According to the census for 1910 in that year 54,579 workmen and 11,507 clerks were employed, who received in wages $64,000,000. The value of the capital invested in this industry amounted to $671,158,000, the value of material used to $96,596,000 and the value of the production to $374,730,000. The establishments of many of the large breweries, such as, for instance, of the **Anheuser-Busch Brewing Association** in St. Louis, the **Pabst-** and the **Schlitz Breweries** in Milwaukee, the **Ehret-** and the **Ruppert Breweries** in New York, and others rank among the industrial wonders of America.

As tobacconists **G. W. Gail** and **Christian Ax** started in Baltimore the firm **Gail & Ax,** which was combined with the American Tobacco Company in 1891. The same city also is the seat of the great tobacco firm of **Marburg Brothers.**

Among Americas great cattle-men **Heinrich Miller,** born 1828 in Würtemberg, and **Carl Lux** from Baden became the most successful and the wealthiest. When they arrived in 1850 in New York, both were poor fellows. But they worked hard and had a keen sight for opportunities. In 1856 they began in California with cattle-raising. Providing the markets of San Francisco and other cities, they became not only the largest land-owners but also the greatest stock-owners in the Far West. In California they owned 800,000 acres, 80,000 heads of cattle and 100,000 of sheep. Also they controlled extensive stretches of land and large herds in Oregon and Nevada. Other great stockmen of German descent are **James C. Dahlman** in Nebraska and **S. A. Knapp** in Iowa.

Among the meat packing houses the firm of **Schwarzschild & Sulzberger** in New York ranks among the most important in America. Founded in 1853 by **Ferdinand Sulzberger** from Baden, it employs at present an army of 10,000 men, and its transactions amount to more than 100,000,000 dollars annually.

As tanners and manufacturers of leather German Americans have been very resourceful and are contributing a material share to the commerce of this country. One of the largest tanneries is that of the firm **Robert H. Foerderer** in Frankford, Pa.; others are **Pfister & Vogel,** and **Trostel & Zohrlant** in Milwaukee, the **Charles A. Schieren Co.,** **Oscar Scherer & Bros.,** and **Charles Hauselt** in New York; **Schoellkopf & Co.** in Buffalo; **Schmidt & Co.** in Detroit; the **Ruepping Leather Co.** in Fond du Lac; **C. Moench & Co.** in Boston; the **Wolff Process Leather Co.** and the **Keystone Leather** Co. in Philadelphia; **Kaufherr & Co.** and **William Zahn** in Newark.

Of German origin is also the **American Felt Company.** Its large factories at Dolgeville, N. Y., were founded by **Alfred Dolge,** born 1848 in Chemnitz, Saxony. He came to America in 1869 and in the town, now bearing his name, began the manufacture of felt, especially of the material used in piano actions. In 1903 he organized in connection with H. E. Huntington extensive felt factories in New Dolgeville, Cal.

That the Germans are entitled to the credit of having established the iron- and steel industries in America, has been shown

THE ANHEUSER-BUSCH BREWERIES IN ST. LOUIS.

in a former chapter. It may truly be said that they laid the foundation to the greatest steel corporation now existing.

Andreas and Anton Klomann from Trier in Rhenish Prussia started in the middle of the 19th century in Pittsburgh a factory for the production of axles for railway cars. In forging these axles, they used a treatment invented by Andreas Klomann, which had so many advantages, that for their superior quality these axles were preferred by all railroads. Among the regular customers of the Klomanns was the Pittsburgh, Fort Wayne and Chicago Railway Company, the purveyor of which, Thomas Miller, bought a share in the Klomann factories in 1859. When the Civil War brought large orders, and, at the same time, an increase in the price for axles from two cents per pound to twelve cents, larger factories became necessary. At the same time the firm was made a corporation, known as the Iron City Forge Company. While its business flourished, the harmony among the partners, however, failed. First, Anton Klomann was bought out in 1863; the same happened to Andreas Klomann, when on May 2, 1864, Andrew Carnegie entered as a member of the company. With the phenomenal growth of this enterprise came consolidations and several changes in name, first to Union Iron Mills Company, then to Carnegie Steel Company, and finally to United States Steel Corporation.

With the history of this concern the names of two Pennsylvania Germans, Henry C. Frick and Charles M. Schwab are closely connected. Frick organized, besides, in 1882 the Frick Coal and Coke Company, which is now the largest coke producer in the world, operating about 40,000 acres of coal and 12,000 coke ovens with a daily capacity of 25,000 tons of coke.

Schwab became president of the Carnegie Steel Company in 1897. When the Carnegie interests were merged in the larger United States Steel Corporation in 1901, he became its first president, remaining until 1904, when he resigned, to become president of the Bethlehem Steel Corporation.

Another German captain of American industries was Heinrich Wehrum, the creator of the great Lackawanna Iron and Steel Works at Buffalo and Seneca, N. Y. The name of F. Augustus Heinze, born in Brooklyn, N. Y., is inseparably connected with the history of the American copper industry. He was to his death president of the United Copper Company, which he had organized. Johann August Roebling, the famous bridge-builder, was the father of the great cable wire spinneries John A. Roeblings Sons Company at Trenton, N. J.

Conspicuous is the record of Germans who founded car building factories of great magnitude. Johann Georg Brill, born in Cassel, created the J. G. Brill Company, whose establishment in Philadelphia is unsurpassed in the production of

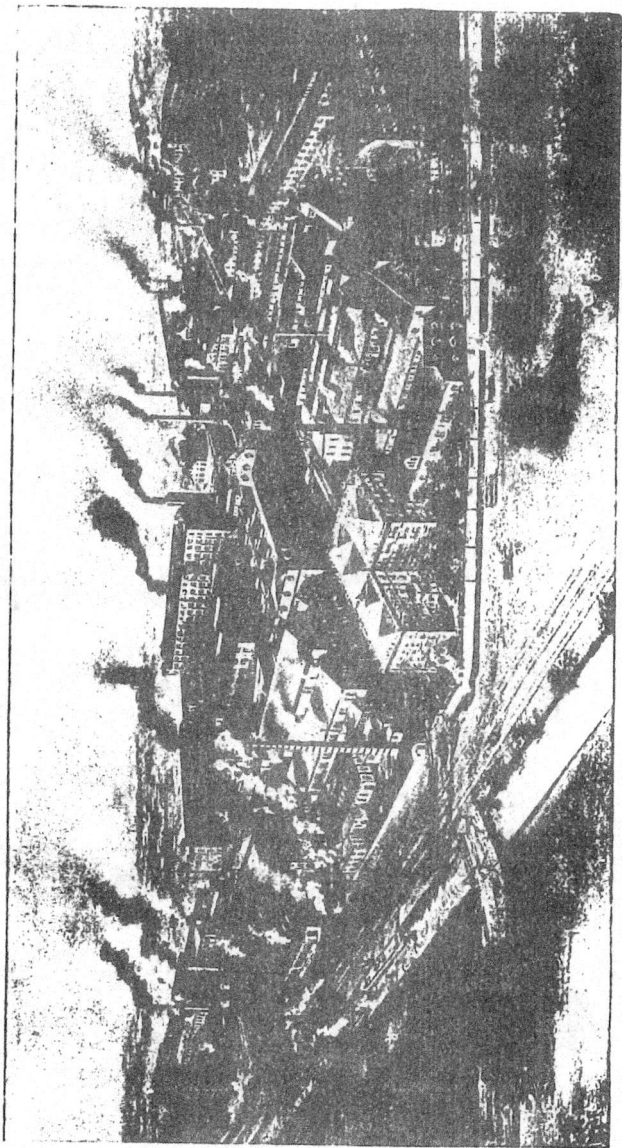

THE CABLE WIRE SPINNERIES OF J. A. ROEBLINGS SONS COMPANY, AT TRENTON, N. J.

electric street cars and trucks. The sons of the founder acquired many additional plants in Elizabeth, N. J.; Springfield, Mass.; Cleveland, O.; Danville, Ill.; and St. Louis.

J. H. Kobusch established an extensive concern in 1887 at St. Louis known as the St. Louis Car Company, which manufactures street and railway cars. Webster Wagner, descending from a Palatine family in Palatine Bridge, N. Y., organized the Wagner Palace Car Company, whose excellent railway cars are unequalled for comfort and beauty.

The largest vehicle factories of America, operated by the Studebaker Corporation in South Bend, Ind., and Detroit, Mich. are the crowning result of untiring work by five Pennsylvania Germans, the Studebaker brothers, whose family name originally was Stutenbäcker. Their annual output amounts at present to over 100,000 vehicles including more than 10,000 automobiles.

In the manufacture of machinery German genius, capacity and efficiency have been so well exemplified that it becomes difficult to single out a branch wherein some German has not pointed the way. The Aultman & Miller Company in Canton and Akron, Ohio, started by descendents of Pennsylvania German families, was one of the foremost producers of agricultural machinery and has lately become a part of the great International Harvester Company.

Large firms in the manufacture of agricultural implements were organized by Orendorff in Canton, Ill., and by Weusthoff & Getz in Dayton, Ohio.

Ferdinand Thun, a native of Barmen, Rhenish Prussia, founded the Textile Machine Works in Reading, Pa., whose output by its excellence has practically transplanted from Europe to America a number of industries which give bread to veritable armies of workmen.

Peter Pauly founded in 1856 the Pauly Jail Building Company in St. Louis, Mo., whose specialty is the construction and furnishing of jails and other houses of correction. At the same place Wilhelm and Friedrich Niedringhaus created the National Enameling and Stamping Company, which converts tinplates into products of endless variety. As producers of fine pottery and art tiles the plant of Balthasar Kreischer in Kreischersville, Staten Island, N. Y., are acknowledged to be the oldest and most extensive in the United States.

As skillful cabinet makers the Germans have been renowned for centuries. Their handicraft has reared in the United States an industry of high order, giving employment to thousands and thousands of busy hands. Among the many firms, devoted to this industry, one of the most notable is the Dubuque Cabinet Makers Association, the founder and president of which is Richard Herrmann, born at Chemnitz, Saxony.

In close relation with cabinet making is the manufacture

116

THE FACTORIES OF THE STUDEBAKER CORPORATION.

of musical instruments. That Germans were the first who made organs and pianos in America, has been pointed out in a former chapter. That was during the 18th century. Since then this industry has been principally in the hands of Germans. In 1833 **Conrad Meyer** constructed the first pianos with full iron frames. This innovation, made with regard to the peculiar climatic conditions of the Eastern United States, proved such a success, that it found acceptance also in all European countries. The 19th century saw the rise of a large number of manufacturers of pianos. **Wilhelm Lindemann** established in 1836 the firm **Lindemann & Sons** in New York. In the ensuing year **Wilhelm Knabe** started manufacturing in Baltimore with an ever growing plant, which in our days became the nucleus of the **American Piano Company.** In 1852 **Albert Weber** founded the **Weber Piano Company**; in 1853 **Heinrich Engelhard Steinweg,** assisted by his sons Karl, Heinrich, Wilhelm, Theodor and Albert established the firm of **Steinway & Sons,** which at present produces not less than 7000 pianos annually, and for the quality of her instruments gained the highest distinctions at the World's expositions held in America as well as in Europe.

Kranich & Bach, Sohmer & Co., Decker & Son, Steck & Co., Strich & Zeidler in New York and many more in other cities may well inscribe their German names as a mark of merit upon their splendid instruments.

The pioneer in making violins in America was **Georg Gemünder,** born 1816 at Ingelfingen, Würtemberg. The instruments made by him and his sons in Astoria, L. I., rival in their wonderful quality of tone the best found anywhere.

What can be accomplished by energy, perseverance and technical skill is illustrated by the great success of German Americans in the various branches of the textile industry, particularly in the Eastern parts of the United States. Thus guided are the **Botany Worsted Mills,** the **Gera Mills** and the **Garfield Mills** in Passaic, N. J., establishments engaged in making worsted goods. Likewise the **Fern Rock Mills** at Philadelphia. **Wilhelm Horstmann,** born 1785 at Cassel, was the pioneer in American silk passamenterie. The concern in Philadelphia, which still bears his name, grew in time to be one of the largest in this country.

Friedrich Baare established the silk spinneries in Schoharie, N. Y., and Paterson, N. J.: **H. Schniewind** those in Sunbury, Pa.; **Robert Schwarzenbach** those in Altoona, Pa., and the brothers **Robert** and **Hermann Simon** those in Union Hill, N. J., and Easton, Pa. **Ludwig Sutro** is the founder of the **Sutro Bros. Braid Company** in New York. **Ferdinand Thun** and **Henry Janssen** established the **Berkshire Knitting Mills** and the **Narrow Fabric Company** at Reading, Pa. At the same place are located also the great glove- and hosiery factories of **Nolde & Horst** and **E. Richard Meinig.**

With the great forward strides of chemistry in Germany the sons of the Fatherland in America are striving to keep pace. There is almost an endless list of firms engaged in the production of pharmaceutical preparations, of artificial fertilizer or of colors for ceramics and the dyer's trade. Among such firms those of **Roessler & Hasslacher, H. A. Metz & Co., Heller & Merz, Maas & Waldstein, Eimer & Amend** in New York, **Louis & Karl Dohme** in Baltimore, **Weightman & Rosengarten** in Philadelphia, **Herf & Frerichs** and the **Mallinckrodt Chemical Works** in St. Louis are regarded as the most important.

The manufacturing of lead pencils was begun in 1849 by **Eberhard Faber,** a member of the well-known Faber family in Nürnberg. The present factories of the firm are located in Greenpoint, L. I., and employ about 1000 men. A rival concern is the **Eagle Pencil Company,** organized in 1865 by **Heinrich Berolzheimer.**

Foremost place in the production of scientific and optical apparatus is held by the firm **Bausch & Lomb Optical Co.** in Rochester, N. Y. The establishment was founded in 1853 by **Johann Jakob Bausch,** born July 25, 1830, in Würtemberg, and **Heinrich Lomb,** born November 24, 1828, in Hessen Cassel. To-day it ranks among the best in America and is unsurpassed for the quality of its products.

As engravers in wood and copper many Germans have won distinction. While in the now abandoned art of wood engraving **Gustav Krüll, Friedrich Jüngling, Henry Wolf, Ernst Schladitz, William Müller** and others were perfect masters, **Louis Prang** in Boston was the pioneer and successful developer of lithography in America. The most admirable of his reproductions were a set of views from the Yellowstone National Park, after water color paintings by Thomas Moran; a series of battle-scenes of the Civil War after paintings of famous masters; and reproductions of the most select Chinese ceramics in the William Th. Walters Collection at Baltimore.

The well-known **American Lithographic Company,** the prominent lithographing firms of **J. Ottmann** and **Julius Bien** in New York, the **Gugler Company** in Milwaukee, the **Hoen Company** in Baltimore, the **Goes Company** in Chicago and many others were established by men of German origin.

The same is true of the **F. A. Ringler Company,** in New York, which is one of the largest institutions for designing, photo-engraving and electrotyping. The founder, **F. A. Ringler,** was born 1852 at Friedwald, Hesse-Cassel.

Of the men, who became widely known for their organizing talents and as leaders of American industries, several are of German origin. **Friedrich Weyerhäuser,** born 1834 in Nieder-Saulheim in Hessen, rose from the owner of a small saw-mill to be a ruler in the American lumber business. Having control over the Weyerhäuser Syndicate, he was commonly known as the "Lumber-king" and it was said of him that his fortune even surpassed that of John D. Rockefeller. This monarch of the Standard Oil Company also acknowledged German origin. His American ancestor, Johann Peter Rockefeller (Roggenfelder) came in 1735 from Bonefeld in Rhenish Prussia and is buried at Larrison Corners, N. J. **John Wannamaker,** descending from a Pennsylvania German family Wannenmacher, is known as the originator of the modern department store. Having opened in 1861 a small store in Philadelphia, he managed by the reliability of his goods to secure public attention to his store in such degree, that he soon could open in Philadelphia as well as in New York establishments on the grandest scale, the transactions amounting to millions in every month. The so-called department stores became the models for countless similar institutions in almost every American and European city.

To the list of such leaders of industry the names of many other men might be added, who at the helm of great corporations and enterprises have built for themselves enviable reputations by upholding German traditions of business probity. In conclusion it should be stated, that this chapter intends to convey only some idea of the enormous activity of men of German birth or lineage in the agricultural, industrial and commercial life of the Uniter States. To do justice to all entitled to have their achievements recorded in this connection, would be an undertaking far beyond the possibilities of this volume.

The North American Turner Bund and Its Influence on the Physical Development of the American Nation.

When in the years 1810 and 1811 the nations of Europe longed to throw off the heavy yoke of Napoleon I., Germany possessed among her patriots a man, who recognized the necessity of preparing the people systematically for the great coming struggle. This man was Dr. Friedrich Ludwig Jahn, a native of the province Brandenburg, Prussia. To make the German youth capable of bearing arms and to harden them for the imminent war of liberation, he resolved to introduce gymnastic exercises among his students and to infuse them at the same time with a patriotic love for freedom. In the spring of 1811, Jahn opened in the Hasenheide near Berlin the first public "Turnplatz," where 500 young students responded to his call and indulged in gymnastic exercises under his direction. In spite of the freedom he accorded his scholars, Jahn was, however, a stern disciplinarian in many other respects, and compelled them to maintain good order and to observe good manners.

Aided by men of like sympathies Jahn founded in the same year the "Deutschen Bund," an organization, the members of which were drawn from students of all German universities. In this way the great movement spread over all Germany. Everywhere the young men banded together for patriotic motives and formed gymnastic societies.

In what enthusiastic manner these Turners responded to the call to arms in 1813, and how great their part was in the liberation of Germany, are facts well known to every student of history.

Three disciples of Jahn, namely **Carl Beck, Carl Follen,** and **Franz Lieber,** introduced Jahn's system of physical training to the United States and incorporated it in the liberal education of the colleges and universities. Supported by John G. Coffin, John C. Warren, George Bancroft, Daniel Webster and J. G. Cogswell, the Germans established in 1826 at Harvard University, in Boston and Northampton, Mass., the first gymnasiums in America based on Jahn's models. Beck also translated Jahn's book "Deutsche Turnkunst" into

English and published it in Northampton. Also through public lectures the three pioneers of gymnastics made it clear, that for a republic the advantages of such exercises consist in that they unite the different elements of the people in common activity and bring classes into close contact, which by their different education and mode of life would otherwise remain apart. Furthermore, they stated that the American climate with its sudden changes, the easiness of travel without physical strain, the free institutions and the dependency of the country on the great masses of the people in case of war demand gymnasiums. "For a time," so Dr. Warren of Harvard stated, "the introduction of gymnastic exercises throughout the country promised to be the beginning of a new epoch of education. As long as they charmed by their novelty these exercises were pursued with zest, but since their value and importance was not generally understood, they were gradually neglected, and finally forgotten. However, the results which these institutions accomplished excelled in my opinion, the most extravagant expectations."

The movement came to new life again when the great tide of the Men of 1848 flowed into this country; these hundreds of thousands of enthusiastic young men, who bore in their breasts the famous motto of the German Turners: "Frisch! Fromm! Fröhlich! Frei!" and were convinced, that a sound body is the necessary preliminary condition for a sound mind.

Eager to conserve their own elasticity and to bequeath to their children the physical and ethical education they had received in the fatherland, these men organized everywhere gymnastic societies, the "Turn-Vereine." The first, established in November 1848, was the Cincinnati Turngemeinde, which still exists. The New York Turngemeinde was organized in the same year and was followed soon by numerous others, which in 1850 centralized in the **"North American Turner-bund"** or "The Gymnastic Union." Its societies endeavor to extend the practice of physical training to all without discrimination as to age or sex. The boy, the man, the girl, the woman, even the father and mother, are not merely tolerated, but are urged to participate in the gymnastic exercises of the society. According to the statistics, compiled January 1, 1915, the Union is composed of 218 societies and a membership of 37,941. The enrollment in the various gymnasium classes was as follows: 4989 Seniors; 3090 Juniors; 2502 Business Men; 7198 Women; 9264 Boys; 7958 girls. The singing and dramatic sections had 2286 members and the women's section 6770. In all the Union had 54,999 members over 14 years, and 17,322 members under 14 years.

Many of the societies also maintain elementary schools, freehand and mechanical drawing schools, schools for the study of German, and girls' industrial schools. From time to time they also arrange free lectures and sessions, in which topics of common interest are discussed. By holding occasionally gymnastic festivals, the attention of the public is kept alive. Every four years the Union arranges national festivals with competitive gymnastics between the societies. At such festivals often more than 3000 active turners participated. They always aroused such interest, that the practice of the German system of physical training was gradually taken up by all large cities in the land.

But the Union was not satisfied with these results.

When in 1880 the Turnerbund held a convention at Indianapolis, the suggestion was made to introduce physical training into the public schools. "We could not conceive of a more beautiful gift," said the first speaker of the executive committee, "than this to bestow upon the American people. It seems to me that this should be a worthy enterprise, for whosoever has conquered the youth has gained the future." After this proposition had been accepted, every favorable opportunity presenting itself was used to petition boards of education to introduce gymnastics. Always ready to co-operate with school boards, the turner societies often gave their teachers gratuitiously for years, in order to let results convince skeptical school boards of the value of school gymnastics.

From the annual report of the Turnerbund for the year 1914 it appears, that gymnastics were introduced into the schools of 76 cities either by the direct efforts of the Turner societies of these cities or through the efforts of the district organizations. Many colleges and universities, also the Military Academy at West Point and the Naval Academy at Annapolis joined the movement, engaging mostly teachers which had received their physical training at the training school, the Union maintains since a number of years in Indianapolis. In nearly all of these institutions the participation in the exercises is obligatory.

As the activity of the North American Gymnastic Union extends now over a period of more than 66 years, it is clear that many millions of American children, men and women have profited greatly by these exercises. As they improved in body as well as in spirit, the whole nation gained immensely.

That the German turners belong to the most loyal citizens of the Union, they demonstrated, as has been told in another chapter, by their participation in the Civil War, during which they fought with heroic enthusiasm for the preservation of our Union.

From all these facts it appears, that the German Turners have contributed their share toward the cultural development of the American nation.

123

The Influence of German Learning and Methods on Education in the United States.

Germany is proverbially known as the land of great thinkers, philosophers and scholars. Through many centuries her brightest intellects have been at work perfecting her educational institutions. From an experience covering a period of over a thousand years of indefatigable research and discriminative investigation, have been evolved superior methods of instruction which cannot but present the highest standards of thoroughness and efficiency.

This ardent love for science, characteristic of the German nation, distinguished also many of those Germans, who in Colonial times made America their home. Numerous teachers were amongst them, as for instance **Johann Thomas Schley,** the ancestor of the family of which Admiral Schley was a distinguished member. Another of such teachers was **Christoph Dock,** who for his excellent methods of teaching has been called "the American Pestalozzi" and whose work on pedagogics, written in 1754, was the first published on this subject in America.

The value of these methods was appreciated by no one more than Benjamin Franklin, in whose printing office many of the schoolbooks used by the Germans were printed. Having become acquainted on a trip through Germany with the splendid institutions of the university at Goettingen, he gave the impulse to a transformation of the Public Academy of Philadelphia into a seat of learning along corresponding lines, creating an institution, out of which developed the present University of Pennsylvania. On his request this university opened a department for German language and literature. Franklin also donated $1000 to the Franklin High School, which was established by the Germans in Lancaster, Pa., and exists still to-day.

Among many other schools, maintained by the Germans, a seminary for female teachers existed in Bethlehem, Pa. How far ahead on the subject of women's education were the views of these Germans over those of the Puritans in New England, may be judged from the fact, that, when a proposition was made in 1793 to establish a similar seminary in Plymouth, Mass., this project was defeated as undesirable on the ground "that in such a school women might become more learned than their future husbands!"

A more liberal spirit took place in the New England States, when during the first half of the 19th century many Americans of high standing went to Germany, to complete their studies. Among these men were Emerson, Longfellow, Bancroft, Everett, Curtis, Ticknor, and the noted pedagogues Griscom of New York, Bache from Philadelphia, and Stowe from Ohio, who travelled to Europe to study the methods of teaching. To these visitors referred Professor Charles W. Eliot, President Emeritus of Harvard University, when he, at a banquet given on May 9, 1913, by the German Publication Society, responded to the toast "The Debt of America to Germany." He said:

"The educational obligations of America to Germany are indeed wide and deep. They relate to literature, science, art, education, and religion. The German gifts were first communicated through a few young pioneers from America, who, after having received a partial education here, went over to Germany to study more deeply and intensively. The universities to which these American students resorted in the early part of the 19th century were in part recent creations, and in part reconstructions on old foundations; but how rich they were, how free, and how strong! — The American pioneers brought back various knowledges, various skills, and many pregnant doctrines. The variety of knowledge and skill which could be procured at the German universities at that early day was something astounding to these American youths, something indescribably rich and various. With their own personal experiences and gains they brought back also to America the structure of the modern German university, then young in Germany and in America not yet conceived of. They had, moreover, absorbed that noble German policy of academic freedom, freedom for the student and the teacher alike. This academic freedom meant emancipation from tradition and prejudice, and from authority, whether governmental or ecclesiastical. They saw, also, how two great doctrines which had sprung from the German Protestant Reformation had been developed by Germans from seed then planted in Germany. The first was the doctrine of universal education, developed from the Protestant conception of individual responsibility; and the second was the great doctrine of civil liberty, liberty in industries, in society, in government, liberty with order under law. These two principles took their rise in Protestant Germany; and America has been the greatest beneficiary of that noble teaching.

The pioneers from New England in the first half of the 19th century have been followed by a stream of American youth, going over to enlarge their experiences, to make new observations, to put in practice the inductive method of arriving at the truth, and to learn to think profoundly and accurately in the German universities. That stream has flowed backward all over this country, fertilizing it with German thought and German methods. These thousands of American students have absorbed in Germany that splendid spirit of scientific research now developed in all fields of knowledge on the same method and in the same spirit. ʿScientific research has been learnt through practice in Germany by thousands of American students and teachers. It is impossible to describe or even imagine what an immense intellectual gift this has been from Germany to America. For this perfected spirit and method of research America is more indebted to Germany than to any other nation, because the range of German research has been wider and deeper than has been seen in any other nation.

There is another bond of union between Germany and America. ·The Teutonic peoples set a higher value on truth in speech, thought and action than any other peoples. They all love truth; they seek it; they woo it. They respect the man who speaks and acts the truth even to his own injury.ʾ The English Bacon said of truth: "It is the sovereign good of human nature." That is what all the Teutonic peoples believe. ·They want to found their action on facts, not fancy; on truth, the demonstrated truth, not on imagination. I say that here is a fine bond of union, a real likeness of spirit, a community in devotion and worship among the Teutonic peoples. Let us hope that at no distant day this common worship, this common devotion, will result in common benefi-cent action."— ·

Of Germans, appointed as teachers at American colleges and universities, **Karl Beck, Karl Follen and Franz Lieber,** spoken of in former chapters, were the first. As among their pupils we read the names of A. P. Peabody, Longfellow, Emerson, and Margaret Fuller. When Follen in 1825 opened the first class at Harvard for German language and literature, there were no German books procurable, and so Follen was obliged to compile text books of his own. Peabody in his "Reminiscences" says about it: "The German Reader for Beginners, compiled by our teacher, was furnished to the class in single sheets as it was needed, and was printed in Roman type, there being no German type within easy reach. There could not have been a happier introduction to German literature than this little volume. It contained choice extracts in prose, and poems from Schiller, Goethe, Herder, and several other poets of kindred if inferior fame. But in the entire volume Dr. Follen rejoiced especially in several battle-pieces from Körner, the soldier and martyr of liberty. I never have heard recitations which have impressed me so strongly as the reading of those pieces by Dr. Follen, who would put into them all the heart and soul that had made him too much a lover of his country to be suffered to dwell in it. He appended to the other poems, anonymously, a death-song in memory of Körner, which we all knew to be his own, and which we read so often and so feelingly, that it sank indelibly into permanent memory; and I find that after an interval of sixty years it is as fresh in my recollection as the hymns that I learned in my childhood." —

It was only a few years later, that a number of eminent American schoolmen, among them Horace Mann from Massachusetts, went to Europe for the special purpose of studying the methods of education in the different countries. Their reports, together with the work on Prussian schools, by the French professor Victor Cousin proved to be of enormous influence in matters of education and led in 1837 to the establishment of the University of Michigan, planned and patterned entirely after German ideas.

To a like extent at the foundation of Johns Hopkins University in Baltimore the principles of German universities were adopted, among them freedom from all denominational influences; high standards and high ideals; encouragement in every manner of the spirit of research in creation of a school for post-graduate studies, etc. Of the earlier members of the faculty nearly all had received their degree at German universities.

The example, set by Johns Hopkins University, was followed by the University of Chicago, Leland Stanford University in San Francisco, Harvard University in Cambridge, Yale University in New Haven, Columbia University in New York, and by many others since.

To make her system of education accessible to the study of all American pedagogues, Germany presented it at the world's expositions at Chicago and St. Louis in the most comprehensive manner, hoping to perform herewith an act of true friendship toward a young nation, to which it had contributed so many of her own children. —

By calling prominent German professors to occupy chairs at American universities, German influence on education has been greatly heightened. At Harvard University on instigation of **Kuno Francke**, professor of German language and literature, a **Germanic Museum** has been established, which aims by means of excellent casts, engravings, drawings, and photographs to acquaint the American student with the best specimen of German art and craft. Another excellent innovation was suggested by the same scholar in 1902. He proposed a regular system of mutual exchange of professors between German and American universities in every branch of science, in order to effect by the interchange of thought, ideas and opinions, resulting from such direct intercourse, a more intimate fusion of the learning of the German and the American people, as well as a more fraternal feeling between them. He expected that this would be brought about by the greater number of students who would be thus afforded an opportunity of coming into close contact with the most eminent scholars of both nations.

This plan, greatly encouraged by Emperor William II. as well as by President Roosevelt, was taken up first in America by Harvard, later on by Columbia and other universities. Carried on from 1904 to 1914, it was crowned with excellent results, for in America as well as in Germany thousands of students, teachers, professors, journalists, statesmen, merchants and industrial workers, all desirous of learning, listened to these emissaries of a friendly nation. Among the notable German scientists, who thus came to America, were the professors Kühnemann, Ostwald, Penck, Clements, Lamprecht, Dähnel, Schumacher and others; among the American professors, who visited Germany, were Burgess, Peabody, Richards, Smith, Adler and others. That this friendly intercourse between the two great nations has been interrupted, is one of the many unfortunate results of the European war.

The influence of German methods of education extended also to the lowest grades in schooling, to the kindergarten. This institution, founded by Friedrich Fröbel, was first brought over to America by the followers of Friedrich Rapp, the sectarian who founded the communistic society New Harmony in Indiana. The kindergarten of this community was started in 1826. The next ones were attempted by **Caroline Frankenberg** in Columbus, Ohio, and by the wife of Carl Schurz in Watertown, Wisconsin. Others rapidly followed, when Miss Elizabeth Peabody, having studied Fröbel's institutions in Germany, organized the "American Fröbel Union" in 1867.

Of great influence on American education were also many private schools, established by able German schoolmen in America. The best known was founded in 1851 by **Peter Engelmann,** a refugee of the revolutionary period of 1848, in Milwaukee. This institution, still existing under the name **"Deutsch Englische Academie,"** received in 1878 a higher mission by its close connection with the **German American Teachers' Seminary,** an institution which is supported by voluntary contributions and gives its pupils a thorough education free of cost. Sending out every year large numbers of excellent teachers, this seminary has become a great factor in education.

Hand in hand with all these institutions go several Germanistic societies, which strive to spread the knowledge of German culture in America by arranging lecture tours for prominent scientists, and by the publication of the works of the best writers. Among the eminent Germans, who followed the invitations of such societies, have been Carl Hauptmann, Ludwig Fulda, Rudolf Herzog, Ernst von Wolzogen, the scientists Sombart, Delitzsch, Paszowski, Bezold, Hötzsch, Lehmann and many others.

It is of course impossible to ascertain in a statistical or any other way the magnitude and importance of the influence of German methods of teaching on American institutions. But certainly the remarks made by Andrew D. White, President Emeritus of Cornell University, are true: "We may well recognize in Germany another mother country, one with which our own land should remain in warmest alliance. For, from the universities and institutions for advanced learning in Germany, far more than from those of any other land, have come and are coming the influences which have shaped and are shaping advanced education in the United States."

Eminent Scientists.

If it were necessary to demonstrate the internationality of science, there is no better evidence than the surprisingly large number of learned Germans who participated in the founding and development of science in America. Indeed, a catalogue of their names and an enumeration of their works would hardly find room in this volume.

Following the German pioneers of science, already mentioned in former chapters, as for instance Lederer, Pastorius, Herrman and Rittenhausen, there appeared in later times a legion of others, many of them the authors of excellent works and regarded here as high authorities in their special lines. We enumerate **Gotthilf Heinrich Mühlenberg** (1753-1815) as the first to publish a series of books on the flora of Pennsylvania. One of the "Latin farmers," **Georg Engelmann,** was the first to describe the unknown vegetation of the Far West. Not less than 112 valuable monographs are the product of his pen and the results of his extensive and often dangerous trips through the swamps, prairies and forests of Louisiana, Arkansas, Missouri, Texas and other states. American scientists acknowledged his labor and perpetuated his memory by naming one of the most beautiful pines of the Rocky Mountains "Albis Engelmanni."

The same honor was extended to **Ferdinand Jakob Lindheimer** in appreciation of his splendid investigations of the flora of Texas. As botanists distinguished themselves also **Adolf Wislizenus, David von Schweinitz, Johann N. Neumann, Wangenheim, Fendler, Römer, Creutzfeld, Bolander, Hoffmannsegg, Rothrock, Hartweg, Kuhn, Metzger** and many others.

The first scientist, who investigated the fishes of American waters, was **David Schöpf,** a physician, who during the war for independence came to this country with the Hessian soldiers. After the war he remained here to study the fishes of New York Bay, of which he furnished splendid descriptions.

The first entomologist was **Friedrich Valentine Melsheimer** (1749-1814). He published the first work about the insects of the Eastern United States. His brother **Ernst Melsheimer** is the author of a voluminous work on the bugs of North America. **Samuel Haldeman** was author of several works about the sweet-water mollusk of our continent.

Gerhard Troost, a pupil of the famous mining academy at Freiberg, Saxony, was the first who lectured in America on geology. From 1810 to 1827 he was professor of mineralogy in the Philadelphia Museum, and was also the founder and first president of the "Academy of Natural Science." In 1827 he went to Nashville, where he was appointed professor of chemistry, geology, and mineralogy, a chair which he held until 1850, the year of his death. He was also State geologist of Tennessee. One of his colleagues, **Karl Rominger**, was State geologist of Michigan. The reports of his explorations, carried on for many years, were published in four volumes in 1873 to 1881.

The famous naturalist **Johann Ludwig Rudolf Agassiz** must be regarded as a German scientist, as he received his training at the universities of Zurich, Heidelberg and Munich. At the latter place he took his degree as doctor and became assistant of the famous naturalists Oken, Schelling, Döllinger, Spix and Martius. When the two last named scientists returned from their celebrated Brazilian tour, Agassiz was selected to describe the fishes, brought home from this expedition. By this work his name became so favorably known, that the king of Prussia in 1846 sent Agassiz to America, to investigate the natural history of the United States.

The lectures he delivered here made such deep impression, that the Harvard University offered him a professorship under so tempting conditions, that Agassiz accepted them and remained in America for the rest of his life. His many expeditions through North America, to the Gulf of Mexico and the Amazonas River form one of the most brilliant chapters in the history of American science. At Harvard the splendid Museum of Natural History, founded by him is a lasting monument to this brilliant scientist. To Agassiz principally is the credit due of having animated immensely the interest of the American public in natural history. His power of describing in lecturing as well as in writing was so inspiring, that he was able to collect great sums for his expeditions and his museum.

German naturalists participated also in many of the exploring expeditions sent out by the U. S. Government. **Emil Bessels** was in 1871 a member of the famous "Polaris Expedition" under Captain Francis Hall. After the leader's sudden death Bessels took charge of the expedition, which, after a terrific trip of 196 days on a huge block of ice, was saved by the steamer "Tigress." Bessel's work about the "Polaris Expedition" appeared in three volumes.

To these able naturalists in recent times the names of many others could be added, as for instance of the paleontologist **Timothäus Conrad**, the biologist **George Eugen Beyer**, the ornithologist **Heinrich Nehrling**, who wrote a splendid volume about the birds of North America. Furthermore, there are the entomologists **Georg H. Horn, Hermann von Bähr, William**

Beutenmüller, the geologist **Eugen W. Hilgard, George Ferdinand Becker, Karl Schuckert** and **Rudolf Rüdemann,** the latter State geologist of New York.

Of German descent is also **George Frederick Kunz,** gem expert and author of the books "Gems and Precious Stones of North America," "Investigations and Studies in Jade," and the "Book of the Pearl," all of which were published in the most luxurious form.

In the wide field of archaeology and ethnology a number of German American scientists have achieved most remarkable results. **Philipp Valentini, Karl Hermann Berendt, Gustav Brühl** and **Karl Rau** wrote splendid monographs and works. **Adolf Franz Bandelier,** born in Bern, Switzerland, spent a life-time in exploring New Mexico, Arizona, Mexico, Central- and South-America in the interest of the "Archaeological Institute of America" and the "American Museum of Natural History." **Franz Boas,** born in Westphalia, made extensive investigations among the Esquimaux of Baffin Land. He was also the originator and director of the so-called "Jesup Expeditions," sent out by the American Museum of Natural History. These expeditions, financially supported by Morris Jesup, began in Spring 1897 and lasted for about ten years, embracing the whole territory of the Northwest coast of North America, Alaska and a great part of Siberia, including the Amur. Their main purpose was the establishment of the connections between the aborigines of Northeastern Asia and Northwestern America. The exceedingly valuable results of these expeditions are laid down in numerous monographs, published in twelve volumes by the American Museum of Natural History, which also owns the rich collections, brought together by the several expeditions.

Of Boas' pupils the German American **Alfred L. Kroeber** became known very favorably by his works on the Indians of California. **William S. Hoffmann,** a Pennsylvania German, made himself known as author of highly interesting monographs about the Menomonee Indians and the Esquimaux.

Important works about different Indian languages have been written by the Moravian missionaries **David Zeisberger** and **Johann Heckewelder,** and by **Albert S. Gatschet.**

As scientific director of several expeditions, sent by the University of Pennsylvania to Asia Minor and Babylonia, **Hermann Volrath Hilprecht** has become widely known. The results of these researches have been published in several valuable works, of which the book "Explorations in Bible Lands During the 19th Century" has found wide circulation.

Of the excellent works of **Franz Lieber** mention has been made in another chapter.

A man of equal eminence was **Hermann Eduard von Holst,** professor of American history in the University of Chicago.

His principal work is "The Constitutional and Political History of the United States," which appeared first in the German language under the title "Verfassung und Demokratie der Vereinigten Staaten von Amerika."

Splendid works on politics, science and political economy have been produced also by **Karl Gustav Rümelin, Friedrich List, Johann Tellkampf, E. R. Seligman, Frank William Taussig** and **Paul S. Reinsch.** Of the German philologists **Alexander J. Schem** produced in 1869-1874 a German-American Conversations Lexikon of eleven volumes.

Many are the works of German scholars of more recent times. Especially noteworthy among these men are **Karl G. von Jagemann, Hermann Collitz, Julius Goebel, Georg Hench, H. G. Brandt, Camillo von Klenze, Hermann Schoenfeld, A. R. Hohlfeld, Ernst Voss, Karl Jessen, Richard C. Schiedt, Friedrich Hirth, Paul Haupt, Hermann Knapp** and **John M. Schaeberle. Albert A. Michelson,** professor of physics at the University of Chicago, well known for brilliant research work in light, won the rare distinction of being awarded the famous Noble Prize of $40,000.

Kuno Francke, since 1884 professor of German literature in Harvard, and since 1903 curator of the Germanic Museum, is author of a number of widely read works, among them "A History of German Literature," "German Ideals of To-day," "Glimpses of Modern German Culture," etc. To the fertile pen of **Hugo Münsterberg,** professor of psychology in Harvard, we owe "Psychology and Social Science," "Eternal Values," and several other valuable works.

Of the works of **Felix Adler,** the founder of the "New York Society for Ethical Culture," the volumes "Creed and Deed," "Life and Destiny," "Marriage and Divorce" deserve mention as of lasting merit.

German scientists have by example and exhortation introduced into the scientific research work of America perseverance, seriousness and thoroughness, qualities which for true science mean infinitely much. "German thoroughness," so said Professor Ira Remsen, President of Johns Hopkins University, "is an expression often used. To the scholar it means everything. Whatever other virtues science may have, they count little without thoroughness. If I were asked, what America owes to Germany most, I would answer without hesitation: **the virtue of thoroughness.**"

Engineers of Distinction.

The United States are admittedly a country of great engineers. This fact is not surprising, as the topographical conditions of no other country offer to engineers so many and extraordinary opportunities to display their abilities and genius. The country abounds with broad rivers and deep cañons; vast prairies and deserts are to be transversed; steep mountain ranges must be overcome. To conquer all these obstacles, where they interfere with commerce and communication, are fascinating problems that call for the exercise of highest mental powers, for rare ability and genius.

Among the masterminds who grew with the solution of such problems, we find so many Germans and German Americans, that it is indeed not said too much, that the history of engineering in the United States is almost identical with the history of the German-American engineers.

When in 1813 **Ludwig Wernweg** built a wooden bridge across the Delaware River at Trenton; when **Albert von Stein** constructed the waterworks of Cincinnati, Richmond, Lynchburg, New Orleans, Nashville and Mobile; when he also made the Appomatox Canal in Virginia; when the Swabian **Gindele** dug a canal connecting Michigan Lake with the Mississippi, and also the great tunnel, through which Chicago is provided with fresh water from the Michigan Lake, all these works were admired as such, doing great honor to the skill of their makers.

But far greater works were still to come. **Hermann Haupt,** born 1817 in Philadelphia, a graduate of West Point, constructed in 1856-1861 the famous Hoosac-tunnel in Massachusetts, having a length of 4¾ miles and costing 16 million dollars. He, too, demonstrated the possibility of carrying coal oil long distances by pipes, effecting thereby to the refineries a saving of enormous sums.

Gifted with equal genius was **Adolf Sutro,** born 1830 in Rhenish Prussia. Having received his training in a German polytechnic school, Sutro came to New York in 1850. Ten years later he transferred his activity to Nevada. Here the Comstock silver mines, discovered in 1859, yielded enormous profits, but the work could be carried on only under enormous difficulties, as the shafts had been sunk to a depth of 2000 feet. In these great depths the miners suffered not only by almost unbearable heat and poisonous gases, but also from large quantities of water, collecting in the shafts. Several of the mines had been flooded and were abandoned.

While visiting the Comstock mines, Sutro conceived the idea

of connecting the widely separated mines by a wide tunnel, which was to serve not only as a ventilator and a drain, but would also be an important factor in cheapening the cost of hauling ore. It took many years, before Sutro succeeded in convincing the mine operators of the feasibility of his plan. And when their timidity and objections had been overcome, he was compelled to defend his project against envious rivals, who were eager to snatch the fruits of his labors from him. After innumerable troubles and disappointments Sutro at last came into position to begin on October 19, 1869, with the gigantic undertaking. 1800 feet below the surface of the earth he constructed a tunnel, 10 feet high, 12 feet wide and 20,489 feet long. In connection with this main tunnel were several lateral ones, leading to the various mines. The total length of all the tunnels was 33,315 feet, or about 6⅓ miles. The difficulties to be overcome were extraordinary, as with the progress of the work the temperature at the face of the rock increased from 72° to 114° Fahrenheit. Two or three hours of work were all the strongest and most experienced miners could endure. The mules often refused to enter the tunnel, and they were dragged by main strength from the air-escapes. Endurance was being strained to its utmost capacity. Man after man dropped down on the rocky floor and was carried to the surface, babbling and incoherent, to slowly recover from the poisonous air.

To the terrific heat came the constant battle with streams of hot water, the temperature of which was never below 100°, and which often entered the tunnel at 130° and even 160° Fahrenheit. To get rid of it, a thousand workmen began to cut a drain channel five feet wide down the middle of the tunnel floor. The amount of flow in 1880 was not less than 1,300,000,000 gallons, and as other mines began to use the tunnel, the total annual drainage rose at times to nearly two billion gallons.

In October 1878 the tunnels were completed and ventilated by several vertical airshafts. Furthermore they were provided with a net of railways and stations, where by immense machines the ore was lifted to the surface. The whole cost amounted to about 6½ million dollars. The tunnel proved to be all that its projector had anticipated, and though in later years it fell in disuse, it was looked upon as one of the greatest triumphs of engineering.

Other mining engineers of note were **Frederick Anton Eilers; Max Boehmer; Albert Arents,** inventor of the lead-mine machinery; **C. W. Kirchhoff; F. Augustus Heinze,** founder of the Amalgamated Copper Company, **C. de Kalb, Herman Gmelin,** and others, who as consulting engineers or presidents of mining corporations rank high in their profession and are known throughout the Union.

Herman Schüssele constructed the great waterwork of San Francisco. His monograph on "The water supply of San Francisco before, during and after the earthquake of April 18, 1906," is a valuable contribution to technical literature.

The greatest achievement in engineering, however, have been accomplished in America by German bridge-builders. The names of **Albert Fink, Adolf Bonzano, Heinrich Flad, Johann August Roebling, Washington Roebling, Konrad Schneider, Gustav Lindenthal, Eduard Hemberle** and **Paul Wolfel** are inseparably connected with the history of engineering in America. Several of these men were rufugees of 1848, as for instance **Albert Fink.** Born 1827 at Lauterbach, he had been trained at the polytechnic school of Darmstadt. In 1849 he emigrated to America and entered the service of the Baltimore & Ohio Railroad, for which he constructed many viaducts and iron bridges, among them the great iron bridge over the Ohio River at Louisville. In the construction of these bridges he employed an invention of his own, a system of girders allowing of a length of span theretofore unknown.

The greatest of these girders are found in the Ohio River Bridge at Louisville, which has a total length of 5,310 feet. Of its 27 spans the largest measure 340 and 360 feet.

Several of the viaducts, constructed by Fink, especially those over the ravines of Cheat Mountain, were considered the most marvellous of their kind. A brilliant test of the abilities of Fink was the Civil War, during which he was charged with the supervision of all military railroads in Kentucky and Tennessee. On this most contested battleground the Confederates made it their rule to destroy all railways, bridges and viaducts they could lay hand on. But as soon as they retreated, Fink followed in their wake, rebuilding with astonishing rapidity what they had demolished, aquitting himself of this task of highest military importance in a most creditable manner.

A factor of no less importance in this regard was **Heinrich Flad**, born in 1824 in Baden. Having studied engineering at the university in Munich, he participated as colonel of a battalion of engineers in the revolution of 1848. In 1849 he arrived in America and was for a number of years very successful in constructing of western railroads. At the outbreak of the Civil War he entered the 3d regiment of volunteers of Missouri, but soon became captain of the Western Regiment of Engineers. In this capacity he rendered services in the reconstruction of destroyed roads, the value of which can be appreciated only by those who know the eminent importance of railroads for the movements and support of armies engaged in actual warfare.

After the war Flad designed in connection with J. P. Kirkwood the plans for the waterworks of St. Louis, and later on, in connection with Captain James B. Eads the plans for the famous Mississippi River Bridge at St. Louis. It was in the execution of this structure, that Flad's skill in the overcoming of technical difficulties and in the application of scientific principles appeared in the most brilliant light.

After the completion of this bridge, which is of classic beauty, Flad was elected president of public works in St. Louis, and in 1890 was appointed by President Harrison as chief of the Mississippi River Commission, which office he held until his death in 1898.

A contemporary of Fink and Flad was **Adolf Bonzano,** born 1830 in Würtemberg. As chief engineer and vice-president of the Phœnix Bridge Company he made the designs for many railroad-bridges. The most interesting of his works was a viaduct across the valley of the Kinzua River in Pennsylvania, which is 1800 feet wide and 270 feet deep. This viaduct, completed in 1882, rested on twenty towers, each constructed of four iron pillars. The aspect of this work, which was completed within only 8 months, was most startling.

A complete revolution in bridge-building was brought about during the midst of the 19th century by **Johann August Roebling,** born June 12, 1806, at Mühlhausen, Thuringia. Soon after his graduation from the Royal Polytechnicum at Berlin he emigrated to the United States and established himself at Saxonburg, Pa. There he developed the manufacture of wire cable for use in bridge construction to a degree unknown before. Bridge-building then was, in comparison to its present perfection, in the first stages of development. Suspension-bridges were known, but the platforms were hung on heavy iron chains, the links of which possessed notwithstanding their weight no great holding capacity. Besides, for spans of more than 180 feet they were impracticable. It remained for Roebling to substitute a system of wire-cables, the enormous carrying capacity of which he demonstrated first in 1845 in a suspended aqueduct of the Pennsylvania Canal carried across the Monongahela River. This was soon followed by the Monongahela suspension bridge at Pittsburg and the suspension railway bridge across the Niagara River.

When Roebling made public the plans for the latter undertaking, the most eminent engineers of America and Europe regarded a bridge of this kind foredoomed to failure, no suspension bridges having ever been built for railway traffic, and the width of the enormous gorge, cut into the rocks by the foaming river, being more than 820 feet. Not discouraged by such apprehensions and dire predictions Roebling went to work in September 1852. Difficulties came with the question of how to carry the first wire across the cañon, as no boatman nor swimmer would risk his life in the terrific whirlpools of the river. After many fruitless efforts

137

Roebling conceived the idea of bringing a strong silk thread from the American to the Canadian shore by means of a kite. This idea proving successful, the first wire was pulled over, and now the spinning of the cables began. There were four of them, every one consisting of 3640 strands. The ends of these cables were attached to cast-iron shoes and anchored in

JOHANN AUGUST ROEBLING.

chambers cut in the rock behind the two towers, which carried the cables. The superstructure of the bridge had two floors, the upper one for railroads, and the lower one for vehicles and pedestrians. The bridge was commenced in September, 1852, and opened for traffic on March 16, 1855. Its cost amounted to only 400,000 dollars.

ROEBLING'S SUSPENSION BRIDGE ACROSS NIAGARA RIVER

The location of this bridge was the most picturesque in the world. With its shapely towers rising from either bank of the Niagara River, and the long, graceful sweep of its cables, it seemed almost a natural part of the surrounding scenery. The famous Falls in the distance and the Whirlpool Rapids beneath lent a particular charm to the airy appearance of the bridge itself.

In 1855, when the first train passed over the bridge, locomotives did not exceed 25 tons in weight, and cars had a capacity of 16 tons; now, engines weigh 100 to 150 tons, and cars carry 30 to 40 tons of material. In addition, the number of trains passing to and fro has increased enormously. In consequence, the bridge in late years was taxed far beyond the capacity for which it was designed, and was taken down in 1897, giving place to a wider and heavier structure proportioned to the requirements. When the bridge was taken apart, the cables, manufactured by Roebling forty-five years ago, were found to be in perfect condition, and as elastic as they had been when originally put into their places.

The completion, in 1867, of the still more remarkable suspension bridge over the Ohio River at Cincinnati with a main span of 1057 feet added greatly to Roebling's reputation. This bridge is carried by two cables, each consisting of 10,360 strands.

The last and greatest masterpiece of Roebling was, however, the famous suspension bridge between New York and Brooklyn. The rapid growth of the two cities and the inability of the ferries to handle the enormous traffic made better connections between the cities an imperative necessity. But an increase in the number of ferries was out of question, as there was no more space for landing slips. The only solution was a bridge. But the local conditions were so extraordinary, that no one believed in the feasibility of such an idea. Not only was the distance between the shores of Manhattan and Long Island very great, but also the East River between was too deep and rapid, to permit the laying of a foundation for a pillar in its midst.

In view of this desperate situation Roebling concluded to apply his system of suspension bridges, which had so far stood all tests, at this place also. It took ten years to design and digest the plans for the gigantic undertaking, as the conditions to be reckoned with commanded the most careful attention to the smallest details, as the slightest error in the calculation of the strength of the cables, towers and foundations might result in terrible disaster. Just as difficult as this preliminary work was the task of procuring the building funds. At many places, where Roebling hoped to receive assistance, he found closed doors. Of the $1\frac{1}{2}$ million dollars subscribed by the City of New York and of the 300,000 dollars subscribed by Brooklyn, large sums disappeared into the pockets of dishonest city officials, who had been entrusted with the administration of the funds. In the end Roebling succeeded in interesting a rich banker in his scheme, who organized the New York Bridge Company with a capital of 5 million dollars.

In spring of 1869 all these preliminary steps had been completed. Now at last the practical work could begin. But an envious fate stepped in to prevent the great engineer from witnessing his highest triumph. While personally engaged in laying out the towers of the bridge, Roebling was unfortunately injured by a falling piece of timber so that several of his toes had to be amputated. The operation was successful; but a few days later tetanus set in, to which the great man succumbed, July 22, 1869.

The grave responsibility of superintending the enormous work now fell to Roebling's oldest son, **Washington Augustus Roebling.** Problems of greatest difficulty came with the providing of secure foundations for the two stone towers, on which the four cables of the bridge were to rest. To give free passage to all vessels, the platform of the bridge had been projected 135 feet above high watermark. Accordingly the two towers were to have a height of 276⅔ feet above high water. As they were to be of granite, it was necessary to construct exceptionally strong foundations. By careful investigations it was found, however, that solid rock, on which the towers could safely rest, was 80 feet below the water level. To reach it, enormous banks of mud, mixed with gravel and stones, must be penetrated. So it became necessary to construct over the places selected for the towers two enormous caissons, boxlike chambers of iron and heavy beams. The caisson on the Manhattan side was 120 feet wide and 172 feet long. Their lower parts formed into air chambers 7 feet high and resting upon the bed of the river. Air was pumped into these sub-aqueous and gas-lighted rooms by powerful machines at a pressure corresponding to their depth below the surface of the water, while the excavating was carried on by men working in the compressed air as in a large diving bell. Day in and out 236 men were here engaged in removing the mud and gravel, while at the same time the building of the towers on top of the caissons went on, forcing with their ever increasing weight the lower end of the caissons deeper and deeper into the river bed.

It cannot surprise, that the daily work in such sub-aqueous rooms, under high pressure, caused serious inconveniences to the laborers. Soon they began to suffer from the dreadful caisson-disease, many cases of which resulting in death. Roebling also was prostrated early in 1872 with it and was compelled for a while to give up active work, but his intellectual faculties remained unimpaired. There were also other unfortunate events. In January, 1871, in the caisson at the Brooklyn side a fire broke out, causing a loss of 15,000 dollars. A fire below the waves of East River!

After many difficulties the fundaments as well as the towers were completed and now the construction of the four cables was to begin. As it would have been impossible to lift their

ROEBLING'S SUSPENSION BRIDGE BETWEEN NEW YORK AND BROOKLYN.

enormous weight to the top of the towers, there was no other way than to spin them between the towers in open air. The first strand was run out May 29, 1876. Others followed and soon the workmen could be seen, hanging at these strands in little boxes, and busy to unite 5296 galvanized steel-oil-coated wires into a solid rope $15\frac{3}{4}$ inches in diameter.

Serious accidents happened here also. When after two years' labor the four cables were finished, on June 19, 1878, suddenly the anchorage of one of the cables broke and the cable fell with tremendous noise into the river, killing several of the workmen. So the difficult work had to be done over again.

At last, on May 24, 1883, the tremendous work was accomplished. The day of its dedication was a national event. All vessels in New York Bay appeared bedecked with flags, while the numerous men-of-war saluted. The President of the United States and more than 100,000 visitors from all parts of the country paid homage to the memory of the genius, whose master mind had conceived this colossal work.

To give an idea of the great work, it may be stated that it measures 5989 feet in length. It consists of a central span 1595½ feet in length from tower to tower, and of two spans of 930 feet, and 1860 feet, respectively, from the towers to the anchorage on either side. The length of the Brooklyn approach is 971 feet, and of the New York approach 1562 feet. The bridge has a width of 85 feet. The roadway is divided into a central promenade with a single track on either side for rapid transit, and a platform for passengers, which is in turn flanked by a tramway for wheeled vehicles.

The actual cost of the bridge, which has withstood in the course of now 33 years harder usage than any other bridge in the world, was nearly $15,000,000.

Another prominent builder of bridges was **Conrad Schneider,** born 1843 in Apolda, Thuringia. While he was not the first man to build a cantilever bridge in the United States, he, however, developed this system to perfection. His most remarkable work is the Niagara Cantilever Bridge, two miles below the Niagara Falls. Spanning the chasm of 850 feet in width, the main body is 210 feet above the surface of the roaring river. The structure has a double track. It consists of two cantilevers, each 395 feet, resting on the towers, the shore end being anchored to the anchorage piers, and the river ends connected by an intermediate span. The work was begun in 1882, but so vigorously pushed, that the bridge was completed and opened for traffic December 20, 1883.

Schneider also constructed the cantilever bridges crossing the Fraser River in British Columbia. Furthermore he designed the plans for the Washington Bridge over the Harlem River at 181st Street, New York City.

Among the most efficient bridge builders of recent times is counted **Eduard Hemberle,** who constructed several railroad bridges across the Hudson, the Ohio, Mississippi and Missouri; furthermore **Paul L. Wolfel,** chief engineer of the American Bridge Company.

A worthy successor of Roebling appeared in 1874 in the

person of **Gustav Lindenthal,** born 1850 in Brunn, Austria, and a student of colleges in Brunn and Vienna. Having been employed on survey and construction of railroads and bridges in Austria, Switzerland and some Western railroads, he moved in 1892 to New York, where he was appointed bridge commissioner during the administration of Seth Low. He completed the construction of the so-called Williamsburg Bridge, a suspension bridge over the East River between New York and Long Island, a short distance north of Roebling's bridge. He also made the original plans for the Blackwells Island Bridge and the Manhattan Bridge.

Lindenthal was also a member of the board of six consulting engineers, which planned the tunnels and terminal of the Pennsylvania Railroad under the East River and the Hudson River. Another of his works is a railway-bridge, which spans the cañon of the Kentucky River at a place where it is 1000 feet wide and 345 feet deep.

Lindenthal is likewise engineer and architect of Hell Gate Bridge, a mammoth steel structure, and the most imposing part of the Connecting Railroad, which is six miles long and forms a link in through transportation between Quebec, Canada, and Tampa, Florida. The whole length of the bridge from the New Haven tracks to the Long Island connection with the Pennsylvania Railroad's passenger tunnel is a little over three and a half miles. The steel arch, rising to 320 feet, has a clear span over the main channel of 1017 feet. The clearing from the high water to the platform is 135 feet, the same as the other bridges across the East River. The arch is able to support not only its own vast weight of 28,000 tons, but the added load of forty-eight of the heaviest locomotives. Unquestionably the bridge can be regarded as the biggest and strongest in the world, for there is no other bridge in existence or proposed that is expected to bear a burden of this colossal character. The structure has four railroad tracks.

For a number of years Lindenthal has been at work on the plans for a bridge across the Hudson River between New York City and New Jersey. According to these plans the bridge will be in all dimensions twice as large as Roebling's Suspension Bridge between New York and Brooklyn. The main span is intended to be 2900 feet long and the height of the two steel towers 660 feet. Unfortunately the plans came to a stand-still when the Pennsylvania Railroad, to which falls the lion share of traffic between New York and New Jersey, decided to built instead of a bridge a tunnel. Still, this does not mean that Lindenthal's scheme will be abandoned. The marvellous increase in the traffic between New York and New Jersey compels the adoption of ever new and greater means of communication. And so it is quite possible that within the space of ten to twenty years from now the two shores of

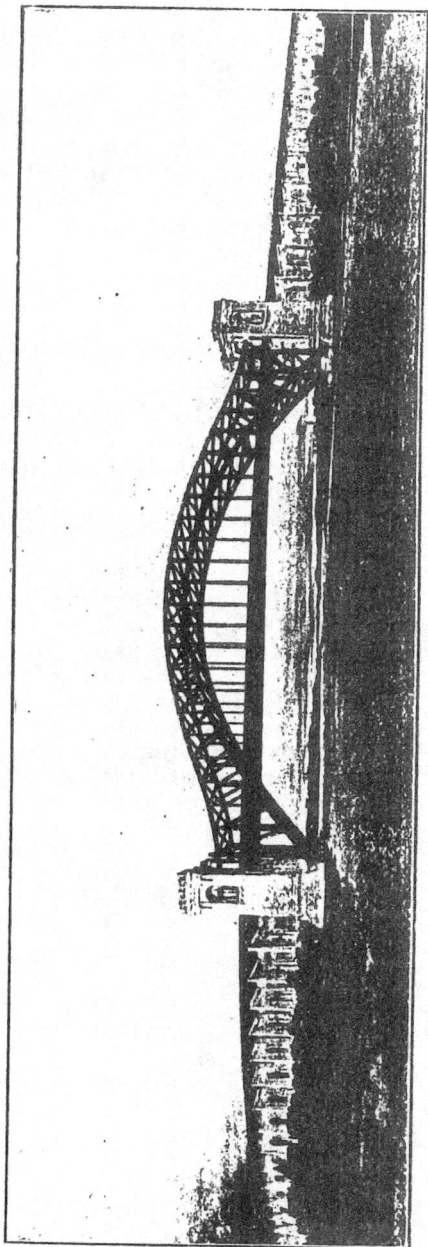

THE HELL GATE BRIDGE AT NEW YORK.

(Constructed by Gustav Lindenthal.)

the Hudson River will also be linked by a wonderful bridge, the masterpiece of a German engineer.

Of electrical engineers, a great number of whom are Germans, **Emil Berliner** should be mentioned, the inventor of the grammophone.   Furthermore **F. B. Herzog,** inventor of automatic switch-boards, elevator signals, police calls, and telephone devices; so also **Bernhard Arthur Behrend,** advisory engineer of the Westinghouse Electric and Manufacturing Company and inventor of electrical machines, which received a grand prize at St. Louis in 1904.

Frank Koester in New York is known as creator of great electric power stations, among them those of the Potomac Electric Power Company in Washington, D. C., and of the Delaware & Hudson Company in Mechanicsville, N. Y.

Most famed of electrical engineers is **Karl P. Steinmetz,** born at Breslau in 1865.   When a student at the university he became soon deeply interested in electricity.   At that time little was known about this mysterious power.   Arc-lights were looked upon as a curiosity.   Of dynamos, motors and other electric apparatus nobody had conceived any idea.   Since his arrival in the United States Steinmetz became one of the most successful investigators of electricity.

His own discoveries and brilliant inventions in this field are too numerous and complicated for description in any but a professional work. Since a number of years Steinmetz occupies the position of consulting engineer at the "General Electric Company" in Schenectady, N. Y. Here he stands at the head of an army of about 35,000 men. In what respect he is held by scientists, appears from a remark made by the president of Harvard University.   When this institution bestowed upon Steinmetz the degree of an honorary doctor, the president said: "I confer this degree upon you as the foremost electrical engineer of the United States, and, therefore, of the world!"

Organizers of Traffic and Transportation.

It is a well known fact that certain important inventions and innovations have been made simultaneously at widely separated places of the globe. So for instance the institution of the railway can be ascribed to England as well as to America. As in England the first railroads were installed for the transportation of coal to the sea, so a Pennsylvania German, **Thomas Leiper** of Philadelphia, constructed in 1806 what is believed to have been the first railroad in America. It was used for the transportation of stone from Leiper's granite quarries in Delaware County, Pa., to a boat landing on Ridley Creek, a distance of about one mile. To facilitate the haul for the horses, Leiper invented special trucks, whose wheels of cast-iron he fitted exactly to two iron rails. This made the hauling so easy, that one horse could draw loads of from three to four times the former weight.

On the further development of railroads in America men of German descent have exerted considerable influence. In the hands of companies of German origin, such as the **J. G. Brill Company** in Philadelphia, the **St. Louis Car Company** and the **Wagner Palace Car Company,** the making of railroad cars of all kinds became a regular science. Their excellent cars are known for comfort and beauty.

An invention of greatest importance for the safety of passengers, the celebrated Westinghouse air-brake, has also been made by an American of German origin, **George Westinghouse.**

As is stated in "Men and Women of America" (edition 1910, page 1571) the Westinghouses came from Germany and settled in Massachusetts and Vermont. Westinghouse's father was an inventor, who moved to Central Bridge, Schoharie County, N. Y., where George Westinghouse was born October 6, 1846. In 1856 the family moved to Schenectady, where young Westinghouse visited the public and high schools. Much of his time he spent in his father's machine shop, and a rotary engine was invented by him before he was fifteen. Going to Troy one day, a railroad accident suggested to him the idea that a brake under the control of the engineer might have prevented the accident. After several trials his first patent was issued April 13, 1869, and the Westinghouse Air-Brake Company was formed on the 20th of July following. In 1883 Westinghouse became interested in the operation of railway signals and switches by compressed air, and developed and patented the system now manufactured by the Union Switch and Signal Company. The "Pneumatic Interlocking

Switch and Signal Apparatus," whereby all the signals and switches are operated from a given point, using compressed air as the motive power and electricity to bring that power into operation, has been successfully introduced. Among the accomplishments of Westinghouse in the electrical field may be mentioned the unit switch system of multiple control for the simultaneous operation and control from one common point of all the motors in a train; and the single-phase motor for street railway service.

Wilhelm Eppelsheimer, a native of Frankfort-on-the-Main, was the inventor of the cable street cars, first used to a great extent in San Francisco and other cities of California.

Most remarkable was also the German influence on the inner organization of the railway traffic in America. Both as civil engineer and organizer no man has rendered more conspicuous service than **Albert Fink,** widely known as one of the pioneers in the construction of iron bridges. Seeing the many evils resulting from the unrestrained and ruinous competition among railroad companies and steamboat lines, Fink recommended that all competing corporations should elect a common board of directors with authority to settle all tariff questions in regard to the transportation of persons as well as of freight.

Fink, not believing in railroad wrecking, but in co-operation, explained that the interests of the transportation companies and the public are not hostile to one another but mutual, and that a regulated tariff with fixed prices, leaving a reasonable profit to the companies, would be much more advantageous to all than a constantly changing one, resulting in disorder and bankruptcy. In consequence of this recommendation the Southern Railway and Steamboat Association was formed, of which almost all railroad- and steamboat companies of the South became members. In 1877 Fink, on invitation of the presidents of the great railroad companies of the East and North, made similar arrangements for a still greater combination. Accordingly he organized the Trunk-Line Commission, which soon embraced nearly all the railroads East of the Mississippi and North of the Ohio, including the railways of Canada. The object of this association was to prevent destructive rate-wars. As chairman of this commission Fink became the most influential factor in all tariff questions of the largest railroad companies of the United States. Fink also initiated the system of through freight and through passenger service now in general use.

Very numerous are the men of German descent who, by keen foresight and by technical knowledge and experiences, have made names for themselves and became presidents and managers of American railroad companies and steamboat lines. Among them have been **Henry Fink,** president of the Nor-

148

folk & Western Railway; **J. Kruttschnitt,** general manager of the Southern Pacific Railroad; **R. Blickensderfer,** general manager of the Wheeling & Lake Erie Railroad; **Karl Gustav Memminger,** president of the Charleston & Cincinnati Railroad; **Heinrich Hilgard** or **Henry Villard,** president of the Oregon & California Railroad, of the Oregon Steamship Company and of the Northern Pacific Railroad, which was completed in 1883 under his direction.

In the field of navigation we find a similar array of prominent men as presidents and managers. **Friedrich Kühne** established in 1872 the Adler Line, which maintained a regular service between New York and Hamburg. **Klaus Spreckels,** the sugar king of California, organized in conjunction with his sons **Johann Dietrich** and **Adolf Bernhard Spreckels** the Oceanic Steamship Company, which made regular trips to Hawaii, Tahiti and ports of Australia. **John H. Gans** has been founder and president of the Gans Steamship Line in New York, which sends vessels to all parts of the globe.

As American director and general manager of the famous Hamburg American Line the late **Emil Boas** was very successful. Till 1892 the line had been represented in New York by the firm **C. B. Richard & Boas.** When the line opened her own bureau at Broadway, **Carl Schurz** became her first American director. After his retirement Emil Boas was appointed his successor. He filled this responsible position up to his death, which happened on May 3, 1912. Since then the Hamburg American Line has been represented in New York by **Karl Bünz,** the former German Consul General in New York and later German Ambassador in Mexico.

The American affairs of the North German Lloyd have been successfully managed for many years by the firm of **Oelrichs & Co.,** of which **Gustav H. Schwab,** born in May, 1857, was the senior-chef. What an enormous amount of business is carried on by the New York Agency of the North German Lloyd may be seen by the fact that it handled during the period from January 1, 1873, to December 31, 1913, 5,588,598 passengers. Since the death of Gustav H. Schwab in November, 1912, **Karl von Helmolt** has been the director of the New York Bureau of the North German Lloyd.

In the interest of navigation also the services of **Ferdinand Rudolf Hassler** and of **Julius Erasmus Hilgard** have proven of the greatest value. While the former was professor of mathematics at the U. S. Military Academy at West Point, he directed the attention of the Government to the necessity of a correct survey of the coasts of the United States as essential for the safety of commerce and navigation. In compliance with this recommendation a special office, the Coast Survey, was established, with Professor Hassler as the head. He remained in office from 1807 to 1843. Hilgard was one of his successors, resigning in 1885. To the Coast Survey the commercial world is indebted for splendid charts, the value of which to navigation can not be over-estimated.

A fact not generally known is that the two families of naval architects, the **Cramps** and the **Herreshoffs**, are of German origin.

The ancestor of the Cramp family was **Johann Georg Krampf,** a native of Baden, who arrived in America at the end of the 17th century and made his home on the banks of the Delaware River. Here the members of his family, the name of which changed to Cramp, took to shipbuilding, which occupation they have continued for several generations. Under the management of William Cramp and Charles Henry Cramp the ship and engine-building enterprise has grown to a very extensive organization.

The American history of the Herreshoffs begins with **Karl Friedrich Herreshoff,** a native of Minden, an accomplished engineer, who in 1800 arrived in Providence, Rhode Island, where he married the daughter of the shipbuilder John Brown. Their son as well as their grand-sons devoted themselves to naval architecture and made a specialty of fast steam- and sailing yachts and of torpedo vessels of high speed. The most interesting figure of the family is **John B. Herreshoff,** who in his fifteenth year became totally blind. In spite of this handicap he brought the business he had inherited to great prosperity. He also made the models for several of those fast sailing yachts which defended the "America Cup" against the English. The Herreshoff Manufacturing Company has its seat in Bristol, R. I.

A name well known to the commercial world was that of **Thomas Eckert,** also a man of German descent. In 1852 he supervised the construction of a telegraph line from Pittsburgh to Chicago, and was superintendent until it became a part of the Western Union Telegraph Company. During the Civil War he was general superintendent of military telegraphy and reached the rank of brigadier-general. He became assistant secretary of war in 1864. After having been appointed in 1866 as general superintendent of the Western Union Telegraph Company, he became, in 1881, president and general manager of this concern and also director of the American Telegraph and Cable Company and several railways, among them the Union Pacific Railroad. The brilliant record of General Eckert assures him a permanent place in the ranks of those who faithfully served the Union.

The German American Press

The history of the German Press in America can be traced for nearly two centuries. When we ask what during this long time has been its essential characteristic, we name the single word: **Truth!**

Truth was the object **Peter Zenger,** the first German journalist in America, fought for in his "Weekly Journal." Publishing nothing but the truth, he won honor and everlasting fame for himself and liberty for the whole American people.

Truth was also the aim of **Christoph Saur,** the printer of Germantown. Nothing grieved him more than to have some news creep into his paper which afterwards proved incorrect.

The example set by these founders of the German press in America has been followed with fidelity by all their successors. Truth has been their guiding star, and by pursuing it the German press of the United States has won for itself among its readers a degree of confidence not enjoyed to like extent by our English press, whose editors do not care as much for the truth as for the sensational effect of their publications.

This contrast between the German and the English press of the United States was never so apparent as during the years 1914 and 1915. While the editors of the German papers endeavored to give to their readers such news only, as in their best judgment seemed reliable and trustworthy — a most difficult task because the British had cut all means of communication with the Central Powers — many editors of the Anglo-American press assisted without restraint and discrimination in the world-wide campaign of slander, inaugurated by London with the deliberate intent to destroy the good reputation of the German nation, its Emperor, army and navy. These editors, ignoring the fact that the people of the United States are drawn from **many** nations and that, therefore, impartiality and fairness to all concerned should be strictly observed, committed, by participating in a systematic poisoning of public opinion, nothing less than hostile act against the vital interests of the United States. For only so long as the various elements of the nation respect each other and work together in harmony, according to the motto "E pluribus Unum," can this country prosper.

No similar act of disloyalty to the interests of the United States can be charged against the German American press. On the contrary, their course has been at all times genuinely American. Collectively and individually its editors have advocated whatever is good in the institutions of our political system, while sharply and relentlessly criticizing its faults; and they have been ready promoters of everything tending to secure order, personal liberty and prosperity. For this reason they never neglected to urge their readers to become good American citizens and as such to contribute to the common welfare.

In accord with many thousands of intelligent Americans, who know Germany and its people from personal observation, the editors of the German American press have always regarded it as their special mission to foster the friendly relations uninterruptedly maintained between Germany and the United States since the latter came into existence. They have done this in the conviction, that these two countries have much in common and that it is to the interests of both to work hand in hand for progress and civilization.

In May 1914 the citizens of St. Louis dedicated a monument to the memory of three distinguished German journalists: **Emil Preetorius, Carl Schurz** and **Carl Dänzer,** who for many years were chief editors of the **Westliche Post,** the leading German paper of Missouri. The front view of this monument shows a naked figure, representing Truth, holding in each hand a torch, the symbol of enlightenment. It is a fit monument indeed, not only for the three journalists named, but for the whole German American press, which, it is our hope, will never forget the inspiring motto of the great German American publicist Franz Lieber: **"Dear is my Country; dearer still is liberty; dearest of all is Truth!"**

*   *   *   *

It may be added here that the printer's art in America is greatly indebted to German inventors. As printing with movable letters was devised by **Johannes Gutenberg** in Mayence, so the rapid steam press was the invention of **Friedrich König,** born in 1774 at Eisleben, Thüringia. The process of making paper from wood-pulp was discovered by **Friedrich Gottlob Keller,** born 1816 in Saxony.

It is due to the enterprise of **Albrecht Pagenstecher,** a prominent paper merchant of New York, that this process was transmitted to the United States. He brought over two wood-grinding machines from Germany and set them up at Curtisville, near Stockbridge, Massachusetts, in 1867. Here he successfully produced a wood-pulp which was immediately pronounced by neighboring paper mills an excellent material for employment in their manufacture. The introduction of this new method of producing paper was without question of momentous import. By providing a raw material offering an enormous saving in cost as compared with rags, the only material theretofore available, the price of newspapers could be reduced to such extent, that a fabulous expansion of the demand resulted. The newspaper of to-day, in its many-paged issues, would not have been possible without it.

Another invention of like importance was made by **Ottomar Mergenthaler,** born May 10, 1854, at Mergentheim, Würtemberg. He came to Baltimore in 1872, where he constructed a type-setting machine, which casts and sets types, while the operator touches letter after letter on a key board.

OTTOMAR MERGENTHALER.

The first "Linotype Machine" was used in 1886 in the composing rooms of the New York Tribune. It proved such a great success as a time- and labor-saving machine, that it is now used in many countries of America and Europe as well as of Australia.

Meisenbach in Munich is the inventor of the so-called "Half-tone process," the cheapest way to reproduce drawings and photographs for newspapers and books. The "Rotogravure-process," used by many American papers for the illustration sheets of their Sunday editions, is an invention of **Karl Klic** in Freiburg, Baden. So also the idea of news-collecting and distributing by special agencies has been conceived and accomplished first by a German, **Paul Julius Reuter,** born 1821 in Cassel, from which the well known Reuter Bureau in London derives its name. It is perhaps not out of order, to bring these facts to the notice of those Anglo-American editors and those professors, who are assisting in the defamation of the German people and who would make the world believe that the Germans are barbarians absolutely devoid of any culture.

MERGENTHALER'S FIRST LINOTYPE MACHINE.

Noteworthy Authors and Poets

Reviewing German poetry in America we must begin with **Pastorius,** the noble founder of Germantown. Like all sectarians disinclined to partake in the noisy vanities of worldly life, he enjoyed the solitude of his flower-garden and praised its peaceful charm in many verses. He also loved to garb his philosophical ideas, his conception of life and his experiences in short rhymes and epigrams, many of which have come down to our days and make interesting reading.

His contemporaries **Johann Kelpius, Konrad Beissel** and other leaders of German sects were prolific in mystic love songs to the Heavenly Bride, to the glorification of whom they devoted many volumes.

Much freer in their conception of life than these visionaries were the non-sectarian German settlers of the 17th and 18th centuries. While they, too, were religious, they never lost sight of the charms of this worldly life, which they held themselves fully entitled to enjoy. Their ideas found a most beautiful expression in a poem, addressed by **William Henry Timrod,** a German of Charleston, S. C., to his little son. These lines, which have a pathetic interest, read as follows:

To Harry.

Harry, my little blue-eyed boy,
I love to have thee playing near;
There's music in thy shouts of joy
To a fond father's ear.
I love to see the lines of mirth
Mantle thy cheek and forehead fair,
As if all pleasure of the earth
Had met to revel there;
For gazing on thee, do I sigh
That those most happy years must flee,
And thy full share of misery
Must fall in life on thee!
There is no lasting grief below
My Harry! that flows not from guilt;
Thou canst not read my meaning now —
In after times thou wilt.
Thou'lt read it when the churchyard clay
Shall lie upon thy father's breast,
And he, though dead, will point the way
Thou shalt be always blest.

They'll tell thee this terrestrial ball
To man for his enjoyment given,
Is but a state of sinful thrall
To keep the soul from heaven.
My boy! the verdure-crowned hills,
The vales where flowers innumerous blow,
The music of ten thousand rills
Will tell thee: 'tis not so!
God is no tyrant who would spread
Unnumbered dainties to the eyes,
Yet teach the hungering child to dread
That touching them he dies!
No! all can do his creatures good,
He scatters round with hand profuse —
The only precept understood,
Enjoy, but not abuse!

The boy to whom these words were addressed inherited the literary gift from his father and became one of the most cherished poets of the South. That he inherited also a profound enthusiasm for all that is beautiful as well as the sense for the high office of the poet, appears from his following verses:

"All lovely things, and gentle — the sweet laugh
Of children, Girlhood's kiss, and Friendship's clasp,
The boy that sporteth with the old man's staff,
The baby, and the breast its fingers grasp —
All that exalts the grounds of happiness,
All griefs that hallow, and all joys that bless,
To me are sacred; at my holy shrine
Love breathes its latest dreams, its earliest hints;
I turn life's tasteless waters into wine,
And flush them through and through with purple tints.
Wherever Earth is fair, and Heaven looks down,
I rear my altars, and I wear my crown."

Enjoyment of life is breathed also by the many poems written by the political refugees who came to America during the first half of the 19th century. As appears from the foregoing chapters, these fugitives were men of vigour and boundless enthusiasm, with open hearts for all the sunshine of this world. For the spirit of American liberty, for the splendor and sublimity of nature, for women's virtues and beauty, they had a warm, receptive mind. They sang of spring, love, wine and song, praised manliness and bravery, oblivious of the cares and hardships of the day, and oblivious of themselves and their surroundings.

Countless are the names of German poets of these and later times, who amidst the restless business life of America cherished their ideals and encouraged others to adhere to them.*) Some of the most impressive poems, written by the "men of 1848," are devoted to the Fatherland. Could it be otherwise? These refugees loved the land of their birth from the bottom of their hearts. For its unity and greatness they had worked many years; to it went their thoughts in time of day and night; to its valleys they hoped to return some future years, and in its sacred soil they wished to be laid at rest. They, who had striven for nothing else but Germany's glory, were banished from it. This caused them bitter grief, but could not change their love.

A deep longing finds expression in the poems of these exiles. In touching tones they sing, such as have not been heard since the strains that floated across the waters at Babylon, as the Jews sang of far away Zion.

Perhaps the most impressive and best known of these poems has been written by **Konrad Krez**, a Palatine, who on account of his participation in the revolution of 1848 had been condemned to death "in contumaciam." Making his escape, he arrived in 1850 in America, practicing law in Sheboygan, Wis. During the Civil War he participated in the siege of Vicksburg and the campaigns in Arkansas and Alabama, and was appointed brigadier-general. His poem "An mein Vaterland," written in America about the year 1860, expressed the feelings of hundreds of thousands of his countrymen, who, like him, were compelled to leave their native country.

An mein Vaterland.

Kein Baum gehörte mir von deinen Wäldern,
Mein war kein Halm auf deinen Roggenfeldern,
Und schutzlos hast du mich hinausgetrieben,
Weil ich in meiner Jugend nicht verstand,
Dich weniger und mehr mich selbst zu lieben,
Und dennoch lieb ich dich, mein Vaterland!

Wo ist ein Herz, in dem nicht dauernd bliebe
Der süsse Traum der ersten Jugendliebe?
Und heiliger als Liebe war das Feuer,
Das einst für dich in meiner Brust entbrannt;
Nie war die Braut dem Bräutigam so teuer,
Wie du mir warst, geliebtes Vaterland.

Hat es auch Manna nicht auf dich geregnet,
Hat doch dein Himmel reichlich dich gesegnet.
Ich sah die Wunder südlicherer Zonen,
Seit ich zuletzt auf deinem Boden stand;
Doch schöner ist als Palmen und Citronen
Der Apfelbaum in meinem Vaterland.

*) For these names the reader may be referred to the Anthologies: "Deutsch in Amerika" by G. A. Zimmermann, Chicago, 1894; and "vom Lande des Sternenbanners" by G. A. Neeff, Heidelberg, 1905.

THE MOST FAMOUS GERMAN POEM WRITTEN IN AMERICA.

(After the original in the possession of Rudolf Cronau.)

‹Land meiner Väter! länger nicht das meine,
So heilig ist kein Boden wie der deine. ›
Nie wird dein Bild aus meiner Seele schwinden,
Und knüpfte mich an dich kein lebend Band,
Es würden mich die Toten an dich binden,
Die deine Erde deckt, mein Vaterland!

‾Oh, würden jene, die zu Hause blieben,
‹Wie deine Fortgewanderten dich lieben,
Bald würdest du zu e i n e m Reiche werden,
Und deine Kinder gingen Hand in Hand,
Und machten dich zum grössten Land auf Erden,
Wie du das beste bist, o Vaterland! ₋

Another gem has been written by **Konrad Nies** in praise of German song, that most beautiful gift, which accompanies the sons and maidens of the "Fatherland," wherever they go.

Das Deutsche Lied.

Als wir entfloh'n aus Deutschlands Gauen,
Durchglüht von jungem Wanderdrang,
Um fremder Länder Pracht zu schauen,
Zu lauschen fremder Sprache Klang,
Da gab zum Segen in die Ferne
Die Heimat uns ihr deutsches Lied,
Das nun, gleich einem guten Sterne,
Mit uns die weite Welt durchzieht.

Wohin auch unsere Wege führen,
Zum Steppensaum, zum Meeresport;
Wo immer wir ein Heim uns küren,
Im tiefen Süd, im hohen Nord:
‹Der deutschen Heimat Segensgabe
Von unsrer Schwelle nimmer flieht,
Und als des Herzens schönste Habe
Bleibt heilig uns das deutsche Lied.›

Es klingt um hohe Urwaldtannen,
Am blauen Golf, am gelben Strom,
Fern in den Hütten der Savannen
Und ferner unterm Palmendom.
Es braust aus frohem Zecherkreise,
Es jauchzt und schluchzt mit Mann und Maid
Und klagt in heimattrauter Weise
Von alter Lust und altem Leid.

Und wo es klingt, da bricht ein Blühen
Und Leuchten auf im weiten Rund;
‹Wie Veilchenduft und Rosenglühen
Geht's durch der Herzen tiefsten Grund.›
Was längst zerronnen und zerstoben,
Was mit der Kindheit von uns schied:
Es wird in Träumen neu gewoben.
Wenn uns umrauscht das deutsche Lied.

Wir schau'n der Heimat grüne Tale,
Der Schwalbe Nest am Vaterhaus;
Wir zieh'n im Morgensonnenstrahle
Durchs alte Tor zur Stadt hinaus;
Wir hören ferner Glocken Klingen
Und deutscher Eichenwälder Weh'n,
Wir fühlen junges Frühlingsringen
Und erster Liebe Auferstehn!

‹Und ob auch Früchte viel und Blüten
Die Hand auf fremder Erde zieht,
Wir wollen hegen doch und hüten
Den Frühlingsspross, das deutsche Lied,
Das uns zum Segen in die Ferne,
Die Muttererde einst beschied,
Und das, gleich einem guten Sterne,
Mit uns die weite Welt durchzieht.

As American artists of German descent were the apostles
of the grandeur of American scenery, so we owe to German
poets many masterpieces of descriptive poetry. Rich in color,
for instance, is **Udo Brachvogel's**

Indianer-Sommer.

Den Hügel noch empor, mein wackres Tier,
Dort lichtet sich der Wald, dort halten wir —
Fühlst du den Sporn? Hinan mit flücht'gen Sätzen!
Schon schliesst sich hinter uns die Tannennacht;
Frei schweift der Blick — ha, welche Farbenpracht!
Erschloss sich Scheher'zadens Märchenpracht,
Rings alles zu bestreu'n mit ihren Schätzen?

Der Himmel leuchtet, ein saphirner Schild;
Es strahlt an ihm die Sonne hehr und mild,
Nicht tödlich, nein, nur schmeichelnd allem Leben.
Am fernen Horizonte rollt der Fluss;
Jedwede Wog' umspielt des Mittags Kuss,
Sie bebt und zittert unter ihm, — so muss
Die Braut am Herzen des Ersehnten beben.

Und schimmernd liegt das Tal, wie Mosaik,
Wie reicher es und blendender dem Blick
Noch niemals unter Künstlers Hand entglommen.
Hin strömt es zwischen dunklem Braun und Grün
Gleich Flammen, die aus Goldtopasen sprühn,
Gleich Purpurmänteln, die um Schultern glühn
Von Königen, die von der Krönung kommen.

Der Ahorn lodert, wie im Morgenhauch
Einst Moses brennen sah den Dornenstrauch,
Gefacht von unsichtbarer Engel Chore.
Dort rankt sich's flimmernd und verzweigt sich's bunt,
Wie die Koralle auf des Meeres Grund,
Und drängt sich um das silberfarbne Rund
Des Stamms der königlichen Sykamore.

Und einsam ragt und priesterlich zumal
Die Lorbeereiche aus dem Bachanal
Von Licht und Glanz, von Farben und von Gluten.
Doch auch von ihrer dunklen Aeste Saum,
Aus ihrer Krone tropft wie Purpurflaum
Die wilde Reb'; es ist, als ob der Baum
Sein Herz geöffnet habe, zu verbluten.

Das Eichhorn springt. Es lockt mit tiefem Klang
Der Tauber seine Taube nach dem Hang,
Wo überreich sich Beere dringt an Beere.
Die Drossel stimmt ihr schmelzend Tongedicht,
Der Falter badet sich im Sonnenlicht,
Und aus der Sumachbüsche Scharlach bricht
Das scheue Reh, des Waldes Bajadere.

"Und dies ist Herbst? So sterben Wald und Flur?
Wie ist dann das Erwachen der Natur,
Wenn noch ihr Tod sich hüllt in solches Leben?" —
So ringt sich's von des Reiters Lippe los, —
Da rauscht's ihm Antwort aus des Waldes Schoss —
Ein Windstoss braust heran und noch ein Stoss,
Und lässt ein Meer von Blättern niederbeben.

Rings quillt es plötzlich auf, wie Schleierflug,
Schneewolken weh'n daher in dichtem Zug,
Vom Norden pfeift's, und trübe wird's und trüber.
Der Taube Ruf verstummt; ein Büchsenknall,
Im Blute liegt das Reh, und in dem Fall
Der Blätter rauscht's wie leiser Seufzerhall:
Noch eine Nacht, und alles ist vorüber!

Der Reiter fröstelt in des Nordwind's Hauch,
Er ruft: "Und dennoch ist dies Tod, ob auch
Gleich Hochzeitskleidern prangt sein Leichenlinnen.
So stirbt ein Tag im reichsten Abendrot,
So küsst die Lippen einer Braut der Tod,
So fühlt ein Jüngling, rings vom Feind bedroht,
Aus Wunden tausendfach sein Herzblut rinnen!" —

One of the most beautiful poems, composed by Germans
in praise of their adopted country, is **Theodor Kirchhoff's** hymn

An California.

Warum du mir lieb bist, du Land meiner Wahl? —
Dich liebt ja der warme Sonnenstrahl,
Der aus Aetherstiefe, azurrein
Deine Fluren küsst mit goldenem Schein!
Dich liebt ja des Südens balsamische Luft,
Die im Winter dir schenket den Blütenduft,
Deine Felder schmückt mit smaragdenem Kleid,
Wenn's friert im Osten und stürmet und schneit!
Dich liebt ja das Meer, das „Stille" genannt,
Das mit Silber umsäumt dein grünes Gewand,
Das dich schützend umarmt, mit schwellender Lust
Dich wonniglich presst an die wogende Brust! —
Wie dein Meer, wie der Lüfte Balsamhauch,
Wie die Sonne dich liebt, so lieb' ich dich auch.
Seine Söhne zumal, — ihr rasches Blut,
Pulsierend in frohem Lebensmut,
Deine Töchter mit Wangen frisch und gesund,
Die Seele im Auge, zum Küssen der Mund.

Warum du mir lieb bist? — Nicht ist es dein Gold,
Du Land, wo die westliche Woge rollt.
Ich wählte zur Heimat diesen Strand,
Weil ich offne, warme Herzen hier fand,
Weil fremd hier der niedrige, kleinliche Sinn,
Der nur strebt und trachtet nach kargem Gewinn,
Weil die eigene Kraft hier den Mann erprobt,
Nicht ererbtes Gut den Besitzer lobt.
Eine Welt für sich, voll Schönheit, trennt
Dich die hohe Sierra vom Kontinent;
Doch schlugst du mit eiserner Brücke den Pfad
Ueber wolkentragender Berge Grat,
Und täglich vernimmst du am goldenen Port
Von den fernsten Gestaden der Völker Wort.
Du bewahrtest das Feuer der Jugend dir,
Den Geist, dem Arbeit des Lebens Zier,
Der wagt und ringet und nie verzagt,
Und wo es sich zeiget, das Glück erjagt.
Ja! ich liebe dich, blühendes, westliches Land,
Wo die neue, die schöne Heimat ich fand.
Wer früge wohl noch, der dich Herrliche sah,
Warum du mir lieb, California!

George Sylvester Viereck at the hundredth anniversary of Bismarck's birth penned the following verses:

The Iron Chancellor

(1915)

Above the grave where Bismarck sleeps
  The ravens screeched with strange alarms,
The Saxon forest in its deeps
  Shook with the distant clash of arms.

The Iron Chancellor stirred. "'Tis war!
  Give me my sword to lay them low
Who touch my work. Unbar the door
  I passed an hundred years ago."

The angel guardian of the tomb
  Spake of the law that binds all clay,
That neither rose nor oak may bloom
  Betwixt the night and judgment day.

"For no man twice may pass this gate."
  He said. But Bismarck flashed his eyes:
"Nay, at the trumpet call of fate,
  Like Barbarossa, I shall rise.

"In sight of all God's Seraphim
  I place this helmet on my brow.
For lo! We Germans fear but Him,
  And He, I know, is with us now."

The dead man stood up in his might,
  The startled angel said no word,
Through endless spheres of day and night
  God in His Seventh Heaven heard,

And answered thus: "Shall man forget
  My laws? They were not lightly made,
Nor writ for thee to break. And yet
  I love thee. Thou art not afraid.

"Bismarck, from now till morrow's sun
  Walks as a wraith amid the strife,
And if thou find thy work undone
  Come back, and I shall give thee — life."

With stern salute the spectre strode
  Out of the dark into the dawn.
From Hamburg to the Caspian road
  He saw a wall of iron drawn.

163

He saw young men go forth to die
   Singing the martial songs of yore.
Boldly athwart the Flemish sky
   He marked the German airmen soar.

A thousand spears in battle line
   Had pierced the wayward heart of France,
But still above the German Rhine
   The Walkyrs held their august dance.

He saw the sliding submarine
   Wrest the green trident from the hold
Of her whose craven tradesmen lean
   On yellow men and yellow gold.

In labyrinths of blood and sand
   He watched ten Russian legions drown.
Unseen he shook the doughty hand
   Of Hindenburg near Warsaw town.

The living felt his presence when,
   Paternal blessing, he drew nigh,
And all the dead and dying men
   Saluted him as he passed by.

But he rode back in silent thought,
   And from his great heart burst a sigh
Of thanks. "The Master Craftsman wrought
   This mighty edifice, not I.

"No hostile hoof shall ever fall
   Upon my country's sacred sod;
Though seven whirlwinds lash its wall,
   It stands erect, a rock of God.

"I shall return unto my bed,
   Nor ask of life a second lease.
My spirit lives though I be dead,
   My aching bones may rest in peace."

Up to his chin he drew the shroud,
   To wait God's judgment patiently,
While high above a blood-red cloud
   Two eagles screamed of victory.

Kuno Francke, who worked so faithfully for friendly relations between America and Germany, is the author of the following lines:

Ich weiss von einem Lande, dem bietet Jahr für Jahr
Des reichen Glanzes Fülle die Hand des Schicksals dar.
Auf Flächen unermessen, aus tiefem Bergesschacht
Reift golden ihm die Ernte, quillt ihm der Erze Pracht.
Gewaltige Ströme rauschen, rings flutet das Weltenmeer,
Aus Urwald und Prairie stürmt mächtiges Leben her,
Und in dem Volke brauset titanenhafter Sinn,
Nach allem Höchsten greifet sein kühnes Wagen hin.
Es rüttelt an den Bergen, es taucht in Meeresschlund,
Es spannt mit Eisennetzen den Fels und Urwaldsgrund,
Es türmet Quader auf Quader bis zu den Wolken grau,
So werkelt es und hämmert an der Freiheit Riesenbau. —
Ein ander Land auch kenn' ich, ein Land gar lieb und wert,
Dort wird vergang'ner Zeiten Geheimnis noch geehrt,
Dort flüstern noch die Wälder manch altes Sagenwort,
Dort rauscht noch in den Wogen der Nibelungenhort,
Dort ragen noch alte Dome dunkel und wundergleich,
Dort sehnen noch Kinderherzen sich nach dem Himmelreich.
O Deutschland, von all' deinen Kindern liebt keines dich so
  sehr,
Als wir, die fremdgeword'nen, die Deutschen überm Meer.
Du bist uns mehr als Mutter, du bist unseres Lebens Ruh,
Du bist unser Weinen und Lachen, unserer Arbeit Segen bist
  du,
Du setzest dem rastlosen Wagen bedächtig Mass und Zeit,
Du weisest dem hastigen Blicke den Weg zur Ewigkeit.

Loyalty to the great cause of liberty can not find a more beautiful expression than in **Friedrich Albert Schmitt's** spirited poem:

Sterne und Streifen.

Im Morgenwind in der Sonne Gold
Der Freiheit heiliges Banner rollt;
Sein Rauschen tönet wie Adlerflug
Um Alpenhäupter im Siegeszug.
Es klingt wie das Rauschen im Urwaldsdom,
Es klingt wie das Brausen im Felsenstrom,
Es klingt wie die Brandung am Klippenstrand;
Von See zu See und von Land zu Land:

Freiheit! Freiheit!

Wie die ewigen Sterne vom Himmelszelt
Herniedergrüssen zur träumenden Welt,
Wie im blauen Aether ihr Licht erglüht,
Erfreuend, erhebend das Menschengemüt,
So grüssen die Sterne des Banners, wenn hold
Es den staunenden Blicken der Völker entrollt,
So kündet ihr Anblick vom heiligen Hort
Dem Lande der Freien das herrliche Wort:
Freiheit! Freiheit!

So zog es voran einst der Väter Heer,
Als die Knechtschaft dräute und Fesseln schwer;
So hat es ermutigt die Völker im Streit,
So hat es die Waffen der Krieger gefeit,
So hat es die heilige Liebe geschürt,
So hat es zum herrlichen Sieg sie geführt,
So hat es gewährt ihnen köstlichen Lohn,
So hat es geheiliget der Union
Freiheit! Freiheit!

Ihr Sterne so hehr und ihr Streifen so hold,
Oh, rauschet zum Feste, oh rauschet und rollt
Und kündet den Kindern und Enkeln es an,
Was einst um die Freiheit die Väter getan!
Oh, rollet und rauschet ein ewiges Lied,
Dass tief in den Herzen es woget und glüht,
Oh, rollet und rauschet, dem Segen geweiht,
Ob dem Lande der Freien in Ewigkeit!
Freiheit! Freiheit!

*　　*　　*　　*

Among the numerous works of German prose writers in
America those treating historical subjects are perhaps of greatest value. During the years 1850 to 1860 **Gustav von Struwe**
wrote a history of the world in eight volumes, published at
New York. This book is of special interest, as the author
reviews events and personalities from a strong democratic
standpoint.

Robert Clemens published a "History of the Inquisition"
(Cincinnati 1849). **Philipp Schaff** wrote a "History of the
Christian Church" (Mercersburg 1851) and "America, and
Its Political, Social and Religious Conditions" (Berlin 1854).
Gustav Brühl, a physician in Cincinnati, was author of the
valuable volume "Die alten Kulturvölker Amerikas."

Ernst Richard is author of a valuable "History of German
Civilization" (New York 1909).

Historical subjects are also treated in several works of
Rudolf Cronau. During the years 1890 to 1892 he wrote his

book "America," which was published simultaneously in German (Leipzig, 1892) and in Spanish (Barcelona, 1892). It gives a review of the discovery and exploitation of the New World from the earliest to the present times. Purposing to acquire authoritative information from original sources and to make himself acquainted with the countries discovered by Columbus, Cortes, Coronado, Cartier, La Salle, Champlain, Pike, Lewis, Clarke and others, the author made extensive journeys through the West Indies, Central America, Mexico, the United States and Canada, following the tracks of the great explorers. Two questions of paramount interest, concerning which wide differences of opinion existed, were the subject of exhaustive investigations by him: the location of the first landing place of Columbus, and that of the actual place of repose of the great discoverer's remains. Cronau's conclusions as to these questions, based on researches made on these trips and included in the above named work, have been accepted as decisive by the most critical authorities.

Another historical work by the same author appeared in 1909 at Berlin under the title "Drei Jahrhunderte deutschen Lebens in Amerika," giving to German readers a comprehensive review of the achievements of the German element in the United States.

A number of able writers have contributed works bearing on this same subject, from various points of view, and collectively presenting an array of facts, which will prove a solid wall against present day efforts to minimize the German as a factor in America. Among these writers are

Franz Löher, ("Geschichte and Zustände der Deutschen in Amerika," Cincinnati, 1847); Anton Eickhoff ("In der neuen Heimat," New York, 1884); Georg von Bosse ("Das deutsche Element in den Vereinigten Staaten," Stuttgart, 1908); Albert Bernhardt Faust ("The German Element in the United States," Boston, 1909); Julius Goebel ("Das Deutschtum in den Vereinigten Staaten," München, 1904); and Max Heinrici ("Das Buch der Deutschen in Amerika," Philadelphia, 1909).

Friedrich Kapp wrote a valuable "History of Slavery" (New York, 1860); furthermore splendid biographies of Friedrich Wilhelm von Steuben and von Kalb; and "Geschichte der deutschen Einwanderung in den Staat New York" (New York, 1868).

Oswald Seidensticker penned "Bilder aus der deutsch-pennsylvanischen Geschichte," a magnetic and finely written work on local history. Very valuable monographs about the German immigrants and sectarians of Pennsylvania have been published by the "German Historical Society of Pennsylvania." Among the contributors are Julius Sachse, Samuel Pennypacker, Daniel Rupp, Daniel Cassel, Oskar Kuhns, Diffenderfer, Hartranft, Schmauk and others. Hermann Schuricht wrote a comprehensive work about the Germans of Virginia; Emil Klauprecht and H. A. Rattermann edited similar books about the Germans of Ohio; Joseph Eiboeck about the Germans of Iowa; Wilhelm Hensen and Ernst Bruncken about the Germans of Wisconsin; Hanno Deiler about the Germans at the lower Mississippi. Gert Goebel described the life of the German backwoodsmen; and Friedrich Rübesamen supplied vivid pictures of the frontier life in Texas, New Mexico and Arizona. Gustav Koerner compiled valuable historical notes in his book "Das deutsche Element während der Periode 1818 bis 1848" (Cincinnati, 1880). Of equal value are the many historical essays of H. A. Rattermann.

A most noteworthy writer during the last century was Karl Heinzen, a refugee of 1848, who as one of the leaders in the United States of the radical German democrats brilliantly advocated their principles. As editor of the weekly "Pioneer" as well as author of the works "Deutscher Radikalismus in Amerika" and "Erlebtes" (Boston, 1864 and 1874) he exerted a remarkable influence on his countrymen in the United States.

Of the German writers, whose mastership of the English language was almost equal to that of their own, Franz Lieber and Carl Schurz are the best known.

Of Lieber's eminent works on international law and social ethics has been spoken in a former chapter. The literary works of Carl Schurz contain magnificent biographies of Henry Clay (Boston, 1887), and President Lincoln (London, 1892). Of greatest interest are also Schurz's "Reminiscences of a Long Life" (New York, 1906), wherein the author reviews the many memorable incidents of his career, so exceedingly rich in struggles, hopes, disappointments and success. For the study of the German revolution of 1848 and the political conditions of the United States during the period from 1850 to 1900 these reminiscences are sources of first order. The same must be said of the collection of his speeches, correspondence and political papers, which in 1913 were edited by the "Schurz Memorial Committee."

A prominent writer of the 19th century was Charles Nordhoff, born 1830 in Westphalia, but brought to this country while still a child. In 1844 he entered the U. S. Navy, serving three years, and making a voyage around the world. He remained at sea in the merchant, whaling and mackerel fishery service until 1853, when he entered journalism and occupied editorial positions on the "New York Evening Post," and later on the "New York Herald." Of his many books the best remembered are "Communistic Societies in the United States" (1875) and "The Cotton States" (1876). The latter provoked a heated controversy, because Nordhoff placed responsibility for the terrible conditions, prevailing then, on the Republican "carpetbaggers," who invaded the South after the Civil War.

The experiences during his former sea-life were described by Nordhoff in the works "Whaling and Fishing;" "Man-of-War Life;" "Stories of the Island World" and others.

In his book "Our Wasteful Nation. The Story of American Prodigality and the Abuse of Our National Resources" (New York, 1908) **Rudolf Cronau** treated the weighty problem of conservation, showing conclusively that the American nation suffers losses amounting to many hundred millions of dollars annually by sheer carelessness and wasteful methods. The twelve chapters of the book bring to view the enormous waste, committed by the American people by the destruction of its forests, the waste of water, soil, mineral resources, the extermination of birds, fishes, game, fur- and great marine animals, the waste of public lands, privileges, money, property and human lives.

To the Travel Literature **Theodor Kirchhoff**, the "Poet of the Golden Gate," contributed highly interesting works in his "Californische Kulturbilder" and "Reisebilder und Skizzen" (Altona, 1875).

Rudolf Cronau published "Von Wunderland zu Wunderland, Landschafts- und Lebensbilder aus den Staaten und Territorien der Union" (Leipzig, 1885); "Im fernen Westen. Eine Künstlerfahrt durch die Prairien und Felsengebirge der Union" (Braunschweig, 1890), and "Fahrten im Lande der Sioux" (Leipzig, 1885).

Robert H. Schauffler, born in Brünn, Austria, became widely known by his attractive books "Romantic Germany" (New York, 1909) and "Romantic America" (New York, 1911), "Through Italy with the Poets" (New York, 1908).

Of the numerous German novelists in America the best known during the midst of the 19th century was **Carl Postel,** who wrote under the pseudonym **Charles Sealsfield.** Having travelled for several years in the Southern States, he published in Philadelphia in 1828 his first great novel "Tokeah or the White Rose," which later on was followed by "Nathan the Squatter-Regulator; "The Legitimate and the Republicans;" "Virey and the Aristocrats" and many others. His prolific pen drew fascinating sketches of the life on Southern plantations, of the lower Mississippi River and the plains of Texas. Endowed with a rich imagination, he unrolled to his readers a new world alive with people never before described. With characteristic strokes he drew the smart Yankee, the light-minded Frenchman, the considerate German, the sensuous Creole and Creoless, the daring trapper and the tough backwoodsman.

Related to the works of this novelist are those of **Friedrich**

Gerstäcker, Balduin Möllhausen, Otto Ruppius and other writers, who travelled extensively in North America and enriched the German American literature by numerous fascinating works of fiction, which found large circulation in Germany as well as in the United States.

Other noted fiction writers are **Friedrich Hassaureck** ("Hierarchie und Aristokratie" and "Das Geheimniss der Anden"); **Friedrich Dresel** ("Oskar Welden;" "Doppelehe oder keine Doppelehe;" "Bekenntnisse eines Advokaten"); **Friedrich Lexow** ("Auf dem Geierfels," "Imperia," "Vornehm und gering"); **Rudolf Lexow** ("Der Rubin"); **Karl Dilthey** ("Die schönsten Tage einer Tänzerin," "Henriette Sonntag"); **Reinhold Solger** ("Anton in Amerika"); **von Jakob** ("The Exiles"); **Adolf Douai** ("Fata Morgana"); **Willibald Winkler** ("Der Sklavenjäger"); **Udo Brachvogel** ("King Korn"); **Adolf Schaffmeyer** ("Ein Phantom," "Auf steiler Höhe," "Die ewige Jagd" and "Im Wirbel der Grossstadt"); **Dorothea Böttcher** ("Der Sohn des Bankiers" and "Der Erbschleicher"); **Hugo Bertsch** ("Bob der Sonderling" and "Die Geschwister"); **Henry Urban** ("Maus Lula," "Lederstrumpf's Erben," "Aus dem Dollarlande," etc.); **Hugo Möller** ("Aus Deutsch Amerika" and "Grand Prairie"); **George Sylvester Viereck** ("The Vampire," "The Candle and the Flame" and "Game of Love").

The great European War brought forth not only numerous pamphlets, but also several noteworthy books, written by Germans in the United States. **Hugo Münsterberg** discussed in his works "The War and America" and "The Peace and America" the essential factors and issues in the great war and their meaning and importance for America. **Edmund von Mach** in his book "What Germany Wants" gives a clear-cut statement of the German side. **Frank Köster** tells in "Secrets of German Progress" (New York, 1915) the fascinating story of Germany's efficiency and her amazing rise to that industrial power, which aroused England to such jealousy, that it made most careful preparations to isolate and crush this new competitor on the world's markets in the same manner as it had done with all former rivals.

The story of these destructive British wars has been given by **Rudolf Cronau** in "The British Black Book" (New York, 1915). Based on historical facts, it shows how England by her machinations has kept the world aflame for centuries, first robbing Ireland, Wales and Scotland of their independence; then successively destroying the power of Spain, Holland, France, Denmark and India; how she poisoned the Chinese with opium and suppressed the free Boers for the sake of their gold and diamond mines; how she conspired with France and Russia to strangle her most successful rival in commerce, Germany, and how in the midst of a mercenary war she seeks to throttle the prosperity of the United States.

170

Alexander Fuehr, doctor of law, in his book "The neutrality of Belgium" (New York, 1915) makes three claims: first, that Belgium was not neutral territory when the German army invaded it; second, that, according to the Law of Nations, the treaty guaranteeing Belgium's neutrality had been void for many years and was considered so by Great Britain, prior to the war; third, that, even if the guarantee treaty had still been in force, International Law fully permitted Germany to invade Belgium under the particular circumstances. To substantiate these claims the author presents large numbers of documents and affidavits, which give full account of the origin and the break-down of Belgium's neutrality.

Among the German American publicists, who came to the front during the great European war, the most notable is **George Sylvester Viereck,** who in the weeklies "The Fatherland" and "The International" wrote numerous strong articles, which imparted to the American public undistorted views of the cause of the great conflict and unvarnished truth about the many serious questions connected with it.

Undaunted fighters for truth have been also **Frederick Franklin Schrader, Francis Dorl,** editor of "Issues and Events," **Bernard Ridder** of the "New York Staatszeitung," **Marcus Braun** of the "Fair Play," and **William Ries** of the "People's Post."

German Music and Song in America

If for no other contribution to its culture and development, the American people owe a debt of gratitude to the Germans for having brought into its social life some brightening rays of sunshine.

Whoever studies the social life of the early settlers, in particular that of the Puritans, Quakers and other sectarians, will find that it was dominated by two aims strangely opposed to each other, the one, an intensive striving for material gain, the other, laying up stores for the life hereafter.

The pursuit of these objects rendered the earthly existence of the Anglo Americans so grave and joyless that visitors to this country were repelled by its melancholic monotony. Such was the experience of the British authoress Mrs. Frances Trollope recorded in her famous book "Domestic Manners of the Americans." Having travelled in this country from 1827 to 1831, she felt herself justified in saying: "I never saw a population so totally divested of gayety; there is no trace of this feeling from one end of the Union to the other. They have no fêtes, no fairs, no merry-makings, no music in the streets."

In confirmation of their own impressions the authoress quotes also the following remarks of another woman: "They do not love music, oh no! and they never amuse themselves — no; and their hearts are not warm, at least they seem not so to strangers; and they have no ease, no forgetfulness of business and care — no, not for a moment. But I will not stay long, I think, for I should not live."—

To have brought a change in this joyless life, is the great merit of the Germans, who made America their home. When they emigrated from the beloved fatherland, their cheerfulness, good humor and love for music and song were the most valuable treasures, they brought with them to our shores. With their sunny mind they enriched our nation, while she was in the process of evolution, to such degree, that the American people should have to the Germans no other feeling but deep gratitude.

There was a great difference in the religious service of the Puritans and Quakers and of that of the Germans. While the first abhorred music and singing the latter enjoyed the wonderful impressive hymns and the great symphonies of Martin Luther, Bach, Händel, Haydn, Mozart and other composers of the 17th and 18th centuries. Visitors who heard these songs in Bethlehem and in the Ephrata cloister, confessed that they were overwhelmed by the impressive cadence of the chorals of the combined choirs, of the angelic or celestial quality of the vocal music.

But these musical exercises were not confined to religious meetings exclusively. From the history of the Moravians we know, that they had songs for their daily work as well. Bishop Spangenberg, head of the community during the middle of the 18th century, states: "Never since the creation of this world have been invented and used such lovely songs for shepherds, farmers, reapers, threshers, spinners, seamstresses and other working people than here. It would be easy, to make up a whole volume with these beautiful melodies."

It did not take long for the conquering power of music and song to make itself felt even in New England. ᴬA Händel and Haydn Society was started in 1786 in Stoughton, Mass. ᵧ In June 1815 it was followed by a similar one in Boston, organized by **Gottlieb Graupner,** a German musician, who founded also the first orchestra, the Philharmonic Society.

Societies with like purposes were formed in New York, Baltimore, Cleveland, Cincinnati and other centres of German life. New York had the Euterpean Society, founded in 1799; the Sacred Music Society, founded in 1823; the Choral- and the Harmonic Society. To these early clubs came in 1842 the famous Philharmonic Society, which still exists. Her members, mostly Germans, aimed not for financial gain, but, to reach in their art perfection. From 1842 to 1865 **U. C. Hill, Georg Loder, H. C. Timm, Theodor Eisfeld** and **Karl Bergmann** alternated as conductors; from 1865 to 1876 Bergmann conducted exclusively and led the society to her triumphant position.

Bergmann was also a pioneer in another direction. He had come to America as a member of the Germania Orchestra, which consisted of fifty political refugees of 1848. Being elected as its conductor, Bergmann boldly began to make concert tours with this orchestra, visiting many of the eastern cities.

After his resignation **Leopold Damrosch** became his successor as conductor of the Philharmonic Society. At the same time he founded the Oratorio Society and the Symphony Society of New York, which under his leadership gave, during May 3d to 7th, 1881, a grand festival in the armory of the 7th New York Regiment. It was a musical event of the highest order. The chorus consisted of 1200 select voices, which were supported by 1000 young ladies of the high schools of New York and by 250 boys of the choirs of several churches. The orchestra numbered 250 instruments. The most important works of the program were Händel's Messias and Te Deum, Rubinstein's Erection of the Tower at Babel, Berlioz's Missa Solemnis and Beethoven's Ninth Symphony. The artistic success as well as the financial results of this festival surpassed all expectation.

Now came a period of great conductors, among them **Theodore Thomas, Karl Zerrahn, George Henschel, Wilhelm Gericke, Anton Seidl, Walter** and **Frank H. Damrosch, Emil Paur, Frank van der Stucken, Ernst Kunwald, Franz H. Arens, Fritz Scheel, Louis Kömmenich** and others, under whose able leadership many of the musical societies reached highest perfection.

Several of these conductors have won, by their genius, an everlasting place in the history of music in America. This is especially true in regard to the Damroschs, Theodor Thomas, Karl Zerrahn and Anton Seidl, all of which were born in Germany. Thomas, a native of Northern Germany, was perhaps the greatest of these leaders. When twenty years old, he started a society for chamber concerts. Several years later he organized also his own orchestra, with which he, from 1864 to 1891, made tours throughout the United States. While these tours were, from a financial standpoint, not a success, their educational value was immense. To hundreds of thousands of people the Thomas-Orchestra was the first wonderful revelation of the power of instrumental music. John C. Griggs says in his "Studies about Music in America": "I can never forget the deep impression the Thomas-Orchestra made upon my mind. It was like a glance into a new world."

Thomas conducted five music festivals in Cincinnati (1873, 1875, 1878, 1880, 1882), one in Chicago (1882) and one in New York (1882). In 1891 he was called to Chicago, to organize a symphonic orchestra, which he conducted with great success. He also distinguished himself as musical director at the Columbian Exposition of 1893.

Indeed, there could be no adequate sketch of the grand orchestra that did not pay a tribute to Theodore Thomas, practically speaking the great missionary of the orchestra in America. He did not create it, but he introduced and developed and extended it, and above all, as Charles E. Russell has correctly said, "he made it intelligible to the public, spreading abroad the understanding of and the taste for orchestral art, patiently teaching its rudiments and by exposition making clear its principles."

A position similar to that held by Thomas in the middle States was held by **Karl Zerrahn** in the New England States. He conducted not only for many years the Philharmonic Orchestra and the Händel and Haydn Society in Boston, but also the concerts of the Oratorio Society in Salem and the famous Worcester festivals in Worcester, Mass. Of him Elton in his work "National Music of America" said: "Zerrahn was the bridge, by which New England travelled to its modern goal in classical music."

174

The names of **Leopold** and **Walter Damrosch** are connected with the brilliant history of the Oratorio- and Symphony Societies of New York, the names of **Karl Bergmann, Anton Seidl, Gustav Mahler** and **Joseph Stransky** with the history of the unsurpassed Philharmonic Society of New York.

Georg Henschel, Wilhelm Gericke, Arthur Nickisch, Emil Paur and **Karl Muck** habe been the leaders of the Boston Symphony Orchestra, that pride of the Hub and America generally. After having been supported by Major Henry L. Higginson for thirty years, this orchestra now plays to paying audiences, and its concerts, given in Boston, New York, Brooklyn, Baltimore and Washington, are financially successful, as they are artistically most brilliant.

No higher encomium could be framed for these orchestras than that the greatest leaders and virtuosos of Germany were glad to come here and as guests take part in performances of genuine worth.

Among such conductors were **Max Bruch, Hans von Bülow, Felix Weingartner, Richard Strauss,** and others; among the virtuosos men like **August Wilhelmj, Rafael Joseffy, Anton Rubinstein, Thalberg, Scharwenka, Louis Maas, Franz Kneisel, Schultz,** and many more, who by the masterly rendition of the works of great composers helped in paving to music, the most pleasing and elevating of the muses, the way to victory.

To-day almost every considerable city has its symphony orchestra, voluntarily organized and maintained not for profit but voluntarily supported by public subscription as a public educator. So rapidly has the number of such grand orchestras grown, that only the specialists maintain any knowledge of this most significant development of our culture. The orchestra is already a feature of American city life, and the cities that have orchestras feel in them steadily increasing pride and interest and give to them steadily increasing support.

* * * *

Vocal music, introduced so effectually by the German sectarians of the 18th century, found great stimulation through the efforts of the political refugees of the period 1820 to 1848. Among these high-spirited heroes of an unsuccessful revolution there were many musicians, enthusiastic followers of their art. Disappointed by the monotony of American life, these men banded together and formed, for their own entertainment, singing societies, in which they cultivated the inspiring songs of liberty, written by Uhland, Herwegh, Freiligrath, Hoffmann von Fallersleben, Lenau and other great German poets.

The first of such singing societies was the Philadelphia Männerchor, founded in 1835, and still flourishing. The next was the Baltimore Liederkranz (1836), followed in 1838 by the Deutsche Gesangverein von Cincinnati; in 1844 the Philadelphia Liedertafel was born, and in 1847 the Deutsche Liederkranz von New York.

Since then the increase of such societies has been enormous. To-day there is hardly any city with a German population, that has not its singing societies.

Occasional visits of one society to others led to the formation of unions for the purpose of holding regular singing festivals with a competition for prizes. The first Sängerfest was held in June 1849 in Cincinnati and resulted in the founding of the **Deutsche Sängerbund von Nordamerika.** Two days were devoted to concerts; on the third day all members, more than one thousand, went in richly decorated steamers up the Ohio River to the romantic Bald Hill, where Sunday was spent with singing and all kinds of entertainments. This festival was for the American press a source of wonder. "The music on the high hill, in the midst of a pleasant grove, by nearly two hundred singers, was grand beyond our power of description." So wrote the Cincinnati Gazette.

Continuing, it said: "Enjoyment seemed to be the object of all, and about the whole assembly there was an air which spoke plainly as words:

> Let us be young again
> And o'er the grassy plain
> Gambol like children,
> And give care the slip.

We do not think the Sabbath under all circumstances a proper day for festivals of this character, but we think they should at proper times be much more frequent than they are now. Americans do not allow themselves enjoyment enough of this kind.

In our too plodding homes, we ponder over tomes,
Ledger and day-book, till we quite forget
That there are fields and bowers and river-banks and flowers.
And that we owe our languid limbs a debt:
A debt most sweet to pay — a needful holiday —
A brain-refreshing truce, 'mid intellectual strife,
That, fought too keenly out, impairs the mortal life."

The example, set by the singing societies of the Central States, was followed by the societies of the East and Northwest, of Texas and the Pacific States. At present we have the **Nordöstliche Sängerbund,** the **Deutsch Texanische Sängerbund,** the **Nordwestliche Sängerbund,** the **Pacific Sängerbund** and the **Nord Pacific Sängerbund.** All hold in regular intervals great Sänger-festivals, combined with a competition for valuable prizes. Among these prizes have been some donated by the German and Austrian Emperors, and it was due to the competition for these trophies of high artistic value, that some of these festivals became events of extraordinary magnitude. There have been such festivals, in which several thousand active singers took part, as for instance in July 1900 in Brooklyn, which was visited by 174 societies with more than 6000 singers. Many of these festivals gained a special splendor by the active participation of famous soloists, as **Henrietta Sontag, Amalie Materna, Etelka Gerster, Johanna Gadski, Ernestine Schumann-Heink** and others, who made the American public acquainted with the most beautiful creations of German song.

Captivated by the magic spell of these songs the Americans began on their part to organize singing societies, with such eminent success, that to-day they are able to compete with their German American fellow-citizens in the perfect rendition of the most difficult compositions of the German masters.

And so the German American Sängerbünde can point with great pride to the work of culture accomplished by them and can say indeed that no other societies have in like manner contributed to the elevation and advancement of the population of our country.

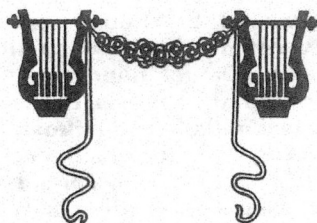

German Drama and Opera in the United States

Together with the oratorios and symphonies of great German composers the dramas of German poets found their way to the United States at an early day. Schiller's "Räuber," "Wilhelm Tell," "Don Carlos," "Cabale und Liebe" were given as early as 1795 in English translations on the stages of New York, Philadelphia and Baltimore. Several dramas of Kotzebue, Zschokke and Halm were given also with great success and brought full houses.

Since these times countless other works of German play-writers have been presented in English to the American public, among them the best pieces of Paul Heyse, Gustav von Moser, Roderick Benedix, Hermann Sudermann, Anzengruber and Gerhardt Hauptmann. That all these great works had a stimulating influence on American playwrights as well as on actors, can not be denied.

This influence was perhaps strongest during the last half of the 19th century, when **Adolf Neuendorf, Carl Hermann, Gustav Amberg, Heinrich Conried** and others founded German theatres in New York, Philadelphia, Baltimore, Cincinnati, Chicago, Milwaukee and St. Louis, and brought the most famous actors of Germany into this country. Among them were **Friedrich Haase, Daniel Bandmann, Bogumil Davison, Ernst Possart, Karl Sontag, Ludwig Barnay, Friedrich Mitterwurzer, Joseph Kainz, Adalbert Matkowsky, August Junkermann, Magda Irschick, Franziska Ellmenreich, Georgine von Januschowsky, Kathi Schratt, Josephine Gallmeyer, Marie Seebach, Hedwig Niemann-Raabe, Marie Geistinger** and others, who, by their excellent play aroused not only the German Americans to enthusiasm, but also the managers and actors of the Anglo-American stage.

"In reviewing these times," so a noted critic said, "it is difficult, to refrain from such language, as not to be suspected of exaggerating. No one in our prosaic days can realize the ecstasy, by which then New York was taken, not simply the Germans, but all New York."

The managers and members of the Anglo-American theatres were the most impressed, because almost every figure, played by these great German actors, was a study, unsurpassable in charm, accomplishment and truthfulness. How deeply interested the best Anglo-American actors became in the play of their German colleagues, can be judged by the fact, that

Edwin Booth, delighted with the acting of Bogumil Davison, invited the German to play with him in "Othello." In this performance, which took place in January, 1867, Davison had the rôle of Jago; Methua Scheller, a German actress, gave the Desdemona, using in the scenes with Booth-Othello the English language, while in the scenes with Davison she spoke German. In the same year Booth also invited Fanny Janauscheck to act with his company "Lady Macbeth" in Boston. Although she spoke in German, she aroused such great enthusiasm, that the houses always were sold out.

Still greater triumphs were achieved by several German companies who visited the United States. The most noteworthy were the "Münchener," the "Schlierseer," and a part of the "Meininger troups."

The Meininger, organized under the protection of the Duke of Saxe-Meiningen, had become famous in Germany for their wonderful ensemble as well as for the great attention they devoted to historic truthfulness in costumes and scenery. In contrast to the American "star-system," by which one particular actor or actress, assisted by some performers of minor grades, glories in the main rôle, the Meininger troupe laid great value on the equality of all actors, in order to accomplish the most harmonious and most artistic interpretation of a dramatic masterpiece.

This idea of ensemble effect had been developed by Richard Wagner, who in the presentation of his operas in Bayreuth secured his triumphs to a great extent by the equality of the most selected singers as well as of the members of the orchestra. As the "Meininger," the "Münchener" and "Schlierseer" observed in their dramatic presentations the same principles, their visits to America made the deepest impression on the public as well as on the managers and members of the American theatres.

Imbued with the same ambitions, which inspired the managers of the above-named troupes, was Heinrich Conried, who, having been an actor himself, assumed the directorship of the Irving Place Theatre of New York City in 1892 and held this position till 1907.

Under his régime numerous other celebrities of the German stage were presented to the American public, among them **Adolf Sonnenthal, Georg Engels, Felix Schweighofer, Rudolf Christians, Ferdinand Bonn, Harry Walden, Agnes Sorma, Helene Odilon, Anna Dierkens, Agathe Barsescu and Mia Werber,** who by their great art won new laurels to the German theatre in the United States.

To interest American students in the great dramas of German literature, Conried also gave a number of high-class performances of Goethe's "Iphigenia," Lessing's "Minña von Barnhelm," Freitag's "Journalisten" and other dramas at several Eastern universities, donating the entire income of such entertainments to the library fund of the respective institutions.

Emulating this munificence **Charles Frohmann** arranged on June 22, 1909, for the benefit of the Germanic museum of Harvard University a similar magnificent performance of Schiller's "Jungfrau von Orleans," with Maud Adams in the title rôle. About 1500 people took part in the pageantry and battle scenes, while the audience, numbering more than 15,000 persons, occupied every seat of the huge semicircle of the stadium, which served as a stage. The great success of this performance on so large a scale was acknowledged by the audience as well as by the critics of the many papers, represented at this occasion.

Conried's successors, among them **Maurice Baumfeld** and **Rudolf Christians,** did their best, not only to keep up the high standard the German drama had reached in former days, but even to surpass it. In similar ways strove the managers of German stages in Chicago, Milwaukee, St. Louis and San Francisco, with the history of which the names of **Leon Wachsner, Alexander Wurster, Ferdinand Welb** and **Ottilie Genee** are insolubly connected.

So the German theatres in the United States have fulfilled their high and sacred mission, to cultivate German dramatic art and to transmit its rich treasures to many millions of Americans and Americans of German descent, to whom the highest performances of German poetry would otherwise remain an unknown realm.

* * * *

Of like great influence with the German Drama has been the German Opera. Overtures and other parts of the "Freischütz," "Martha," "Czar und Zimmermann" had been played by American orchestras as early as 1839. But the first performances were not given before 1855, when twelve evenings were arranged in Niblo's Garden in New York by **Julius Unger.** Four years later **Karl Bergmann,** the leader of the Philharmonic Society, introduced Wagner's "Tannhäuser," which was followed in September 1862 by a season, during which **Karl Anschütz** produced the "Zauberflöte," "Don Juan," "Stradella," and other German operas.

Soon afterwards **Adolf Neuendorff** brought for the first time Wagner's "Lohengrin," "Der fliegende Holländer" and "Rienzi" before the American public. Assisted by such eminent singers as **Theodor Wachtel, Theodor Habelmann, Wilhelm Formes, Eugenie Pappenheim, Pauline Lucca, Ines Lichtmay** and others these performances were such brilliant artistic and financial successes, that it was easy for **Leopold Damrosch,** leader of the Philharmonic Society, to persuade the directors of the Metropolitan Opera House, to arrange in 1884 a series of German operas in place of the Italian operas, which had resulted in serious financial loss. During this season, which consisted of 57 evenings, the American public became acquainted with the operas "Fidelio," "Die Hugenotten," "Die Stumme von Portici," "Der Prophet," and, last but not least, "Walküre."

In selecting his artists Damrosch, breaking with the American star-system, followed the example set by Wagner in Bayreuth. Without regard to cost, he brought together a magnificent ensemble of first-class singers, of whom **Amalie Materna, Marianne Brandt, Marie Schroeder - Hanfstängel, Auguste Seidl-Kraus, Joseph Staudigl, Adolf Robinson** and **Anton Schott** were the most notable. While the artistic success of this season was overwhelming, the financial result was also such as to induce the directors of the Metropolitan Opera House to make plans for a second, still greater season. But the enormous strain of the work had proved fatal to the inspirer of the new venture. Leopold Damrosch suffered a complete break-down and died on February 10, 1885, just when his triumphs were brightest. The season was brought to a successful close by Walter Damrosch, the son of the deceased leader.

In the next season he was followed by Anton Seidl, a member of Richard Wagners household, who had also conducted many of his operas in Italy and at the theatre in Bremen. While almost all of the great singers of the first season were re-engaged, Seidl brought with him several other accomplished artists, such as **Lilli Lehmann, Albert Stritt, Emil Fischer, Gudehus** and others. With such an army of most accomplished singers victory was assured. And indeed, the interpretation given by Seidl to the great works of the master, Richard Wagner, and to other operas, aroused an enthusiasm never before experienced. And when during the seasons of 1885 to 1891 Seidl presented all the other great operas of the Nibelungen Ring, "Rheingold," "Siegfried," "Götterdämmerung," and when he brought also the eminent **Fanny Moran-Olden,** the matchless Albert Niemann, the brilliant **Theodor Reichmann,** and the ideal Max Alvary (Achenbach) into play, the unbelievable became a fact, that all the dried-up business-men of New York became "Wagner-fiends," and that on afternoons they deserted their offices, hastening to the Opera House, to delve into the mystic world of ancient German gods and heroes. No wonder that, when Seidl suddenly died, on March 28, 1898, every lover of art felt this as a personal loss.

Several seasons, started by Walter Damrosch and the managers Abbey and Grau, brought other numbers of eminent German singers to America, among them Rosa Sucher, **Johanna Gadski,** Marie Brema, Olive Fremstadt, Ernestine **Schumann-Heinck,** Ernest van Dyck and Andreas Dippel, which were joined by Marie Rappold, Katharine Fleischer-Edel, Marie Mattfeld, Alois Burgstaller, Albert Reiss, van Roy, Karl Burrian, Heinrich Knote, Otto Goritz and others, when in 1903 Heinrich Conried became manager of the Metropolitan Opera House. Assisted by these brilliant singers and the eminent conductors Felix Mottl, Gustav Mahler and Alfred Hertz Conried presented to the public not only the entire "Nibelungen Ring" several times, but also Wagner's "Meistersinger," Strauss' "Salome," Humperdinck's "Hänsel und Gretel," Goldmark's "Königin von Saba," and Wagner's last great work, "Parcifal." This consecrational festival play was enacted for the first time in America on Christmas Eve 1903. Never before had such great care been devoted to any opera. While the corps of artists was the most select, utmost attention had been given also to the costumes as well as to the sceneries. The result was a performance which, as was stated by the most able critics, even surpassed those given in Bayreuth. Thousands listened to the last message of the great German master in deep devotion, and all agreed that this sublime play left with them a most ennobling impression. In the history of music the event was epoch-making, as it was for the first time that "Parcifal" was given anywhere outside the sacred temple of Bayreuth, and for this reason the attention of all Europe was directed on New York.

Under Conried's régime the members of the Metropolitan Opera made also several tours through the western parts of the United States, visiting Pittsburgh, Chicago, St. Louis, Kansas City and San Francisco.

After the resignation and death of Conried the management of the Metropolitan Opera House became a double one. While the Italian Gatti Casazza was general manager, the care of the German opera was turned over to Andreas Dippel, who deserves great credit for the institution of a German chorus. After two successful seasons Dippel resigned, to organize the Philadelphia-Chicago Opera Company, which he led to many triumphs.

Under the régime of Gatti Casazza the public became acquainted with Richard Strauss' "Rosencavalier" and Humperdinck's "Königskinder." Also a number of new brilliant German singers were engaged, among them Frieda Hempel, Margarethe Ober, Geraldine Farrar, Karl Jörn, Herman Weil, Johannes Sembach and Karl Braun, who, with Alfred Hertz and Arthur Bodanzky as leaders, brought the performances to the highest degree of perfection. And so the German stage in America has never failed to inspire the love for works of standard literary merit and of the highest educational value.

Well Known Artists, Sculptors and Architects.

A history of American Art would be imperfect without giving credit to a large number of German painters, sculptors and architects, who made the United States their home or were born here from German parents.

The first examples of German art in America date back as far as the middle of the 18th century. There lived among the Moravians at Bethlehem, Pa., a painter, **Johann Valentin Haidt,** born at Danzig, Eastern Prussia, in 1700. Attracted by the pious life of the Moravians, he joined their sect and made his home in Bethlehem. Here he painted numerous Biblical scenes, some of which may still be seen in the archives of the Moravians.

At the end of the 18th century **Jacob Eichholz,** born 1776 in Lancaster, Pa., a pupil of the famous Gilbert Stuart, ranked among the best portrait painters of Philadelphia. Several of his works, among them a portrait of the Moravian Missionary Johann Heckewelder, are in the collection of the Pennsylvania Academy of Fine Arts.

Public interest in arts at that time was very low. Just as Muther stated in his "History of Modern Painting: "people ate and drank, and built and reclaimed the land and multiplied. A large bar of iron was of more value than the finest statue, and an ell of good cloth was priced more highly than the "Transfiguration" of Raphael."

J. L. Krimmel and **Paul Weber** are the names of two artists who lived during the first half of the 19th century. While of their work but little is known, we are much better informed about three artists, of whom each one became a pioneer in some distinct line of painting in America. These men were **Emanuel Leutze, Karl Friedrich Weimar** and **Albert Bierstadt.** Born in Germany, these three came in their early years to America, received here the first stimulus for art, then going abroad to complete their studies at Düsseldorf, the famous art center situated at the lower Rhine. Leutze arrived there in 1841; Weimar in 1852, and Bierstadt in 1853. It cannot surprise that their paintings show in composition, color and technique the unmistakable stamp of the Düsseldorf school at that time. But in their subjects they are entirely different. Instead of choosing for themes the scenes of happy family life, or romantic knights, or peaceful landscapes of the Rhine and Switzerland, they present men and sceneries of an entirely

WASHINGTON CROSSING THE DELAWARE.
(After the painting by Emanuel Leutze.)

different world, scenes from the lives of great discoverers, of Indians and trappers, and of the battles, in which the Americans fought for their liberty. Their hearts beat with enthusiasm in admiration of the heroes whose bravery and patriotism had won the war for independence. Again, their skillful brush portrayed the sublimity of nature not yet touched by man. To them the picturesque aborigines no less than the men who formed the vanguard of the white races were neverfailing founts of inspiration. It is a peculiar fact, that these German American artists proved in spirit as well as in their choice of subjects far better Americans than any of their colleagues born on American soil.

Leutze was greatly interested in the figure of Columbus. He painted the great discoverer explaining his ideas to the High Council of Salamanca; in audience with his noble patroness Queen Isabel; and in the brilliant entrance at Seville after the return from his first successful voyage. Again he portrayed him loaded down with chains in the dungeon, suffering the abuses heaped upon him by an ingrate government.

The last painting, which won him a gold medal at Brussels, was followed by another historical subject, "The Landing of the Norsemen in Vinland." While Leutze established his fame with these paintings, he will, no doubt, be remembered longest by his large painting "Washington crossing the Delaware." Executed 1851 in Düsseldorf, it is now one of the gems of the Metropolitan Museum of Art in New York.

The episode is depicted in the early hours of a cold winter morning. The last star still is gleaming in the sky. A little flotilla of boats, rowed by sturdy men, seeks a way through the heavy packs of ice, floating on the river. In the leading boat the hero of those stirring times stands erect, his clear eyes seeking to pierce the distant haze.

When exhibited in Germany this painting made such deep impression, that the Prussian Government honored the artist by bestowing on him the great medal for science and art. In America it has been reproduced more often than any other picture. Making its way into hundreds of thousands of humble huts as well as into rich palaces it became indeed a national possession of the American people.

Among the numerous paintings following, the most notable were "Washington at Monmouth;" "The Settlement of Maryland by Lord Baltimore," and "Westward the Course of Empire Takes Its Way." The last one, finished in 1862, is a large mural painting in the Capitol at Washington and shows a caravan of those emigrants who, enticed by the discovery of gold in California, made with their linen-covered "prairie-schooners" the long journey from the Mississippi to the Pacific, to establish there new homes. The picture presents the weary travellers as having crossed a pass on the Sierra Nevada. In the far distance they see the New Canaan, stretching like a mirage of hope before their eyes and bathed in the glorious lights of a Western sunset.

Of the few American artists of the 19th century who created historical paintings, Emanuel Leutze was the greatest. Imbued with a patriotic love for America, its history and the spirit of its institutions, he was at the same time a man of large mould, capable of grand enthusiasm, and aspiring to grasp soaring ideals. Although his art was often at fault, it makes us feel, notwithstanding, that in contemplating his works we are in the presence of a gigantic mind. He drew from wells of seemingly inexhaustible inspiration. He was Byronic in the impetus of his genius, the rugged incompleteness of his style, the magnificent fervor and rush of his fancy, the epic grandeur and energy, dash and daring of his creations. To him is well applied the German motto:

> "Wer den Besten seiner Zeit genug gethan,
> Der hat gelebt für alle Zeiten." —

How much men are the products of environment and impressions, is shown also by the life of **Karl Ferdinand Weimar,** or, as his name is Americanized, Wimar. Born 1828 in Siegburg he came in 1844 with his parents to St. Louis, then a regular frontier town and a station of the American Fur Company, from where large trading expeditions went to New Mexico, California and Oregon. To this place the Indians and trappers of the upper Mississippi and Missouri made annual pilgrimages for the purpose of exchanging furs for guns, ammunition, cloth and such other commodities as were needed in their wild life. Greatly attracted by these picturesque figures, Weimar began to sketch them, but feeling his shortcomings he went in 1852 to Düsseldorf to study. Here he enjoyed the instruction of such famous artists as Oswald Achenbach and Emanuel Leutze, who just then were at their height. In Düsseldorf Weimar finished several paintings, of which "The captive Charger" was the most impressive. It shows several Indians in possession of the beautiful horse of an American officer, who has been killed in battle.

Having acquired the technique of his art, Weimar returned in 1856 to St. Louis. Taking part in several expeditions of the Fur Company to the upper Missouri, he made studies for several paintings, among them "Indians hunting buffaloes." He had just begun to make the drawings for a number of mural paintings for the cupola of the courthouse in St. Louis, when he fell a victim to consumption.

His desire to portray to later generations faithful scenes of the fast vanishing Indian life Weimar could fulfill only to a small degree. But he is entitled to recognition for having been the first to discover and utilize in worthy manner the superb

IN YOSEMITE VALLEY.
(After a painting by Albert Bierstadt.)

picturesque qualities of the Indian, while this theme was practically ignored by contemporary artists. As Wm. R. Hodges says in a biography of Weimar: "It is most strange that none of our early painters seemed conscious of the existence of the Indian save as the blood-thirsty and implacable enemy of the white man. It is possible that race hatred blinded their eyes to his pictorial value, and that it was reserved to one foreign born, with a mind unclouded by the recollection of centuries of relentless warfare to perceive with an artist's eye a virgin field unequaled in dramatic and pictorial interest."

So Weimar was the forerunner of Remington, Schreyvogel, Demming, Leigh and other artists, who in our times by representations of Western life have recorded such great success.

While thus Leutze was a pioneer on historical and Weimar on ethnological subjects, so **Albert Bierstadt** is entitled to the honor of having disclosed first to the Americans the grandeur of Western sceneries. Born 1830 at Solingen, Rhenish Prussia, he went in 1853 to Düsseldorf, where he was a pupil of Lessing and Andreas Achenbach.

On his return to America he accompanied an exploring expedition under command of General Lander to the Rocky Mountains. The results of this venturesome journey consisted in several powerful paintings, which were revelations throwing beholders into an ecstacy of delight. These landscapes were no prosaic copies from nature, but poems in color, wherein the author expressed with great effect the overwhelming grandeur of his scenes.

This first trip into the sublime wildernesses of the Far West were later on repeated many times. 'Landers Peak," "Mount Corcoran," "Mount Hood," "The Domes of Yosemite Valley," "Evening at Mount Tacoma" are the titles of a few of Bierstadt's canvasses, which may be justly ranked with the best examples of landscape painting of the 19th century.

The influence of Bierstadt on American art was very remarkable. Among his followers were Thomas Hill, Thomas Moran, Julian Rix, William Riess, and others, who in their spirited works glorified the wonders of our Far West. —

< A contemporary of Leutze was **Christian Schüssele,** born 1824 in Gebweiler, Elsass. He came to America in 1848 and was appointed professor of drawing and painting in the Pennsylvania Academy of Fine Arts in Philadelphia. Attracted like Leutze by the great figures of American history, he painted among other scenes "Franklin before the Lords in Council;" "Washington at Valley Forge;" "McClellan at Antietam;" "Men of Progress" and "The Moravian Missionary Zeisberger preaching to Indians." (See page 24.) All were reproduced by eminent engravers and largely circulated.

Theodor Kaufmann, a Hanoverian, selected scenes of the

DEFENDING THE STOCKADE.
(After a painting by Charles Schreyvogel.)

Civil War for his canvasses. His paintings "General Sherman at the Campfire," "Farragut" and "Lincoln's Death" have also been reproduced in engravings.

The Pennsylvania German **Peter Rothermel** is represented in the collections of the Pennsylvania Art Society by the painting "The Statehouse on the Day of the Battle at Germantown." He also produced a gigantic canvass "The Battle of Gettysburg," which was one of the attractions of the Centennial Fair at Philadelphia in 1876.

Thomas Nast, born 1840 at Landau in the Palatinate, is the author of two well known paintings: "Lincoln's Entrance Into Richmond," and "The Departure of the 7th New York Regiment on April 19th, 1861." (See page 100.) This brilliant canvass adorns the armory of said regiment.

A real "Painter of the Western Frontier" was **Charles Schreyvogel**, of New York. Having studied under Karl Marr

A SURE SHOT.

and Kirschbach in Munich, he leaped after his return in 1890 into fame at one bound with his spirited picture "My Bunkie." It shows a handful of U. S. cavalrymen in a running fight with Indians. One of the troopers, dismounted, is seen by his "bunkie" and drawn up on the latter's mount. Everything is on the gallop. The free action of the horses and the strain of the soldiers are superbly reproduced. But the great points of the picture are its immense nerve and its atmosphere. At a glance it is seen that "My Bunkie" is true to life.

In rapid succession this painting was followed by others, reflecting with admirable fidelity the strenuousness of Western life. "Defending the Stockade" is the title of one of these canvasses. The scene is the interior of a fort, which is held by hardly a score of men. Everywhere is passionate action and hot fight, everywhere curls the yellowish smoke of powder. Already the redskins are mounting the palisades, eager to drive the soldiers away by the flames of burning brushwood thrown at them. In desperate desire for combat the gallant soldiers hurry, to repel once more the bloodthirsty enemy, which seems to be in overwhelming majority.

"The Fight for the Waterhole" is a similar painting, full of action. In the middle of a desert, overflowed by the setting sun with magic light, stretches a little pool of water. Its possession means life or death, as animals and men have suffered terribly under the intense heat of the day. But a band of hostile Indians occupies the place, determined to hold it to the last man. Upon them breaks a troup of cavalry with irresistible vehemence. The horse of the officer rears up like a bolt, as the deperate struggle for the precious liquid grows in violence.

Many other paintings of equal value followed in rapid succession, among them "How Cola," "The Despatch Bearer," "A Sure Shot" and others, reproductions of which have found wide distribution. Unfortunately the prolific artist met a premature death in 1911.

Rudolf Cronau, born in Solingen, Rhenish Prussia, in 1855, painted "A Rencountre in the Far West." The canvass shows the weird scenery of a valley of the Green River, Utah. Gigantic rocks rise to towering height, like sentinels guarding the entrance of the valley for ages past. A band of hostile Indians has surprised a group of prospectors, encamped in an exposed position, and it is left to the beholder to picture to himself the outcome of the combat about to develop.

"Sunset of the Red Race" is the title of another work of the same artist. A Sioux Indian, seated at the foot of some burial scaffolds of his ancestors, glances over a wide river-valley, flooded with the rays of the setting sun. Once this valley belonged to the hunting grounds of his tribe, but now it is traversed by the locomotive, the yelling whistle of which sounds the doom of the red race. —

Cronau painted also numerous sceneries of the West Indies, Southern Spain and Morocco, among them a series of water colors from the Alhambra.

Albert Groll is an artist whose brush conveys glorious pictures of the deserts of Arizona, so wonderful in color.

Friedrich Dielman, born 1847 at Hanover, is like many American artists a former student of the Royal Academy of Munich. Living since 1876 in New York, he devoted himself to historical and mural painting. Examples of his work are

A RENCOUNTER IN THE FAR WEST.
(After a painting by Rudolf Cronau.)

SUNSET OF THE RED RACE.
(After a painting by Rudolf Cronau.)

to be found in the Congressional Library, in the building of the "Washington Evening Star" and in the building of the Savings Bank in Albany, N. Y.

The same specialty has been selected by **Arthur Thomas** in New York. He decorated the City Hall at St. Louis, the Memorial Hall at Columbus, Ohio, the Court House at South Bend, Indiana, and other public buildings with historical and allegorical paintings, distinguished by clear conception, excellent design and brilliant color.

Among the noted painters, who in their subjects confined themselves to sceneries of the East and of the Middle States, were **Wilhelm Sonntag, Hermann Füchsel, Heinrich Vianden** and **Gottfried Frankenstein**. The latter's paintings of the Niagara Falls conveyed to Europe an estimate of this marvel in nature with compelling force.

A highly esteemed landscape painter was also **John Henry Twachtman,** born in Cincinnati in 1853. He studied in Munich, Venice and Paris. In his contemplative attitude toward nature, in his almost ethereal character of his technic, in the purity and simplicity of his emotion he reminded much of Corot and Whistler. He spiritualized the objects he painted and at the same time he has spiritualized his paint. It has been said of him, that "ethereal color and form seem to have blown into the canvas, and that his art was a victory of the creator over his materials." He died in Gloucester, Mass., in 1902.

Another splendid artist, carried away much too soon, was **Robert F. Blum,** born 1867 in Cincinnati. His excellent scenes of Venice and Japan are full of sunlight and lustrous color. Also they are distinguished by careful drawing. His "Japanese Sugar-Huckster" is one of the gems of the Metropolitan Museum of Art in New York. At the same museum we find two remarkable paintings of **Charles F. Ulrich,** born 1858 in New York: "The Glass-Blowers in Burano," and "The Promised Land." The Corcoran Gallery in Washington has a painting showing the arrival of immigrants in Castle Garden, the former landing place in New York. These pictures are distinguished by a mild lustre of color and sobriety in tone.

A very productive genre painter was also **Henry Mosler,** born in 1841 in New York. One of his best, "A Wedding in the Bretagne," is in the Metropolitan Art Museum. "The Dawn of Our Flag," a symbolic glorification of the Star-spangled Banner, is owned by the Corcoran Gallery in Washington.

Several of the most noteworthy of American artists of German descent who went to Germany to study, have made that country their permanent home, feeling that they would enjoy there a much richer artistic atmosphere and greater appreciation than in their native country. Among these artists were **Carl Marr, Toby Rosenthal, Gari Melchers** and **Hermann**

Hartwich. Marr was born at Milwaukee, in 1858. Having studied in Munich he has remained there ever since, honored by being appointed as a professor at the same Royal Academy where he had pursued his studies. One of his first paintings was "The Mystery of Life," showing Ahasver, the wandering Jew. Tired of life, he meditates, his gaze fixed on the lifeless body of a beautiful young girl, which has been tossed up by the sea on a gloomy shore. ‹This painting as well as another, "Gossip," showing two girls spinning, are owned by the Metropolitan Museum of Art in New York.

‹ Perhaps the most powerful painting of Marr, the "Procession of Flagellants" is owned by his native town, Milwaukee, to which it was donated by some of her citizens. When this painting was first shown in the Munich Exhibition of 1889, it was placed most effectually. Entering the exposition building from the street, one passed through a vestibule which by the aid of Oriental rugs had been converted into a mass of soft, richly subdued harmonies. From this vestibule one entered a room, where a screened skylight diffused a twilight effect on groups of palms. From this dimly lit apartment a door ten feet wide gave entrance to the picture gallery, and on the wall opposite was the painting, the only one that could be seen. The whole arrangement gave the effect of looking from a window on the self-tortured, fanatical wretches, who, scourge in hand, led by the hermit Rainier, overran Italy in the 13th century. So strong was the illusion, so intensified by the picture's realism, that it required only a slight exaltation of the senses to hear the hiss of the scourge as it fell on the lacerated and bleeding back of the devotee, the praying, the groaning and the weeping. It was certainly no small honor to the picture to place it thus in an exhibition which represented not only the best of German, but also much of the best of French art. But it was, together with the gold medal awarded the painting, an honor which was well deserved. An excellent composition containing over two hundred figures, all well drawn; a story requiring much historical research, well told, although not without some warrantable artistic license; stirring and dramatic action without a suggestion of the stage; the whole, if not vigorously, at least well painted — the artist had produced in this work a picture which in its technical qualities easily took rank with the average in the exhibition, and in its quality of invention stood almost alone.

The "Flagellants" have been followed by many other paintings, very few of which, however, found their way to America, as they have been mostly acquired by German galleries and connoisseurs.

Munich became also the home of **Toby Rosenthal,** born in 1848 at New Haven, Conn. He created numerous paintings, showing scenes of every-day life, many of which breathe a delicious humor.

Gari Melchers, born in 1860 at Detroit, is of all the American artists, living abroad, the best known in this country, as many works of his virile art have been included in American galleries. "Skaters" is in the possession of the Pennsylvania Art Academy in Philadelphia; "Penelope" belongs to the Corcoran Gallery in Washington; a portrait of ex-President Roosevelt is in the National Gallery, Washington; others are to be found in the Art Museums of Detroit, Chicago, and Pittsburgh; one of the very best, "Madonna," is owned by the Metropolitan Museum of Art in New York.

All the paintings of Melchers, who occupies since several years a professorship at the Academy of Art in Weimar, Ger-

A MONARCH OF THE NORTHERN FORESTS.
(From a painting by Karl Rungius.)

many, are extremely interesting in the charming play of light and color, and no one can imagine a more wholesome corrective against the excrescences of the so-called "modern art," as futurism, cubism and other insane "isms."

Among the best American portrait painters we' find **Adolf Müller-Ury, Emil Fuchs, Paul Selinger, Karl L. Brandt, W. J. Baer, Wilhelm Funk,** and **Karl Gutherz,** the latter also the author of a painting in the Congressional Library, "The Light of Civilization."

An excellent painter of animal life is **Karl Rungius.** The majestic Wapiti of the Rocky Mountains, the graceful antelope

196

of the plains, the shaggy moose of the Northern forests have been presented by this artist in unsurpassable manner. A specialty of **Edmund H. Osthaus** in Toledo is the dog.

The number of first-class illustrators of German origin is very large. Among them are **Max F. Klepper, Joseph Leyendecker, Charles Reinhardt, L. W. Zeigler, Blumenschein, Julius Loeb, A. B. Wenzell, Benjamin W. Clinedinst, Erich Pape** and others, many of whom are former pupils of the Art Academies of Germany.

* * * *

While at the beginning of the 19th century the interest of the young American nation was very low in regard to paintings, it was entirely absent in regard to sculpture. The Puritans and Quakers in their prudishness abhorred all representations of the human body, with exception perhaps of some sexless cherubs. So the meagre orders given to the masters of the chisel were confined to the execution of tombstones, and, after the Civil War, to a few soldiers' monuments.

Such unfavorable conditions embittered the life of several German sculptors, born in the United States or drifted to this country by some caprice of fate. There was for instance **Ferdinand Pettrich,** a former pupil of the famous Thorwaldsen. Born at Dresden, he came in 1835 to Philadelphia, hoping to find work. But the only commissions he succeeded in getting were some monuments for tombs. The figures of an "Amor defeated" and of "Mephistopheles," done in the sculptor's all too many leisure hours, induced President Tylor to commission Pettrich with the execution of four large reliefs for the base of a monument to Washington. Congress, however, could not be induced to grant the money for the work, which had already been finished in clay. Disappointed the sculptor returned in 1845 to Germany.

Francis Dengler, Franz Meinen, Christoph Paulus, Heinrich Baerer, Georg Hesse, Ephraim Kaiser and **Caspar Buberl** suffered greatly under similar difficulties. Few and far between were the opportunities for them to exhibit their ability, such as was shown by Buberl in five great reliefs for the Garfield monument in Cleveland. These reliefs, showing the martyr-President in different phases of his life, contain more than one hundred figures in full life size. The Patent Office in Washington has, by the same artist, several allegorical groups: "Electricity and Magnetism;" "Fire and Water;" "Invention and Industry;" "Agriculture and Mining." The National Museum is in possession of a colossal group "Columbia as Protectoress of Science, Art and Industry."

William Rinehart, the son of a German farmer in Maryland, had the good fortune, to be sent by the great art collector W. S. Walters in Baltimore to Italy, where he studied and made two bas-reliefs, "Night" and "Day." For a short time he

197

came back to Baltimore, but, missing here the atmosphere so necessary for artists, he returned to Rome, where he made many beautiful sculptures, of which "Clytie," a life-sized nude marble, is in the Peabody Museum, while "Latona and her Children" is in the Metropolitan Museum.

Joseph Sibbel and **Joseph Lohmüller** in New York were very prolific during the latter part of the 19th and the beginning of the present century in beautifying the cathedrals and churches of America with reliefs of Biblical scenes and the statues of Madonnas, Martyrs, Saints and Apostles.

More favorable times for the masters of the chisel came with the great expositions in Chicago, Omaha, Buffalo, St. Louis, Portland and San Francisco. To break the tiresome monotony of the enormous palaces and temples, of the wide courts and endless colonnades it was necessary to adorn them with allegorical groups and statues, such as had been seen at the exposition grounds of Europe. Here, at last, came for American sculptors welcome opportunities to show their abilities. No one answered the call with greater enthusiasm than **Karl Bitter**, born in 1867 at Vienna, and a former student of the Academy of Fine Arts of his native city. He arrived in New York in 1889, at a time, when architects prepared plans for the great Columbian Exposition in Chicago. To Richard M. Hunt, one of the foremost architects in New York, had fallen the task of designing the stately Administration Building. On his invitation Bitter executed the elaborate sculptural decorations for this building with such success, that he was requested to furnish also the sculpture works for the Liberal Arts Building and other palaces. They were done in such masterly way, that several years later, when Buffalo prepared for the Pan-American Exposition, the National Sculpture Society nominated Bitter as the director of sculpture. In this position Bitter, with an inspiration that captured the Board of Architects, conceived a scheme of sculpture, which illustrated the purposes and objects of the exposition as an inherent revelation of the delevopment and various forms of energy and activity of the Western Hemisphere. That it should be merely ornamental did not satisfy him. Hence his scheme was a progressive composition: first, Nature; then, Man; and then the Genius of Man. Nature was expressed by fountains and groups entitled Mineral Wealth, Animal Wealth, and Floral Wealth. The Fountain of Nature was balanced by such subjects as the Savage Age, the Age of Despotism and the Age of Enlightenment. In the division showing the Genius of Man, there were groups representing the human emotions and the human intellect; the birth of Athene typifying the intellect.

Science, Agriculture and Manufacture were counterparts on the Fountain in the center, and the great tower was surmounted by the Goddess of Light. The main approach to the exposition, called the Triumphal Causeway, was symbolical of the National spirit. The groups in the niches represented Courage, Patriotism, Truth and Benevolence; the fountains between which one paused symbolized the Atlantic and Pacific; and the mounted standard bearers crowning the four pylons of the causeway were, with their accessories, designed to express Power and Peace. There were more than five hundred of such groups and figures. In selecting his collaborators, in supervising the tremendous work and in placing the finished groups in position, Bitter displayed such infinite tact, thorough knowledge, and extraordinary executive abilities, that this part of the Pan-American Exposition was its greatest success.

So it was only natural, that, when the projects for the Louisiana Purchase Exposition at St. Louis and for the Panama-Pacific Exposition at San Francisco were discussed, Bitter's services as director of all sculpture work were regarded as indispensable. His general schemes for these expositions manifested again the boundlessness of his inventive spirit, the breadth of his mind and the wide range of his powers. They illustrated the marvellous natural gifts of the Western regions, their development by men, the rise of the West, the contact of American culture with that of Asia, and the great benefit mankind will derive from the completion of the Panama Canal. —

While Bitter was engaged in all these herculean works, he found nevertheless time to create a large number of statues, monuments and portrait-busts. (The most remarkable of these works are an equestrian statue of General Franz Sigel (see page 103) and a Carl Schurz Monument. Both have been made for New York and are notable for their dignity.) Besides, Bitter made for the University of Virginia a wonderful figure of Thomas Jefferson; furthermore the beautiful Villard Memorial in Sleepy Hollow at Tarrytown, N. Y., showing a workingman at evening's rest, having forged great things on the anvil of life.

When Bitter in 1915 lost accidentally his life in his forty-seventh year, America lost a genius, who had gained the unbounded admiration of all his fellow-craftsmen.

The expositions at Chicago, Buffalo and St. Louis were also the grounds, where **Isidor Konti,** coming from Vienna, found opportunities to give full rein to his rich imagination. In St. Louis the Great Cascade with an abundance of water-gods, nymphs and phantastic creatures of the ocean was his work. At the same place he exhibited a group "The Despotic Age." It showed some workmen who, loaded with chains and almost breaking down, pull a heavy triumphal car, on whose platform sits a brutal despot, whose hard cruel eyes betray, that pity is a virtue unknown to him. At the side of the car walks a fury, driving on with her whip the groaning human beasts of burden to still greater efforts.

A tragedy of life was also the subject of **Alexander Wein-man's** most impressive group "Destiny of the Red Race," symbolizing the irrevocable fate of the North American Indians. As their existence was depending upon the existence of the buffalo, which provided them with food, clothing and even shelter, the artist placed this now almost extinct animal at the head of a small group, consisting of a chief, a warrior, a squaw and a boy. With them vanishes Manitou, the Great Spirit, to whom the red men directed their prayers and hopes.

Frederick W. Ruckstuhl, born in 1853 in Alsace, executed two colossal marble statues, "Wisdom" and "Force," placed at the steps of the Appellate Court House, New York City.

Other works are "Defense of the Flag" at the Confederate Monument at Little Rock, Ark.; "Solon," "Macauley," "Franklin" and "Goethe" in the Library of Congress; several soldiers' monuments and statues, among the latter an equestrian statue of General Hartranft, at Harrisburg, Pa.

Max Mauch, A. Schaff, Bruno Louis Zimm, Carl Heber, F. E. Triebel, Henry Linder, Theodor Baur, Gustav Gerlach, Max Bachman, M. Schwarzott, Rudolf Schwarz, Frank Hap-persburger, Leonard Volk, Carl Gerhart, A. Weinert, E. Wuertz, C. F. Hamann, Charles Henry Niehaus, Otto Schwei-zer, Albert Jaegers, Friedrich Roth, and **Charles Keck** are American sculptors of German descent, all of whom have done very creditable work.

Niehaus, born in 1855 at Cincinnati, studied also in Munich. After his return he opened a studio in New York, where he created numerous statues of noted Americans, among them those of the Presidents Lincoln, Garfield, Harrison and McKin-ley. At the Louisiana Purchase Exposition he was represented by a powerful equestrial statue of Louis IX, King of France, from whom Louisiana derived its name.

The city of Indianapolis owns perhaps the most imposing soldiers' monument in the United States. While its architectural part was designed by the famous architect Bruno Schmitz in Berlin, the four magnificent groups of warriors and sailors have been modelled by **Rudolf Schwarz,** who immigrated in 1897 from Vienna. The same artist made also the soldiers' monuments in South Bend, Terre Haute, Dayton, and other cities of Indiana and Ohio.

Otto Schweizer in Philadelphia is engaged in the same line of sculpture. In front of the City Hall of Philadelphia we find his statue of General Peter Mühlenberg (see page 51): Utica, N. Y., and Valley Forge have Steuben monuments; Buffalo a Schiller monument. Also he created numerous statues of American statesmen. Among his recent works is a monument to the memory of Molly Pitcher in Carlisle, N. J.

Albert Jaegers, born at Elberfeld, Germany, 1868, came to Cincinnati while still a child. Entirely self-taught in his

200

profession, he won a number of competitions inaugurated and decided by the National Sculpture Society. He was also the winner in a competition for a monument of Major-General Baron von Steuben. This statue, standing at the northwest corner of the famous Lafayette Park in Washington, D. C., shows the general as standing on an eminence inspecting the great maneuvres held by him in Valley Forge in spring of 1778. He is heavily cloaked; the hand lightly at rest on the hilt of his sword. So he follows with keen interest the unfolding movement of the troops (see page 56). At the base of the statue are two groups, the one, "Military Instruction," representing Steuben's life work, the drilling and training of the American Army. An experienced warrior is shown instructing a youth in the use of the sword. In the second group, "Commemoration," America is teaching youth to honor the memory of her heroes. A foreign branch is grafted into a tree of her national life. She welds to her heart the foreigner who has cast his life and fortune with the weal and woe of her people, embodying the idea of unity and fraternity of all nationalities under the guidance of a great republic.

The statue was unveiled in presence of President William Taft and of almost 20,000 delegates of German American Societies on December 7, 1910. A chorus of 1000 members of the Northeastern Singers' Association, accompanied by the United States Marine Band, sung the "Star-Spangled Banner" in a most inspiring manner. Then followed a salute of honor fired by a battery, amid the cheers of a delighted multitude gathered to do honor to the great hero, who had contributed so generously to the success of the Continental Army.

· A second great success was achieved by Jaegers in the competition for a monument in commemoration of the landing of the German settlers of Germantown.

The main statue of this monument represents, throning high upon a rock, the sacred light bearer, whose escutcheon, Siegfried killing the dragon, typifies the eternal warfare against the powers of darkness. Reposeful and mighty, the goddess leans toward the oak, that fine emblem of German sturdiness.

This statue, as the crowning feature, viewed from a certain distance, assumes the importance of the monument proper; but upon nearer approach the center figures of the main group below, the German Pilgrim Father, absorbs the attention until it is realized that this is the great note of the monument. Fearless and true, this Pilgrim steps forth into the New World, a prayer in his heart, his protecting arm around his mate — to face his labor and his destiny (see frontispiece). Ever at his side walks the spirit of joy and music, the spirit that points to ideals.

On the sides and rear of the pedestal reliefs reveal the important part the German Americans have taken in the making and development of their adopted country. In the one physical labor is shown as the fundamental principle upon which art and science arise. Another shows the war volunteer, who freely sheds his blood for the independence and union of his country. The last one commemorates the protest against slavery made by the inhabitants of Germantown in 1688.

* * * *

As conspicuous as is the influence of German painting and sculpture on American art, so the influence of German architects on American architecture has been very remarkable. Indeed, it can be said, that the most beautiful buildings of our United States have been designed by architects of German origin.

To begin with the most prominent building of our country, the Capitol at Washington, D. C., it can be stated, that its grand dome as well as the extensions of the Houses of Senate and Representatives have been designed and executed by Thomas U. Walter, the grandfather of whom, Jacob Friedrich Walter, had immigrated from Germany.

The dome is an object of imposing beauty, to be seen for miles around. No edifice in the world possesses one equal to it in classic symmetry. Of cast iron, great engineering skill was required in its erection. The walls had to be trussed, bolted, girded and clamped in every conceivable way to hold in position the immense superstructure. To appreciate its immense weight is scarcely possible. Walter calculated its 8,909,200 pounds of cast and wrought iron as giving a pressure of 13,477 pounds to the square foot at the basement floor, and the supporting walls as capable of holding 755,280 pounds to the same area. The pressure upon the walls of the cellar floor, exclusive of the weight of the bronze statue of the Goddess of Freedom, on top of the dome, weighing 14,985 pounds, is estimated at 51,292,253 pounds. The dome is composed of two shells, one within the other, which expand and contract with the variations in temperature; between these the stairway winds in its ascent. The greatest diameter at the base is 135 feet 5 inches.

The lower portion of the exterior is surrounded by 36 columns representing the 36 States in the Union at the time it was designed. The 13 columns which encircle the lantern above the tholus are emblematic of the 13 original States. This lantern is 24 feet in diameter and 50 feet in height. Its light notifies the surrounding country for miles of a night session in either House. The cost of the dome was $1,047,291.

Walter constructed also the U. S. Treasury Building, the east and west wing of the Patent Office, and the beautiful Girard College in Philadelphia.

202

A CORRIDOR IN THE CONGRESSIONAL LIBRARY AT WASHINGTON, D. C.

‹ In the immediate neighborhood of the National Capitol is the impressively beautiful Library of Congress, also a work of German architects, namely **Johann I. Schmitmeyer,** a native of Vienna, and **Paul Johannes Pelz,** born at Seitendorf Prussish Silesia. The latter, a pupil of **Detlef Lienau,** a noted architect in New York, had, previous to his work on the Congressional Library, been connected with the U. S. Lighthouse Board, for which he made the designs for many lighthouses, who in 1873 won the first prize at the World's Exposition in Vienna. In the same year he formed with Schmitmeyer in Washington a business agreement, to participate with him in the competition for the architectural plans of the Congressional Library. Of twenty-eight designs, submitted by the foremost architects of America as well as Europe, Schmitmeyer and Pelz were the winners, holding the ground also in a second competition, in which the number of participators rose to forty. Having gained final victory, the two Germans remained for thirteen years at work, furnishing the designs for every detail. By making several trips to Europe, they studied also the arrangements of all great libraries existing. Merging the practical knowledge of former centuries with modern innovations, the two architects created thus the magnificent palace which stands in all respects among the libraries of the world unequalled.

Without question this building is the most beautiful in America. Finished in Italian Renaissance style, it is with its numerous spacious halls, stairways, corridors, assembly rooms and its magnificent reading-rotunda a triumph of architectural art.

In view of this fact and considering the diligent work of the architects, who spent almost a lifetime in their efforts to reach in every point highest perfection, it is deeply to be regretted, that the two masters neither received an adequate material compensation, nor the artistic recognition to which they were entitled. After their designs had been finished, the Library-Committee, appointed by Congress, removed the two architects and assigned General Thomas L. Casey, chief of the U. S. Corps of Engineers, to take charge of the actual building of the structure. As he commanded a military education only and was unable to supervise also the artistic part, his son Edward, a young man twenty-five years of age, who had studied for a short while at Ecole des Beaux Arts in Paris, was made artistic supervisor, receiving a salary twice as high as that paid to Mr. Pelz, the real architect. Not enough yet. To crown these foul tricks a plate of marble was inserted over the main entrance of the building, bearing the following inscription:

Erected under the Acts of Congress of April 15, 1866,
October 2, 1888 and March 2, 1889, by
Brig. Gen. Thos. Lincoln Casey, Chief of Engineers,
U. S. A.

Bernhard R. Green, Supt. and Engineer.
John L. Smithmeyer, Architect.
Paul J. Pelz, Architect.
Edward Pearce Casey, Architect.

Thus the chief engineer of the U. S. Army was stamped as the creator of the library. The real designers were to contend themselves with the third and fourth place and to share their just title with an inexperienced young man, who had contributed hardly anything toward the artistic design or finish of the whole building. Messrs. Schmitmeyer and Pelz remonstrated against this diminution of their credit, nevertheless the marble plate was inserted and is still there, a visible monument of influences at work upon a Congress of our United States.
How professional men judged of this matter appears from the following declaration of the president and the secretary of the "American Institute of Architects": "We are familiar with this building, from the beginning to the present time, and feel that no one can, with propriety or honesty, be entitled to the credit as architects of this building except J. L. Smithmeyer and Paul J. Pelz. They have devoted the best years of their lives, from 1873 to 1893, in perfecting the plan and in designing the exterior and interior of that building." —
And the magazine "Architecture and Buildings," in its number of April 3, 1897, explained: "It looks queer to professional men that the names of the paymaster who drew the money for the building out of the Treasury on his signature, and the clerk of the works or superintendent, with the supernumerary and superfluous title of engineer (as if there had been anything to "engineer" in the building, save the appropriations in Congress) appear above those of the architects, who created it in their minds and who are in truth the fathers of the structure. Why does there appear a line of demarkation below the Chief of Engineers, putting the architects "below the salt" as it were? — It must be remembered here that the advent of General Casey was at a time, when Messrs. Smithmeyer & Pelz had, like Columbus, already discovered America: their plans were complete and ready to be proceeded with."—

205

German American architects furnished also the designs for many other important public buildings. **Hornbostel** designed the beautiful Technical High School in Pittsburgh; also the Memorial Building and the Educational Building in Albany, N. Y. **Alfred C. Clas** erected the Public Libraries of Milwaukee and Madison, Wisc. **H. C. Koch** made the plans for the City Hall in Milwaukee; **Theodor Karl Link** made the plans for the City Hall and the Union Station in St. Louis; **Otto** and **Cyrus Eidlitz** are the architects of the New York Times Building, the Public Library in Buffalo and many business buildings. The brothers **Hertel** erected the beautiful palace of the Vanderbilts on Fifth Avenue, New York; **Henry J. Hardenbergh** constructed the Waldorf-Astoria Hotel, the Plaza, Manhattan, Dakota Hotel and others. **G. L. Heins,** as member of the firm **Heins & La Farge,** designed many churches and the magnificent Protestant-Episcopal Cathedral of St. John the Divine in New York. Heins, born in 1860 at Philadelphia, has been also the State architect of all New York State buildings since 1898.

No pretense is made of the completeness of this chapter, outlining the works of American artists, sculptors and architects of German descent. To do justice to all is impossible here. But enough has been shown to prove, that in all the different realms of art, representing the highest stages of human culture, America is deeply indebted to German Americans. Among their works are many, that for their noble conception and artistic execution deserve a place of honor among the art treasures of the New World.

German American Women and their Works.

A history of the German Women in America has not yet been written. But the theme is such an attractive and superb one that, we hope, only an incentive like this is needed, to direct the attention of some competent authoress to this task and inspire her to take it up. What more beautiful theme could she find than to collect all the scattered evidences of heroism, greatness, fortitude, perseverance and compassion the German women have exhibited during the three centuries of German participation in the development of this country?

Imagine the indescribable hadships and perils the wives of those German pioneers had to face, who in the 18th century were placed by the British Government at the most exposed localities on the frontier, where they formed bulwarks for the English settlements against the French and Indians. And imagine the horrors these women were subjected to, when during the period from 1777 to 1782 the British, to annihilate their own subjects, engaged Indians as allies and inflamed their bloodthirstiness by offering prizes of 8 to 20 dollars for every American scalp, be it of man, woman or child. What tragedies may have been linked with the 1062 scalps of American country folks, found by Captain Gerrick among British booty, and intended to be sent by the Indians as a token of their loyalty to the king!*)

It is necessary to remind of these dreadful times and such events, that we may recognize what German women endured and suffered. That among them were many heroines, we know

---

*) The report of Captain Gerrish was published by Benjamin Franklin. It refers to a skirmish, in which the Americans captured from the British a large quantity of furs. the report has the following passage: "The peltry amount to a good deal of money, and the possession of this booty at first gave us pleasure; but we were struck with horror to find among the packages eight large ones, containing scalps of our unhappy country folks, taken prisoners in the three last years by the Seneca Indians from the inhabitants of New York, New Jersey, Pennsylvania, and Virginia, and sent by them as a present to Colonel Haldimand, Governor of Canada, in order to be by him transmitted to England as a token of the loyalty of the Indians to the king." The packages contained 1062 scalps. In accordance with the well known policy of the British Tories in the United States to eliminate from American histories and school books everything avers to English interests, great efforts have been made to discredit the report of Captain Gerrish and make it appear as a fabrication of Benjamin Franklin!

from the lives of the wife of Christian Schell, of Elisabeth Zane, Emilie Geiger, Molly Pitcher and many others.

The praise conferred by Dr. Rush on the German women of the 18th century is due also to the German wives and mothers of to-day. But to the virtues of bygone times have been added other charms, which make these wives in fact comrades to their husbands in the highest meaning of the word. Having entered the wide avenues, opened for their sex by such intellectual pioneers like Susan Anthony, their minds and characters extended in greatness as well as in richness and diversity.

Many highly gifted German women arrived in the United States with the political refugees of 1848. One of the most remarkable was **Mathilde Franziska Anneke,** who at the side of her husband, a former Prussian artillery-officer, had gone through all the hardships of that stormy period. While in Germany, she had argued for equality of the sexes and the opening of channels for woman's work, but the journals she published in this behalf, were suppressed by the reactionary government. After their arrival in America Mrs. Anneke became one of the most enthusiastic champions for women's rights. In delivering the many lectures in behalf of this movement, she was frequently interrupted in the beginning by howling mobs, but, by the forcefulness of her arguments, remained victorious and was listened to with respectful attention. Making her home in Milwaukee, the German-American Athens, she was appreciated as a poetess and fiction writer as well as leader of a private school, in which she distributed freely of the great wisdom and beauty of her noble heart.

Well remembered are also Mrs. **Carl Schurz,** neé **Margarethe Meyer,** who in 1855 instituted in Watertown, Wisc., a Fröbel Kindergarten. The memory of **Anna Uhl-Ottendorfer** is also alive, who, after the death of her first husband, successfully managed the New Yorker Staatszeitung for a number of years.

Among German American women notable for their abilities in the realms of literature, science and art, one of the best known during the first half of the 19th century was **Therese Albertine Louise von Jacob,** better known by her nom de plume "Talvj," formed of the initials of her name. She was born in Halle, Germany, the daughter of the eminent professor von Jacob. In 1830, when she became the wife of the American Orientalist Edward Robinson, professor at Andover, she had already attained fame by her splendid translations of Slavic folk songs into German. In America she became interested in the colonial history of the United States and in Indian folk lore, and wrote among numerous other works "A History of Captain John Smith" and "The Colonization of New England." In New York the home of the Robinsons was the place where the literary life of that time focussed.

A similar rendezvous for all intellectual people was the home of Mrs. **Bayard Taylor**, the daughter of the distinguished German astronomer Peter Andreas Hansen. Her memoirs have been published in America under the title "On Two Continents." They are full of interesting reminiscences of the most prominent authors and authoresses of the middle of the 19th century.

That among the German-American women are many highly gifted priestesses of poetry, may be learned from the beautiful contributions of **Dorothea Boettcher, Minna Kleeberg, Marie Raible, Pauline Wiedenmann, Bella Fiebing, Marianne Kuenhold, Fanny Gumpert, Amalie von Ende, Elisabeth Mesch, Anna Kirchstein, Edna Fern, Laura Wilhelmine Krech, Sophie Neeff, Anna Nill, Elisabeth Rudolph, Henni Hubel, Martha Toeplitz and Carrie von Veltheim-Huelse** to the two anthologies "Deutsch in America" (by Dr. G. A. Zimmermann, Chicago, 1892) and "Vom Lande des Sternenbanners" (by Dr. G. A. Neff, Ellenville, N. Y., 1905). Several of these women are also widely known for their novels, short stories, travelogues and other prose works.

The four sisters **Klumpke** of San Francisco, daughters of an early German pioneer in California, distinguished themselves in different lines of activity. **Anna Elisabeth Klumpke** became a noted artist, following the footsteps of her friend, the famous Rosa Bonheur, who, in appreciation of her great talent, bequeathed to her her chateau as well as her fortune. **Augusta Klumpke** devoted herself to medical work and became professor in the medical faculty of the University of Paris. **Julia Klumpke** distinguished herself as violinist, and **Dorothea Klumpke** won laurels as an astronomer, by performing such spendid work at the Observatory at Paris, that she was made an officer de l'Académie of France.

As dramatic artists **Helene Hastreiter**, born in Louisville, and **Marie von Ellsner**, born in New York, belonged to the great stars of the latter part of the 19th century. **Helene Louise Leonard**, better known under her stage name **Lillian Russell**, is also of German origin.

One of the most famous of the great singers America produced was **Minnie Hauck**, born in New York in 1853 as the daughter of one of the German refugees of 1848. During her many European and American tours she was everywhere received with great enthusiasm and won the rarest distinctions ever bestowed upon such artist. Her most fortunate rôle, in which for a long time she was unapproached, was "Carmen."

Other great German singers who made America their home are **Emma Juch, Johanna Gadski, Fritzi Scheff** and **Ernestine Schumann-Heink**, all of whom have on their frequent tours throughout the United States won the hearts and souls of their enchanted hearers with their beautiful voices.

The American people are indebted also to the German

women for making them acquainted with the German idea and celebration of Christmas, the sweetest festival of Christianity. By introducing the Christmas-tree and the custom of exchanging gifts to one another, they made the day of the birth of the Saviour from one of solemnity to one of joy, as Christmas should really be to us, at which we more fully live up to "Peace on Earth and Good Will to Men."

Most influential in this direction have been the efforts of Miss **Carla Wenckebach**, Mrs. **Elise Traut** and Mrs. **J. B. Herreshoff**. Miss Wenckebach, professor of German language and literature at Wellesly College, in 1898 published the charming essay: "A Christmas Book. Origin of the Christmas Tree, the Mistletoe, the Yule Log, and St. Nicholas." Mrs. **Elise Traut**, living in New Britain, Conn., is authoress of a similar work, having the title: "Christmas in Heart and Home." In this book she speaks on the deep significance of Christmas and the most inspiring manner of its celebration. Mrs. **J. B. Herreshoff**, a descendant of the famous ship-builders family, succeeded in 1912 in making a profound sensation by having shipped a gigantic fir of 80 feet from the Adirondack Mountains to New York City, where it was erected in Madison Square. On Christmas eve, when darkness came, the chimes of the Metropolitan Tower began to play sweet melodies, and then at once the gigantic tree, which had stood in mysterious gloom, burst forth in the splendor of thousands of electric lights, in red, white and blue. The effect was so overwhelming, that the immense crowd, assembled there, broke into shouts of delight. The joy increased, when one thousand poor children were presented with Christmas gifts.

The deep impressiveness of this celebration caused its repetition on all the following years. Boston, Philadelphia, and many other cities imitated the example set by New York, and so the Christmas celebration was successfully introduced in American civic life. —

The philanthropic character of German-American women was manifested in many splendid works of charity. The names of **Anna Ottendorfer** and **Anna Woerishoffer** are inseparably connected with the German Hospital, the German Dispensary and the beautiful Isabella Home in New York. **Catherine L. Wolfe**, whose ancestors came from Saxony, is known as the founder of the Home for Incurables at Fordham, New York. Also **Eleonore Ruppert** in Washington and **Lauretta Gibson**, neé Bodman, in Cincinnati are remembered for their great liberality toward similar institutions.

Mrs. Catherine L. Wolfe was one of the patrons of the Metropolitan Museum of Art, in New York, to which she donated not only her beautiful collection of paintings, but also a fund of 200,000 dollars for their preservation and increase. And another million dollars were bequeathed by her to several educational institutions founded by her father and herself.

Another proof of the benevolence of the German-American women is the success of the many grand bazaars held since the outbreak of the European War in all United States cities having a percentage of German population. Although the general management of these affairs was in the hands of men, the greater amount of work was, however, performed by women, who with wonderful enthusiasm labored for many weeks in advance to secure the desired financial success. That their unbounded inspiration was not transient, but deeply seated, has been shown by the repetition and increasing results of these affairs. The great German Bazaar, held in New York during December, 1915, brought 350,000 dollars, and the financial result of the bazaar held in Madison Square Garden from March 11th to 23d, 1916, amounted to more than $725,000.

But far more elevating than these splendid results was the spirit, with which the enormous amount of work was accomplished during these weeks by delicate women and girls. From noon until late into the night they worked with untiring zeal, and when at midnight the legions of these volunteers, thoroughly exhausted, hurried to their far away homes, their eyes nevertheless brightened at the thought of the opportunity which enabled them to join in such a noble work of charity. That these bazaars became such wonderful demonstrations of self-sacrifice, was in the first line due to the German-American women, who by their efforts added another leaf to their wreath of gold.

Monuments of Philanthropy.

As glorious as are the physical and ethical contributions of the German element to American culture, so glorious are also the many works, which manifest their benevolence as well as their public spirit and love for justice.

The origin of several of these philanthropic institutions goes back to the 18th century.

It was on Christmas Day of 1764, that in the little Lutheran schoolhouse in Philadelphia a number of German citizens organized the **German Society of Pennsylvania,** in order to fight the horrible abuses, which had arisen with European immigration. To review these evils means to open the blackest pages of our Colonial history. English and Dutch shippers, not supervised by the authorities, who took no interest in the proper treatment and future of emigrants, committed the most abominable crimes against these poor people. Pretending to be willing to help all persons without means, they offered such people credit for their passage across the ocean, on condition that they should work for it after their arrival in America, by hiring out for a certain length of time as servants to colonists, who would pay their wages in advance by refunding the passage money to the ship-owners. As these persons were redeeming themselves by performing this service, they were therefore called "Redemptioners."

With this harmless-looking decoy many thousands of poor human beings were lured to sign contracts, only to find out later that they had become victims of villainous scoundrels and had to pay for their inexperience with the best years of their lives.

. The abuses of this system grew in time to such an extent, that the redemptioners were in fact not better treated than slaves and were often literally worked to death, to say nothing of insufficient food, scanty clothing and poor lodging. Of the right to punish redemptioners, many heartless people made such frequent and cruel use, that laws became necessary whereby it was forbidden to apply to such servants more than ten lashes for each "fault." Female redemptioners were quite often by all kinds of devilish tricks forced to lives of shame, conditions, which some of the peculiar laws of the colonies even invited.

' Incidents of such character stirred the German citizens of Philadelphia to revolt against such infamous treatment of immigrants. Forming the German Society of Pennsylvania, they secured in time laws by which ship-owners as well as the captains and other officials became subjected to strict control and many of the worst abuses were successfully stopped.

The German Society of Pennsylvania became the model for many similar institutions in the other parts of our continent, as for instance in New York, Charleston, S. C., Baltimore, Birmingham, Boston, Pittsburgh, New Haven, Rochester, Hartford, St. Louis, New Orleans, Chicago, Kansas City, San Francisco, Portland and Seattle. By uncovering evils and vigorously persecuting guilty persons, by continuously framing and recommending efficient laws, these societies secured at last a better treatment of the immigrants on the ocean as well as after landing. ‹ With full justice these German Societies may be called the true originators of our modern immigration laws.

When in time the regulation and enforcement of these laws became national affairs, the German Societies, thus released of a part of their work, directed their efforts to other problems, that became more important and difficult to solve, as the exodus to America gained tremendous proportions.

To give an idea of their benevolent work, no better illustration can be found than the German Society of New York, which grew to be the most important of all when New York became the principal immigration port of the United States. Founded in 1784, the society has at present about 1200 members who pledge themselves to contribute each at least $10 annually. It directs its efforts principally to relieve the distress of such immigrants who are unable to find work, or are reduced by sickness or other unfavorable circumstances. Meals, coal and other necessities are distributed among the needy. Numerous physicians in the service of the society make free calls among deserving families and provide free medicines. A special department secures positions for persons looking for work; an information bureau gives practical advice and information either personally or by letter. A banking department offers cheap and safe ways for the transaction of money matters, procures railway and steamboat tickets, performs notarial acts and other services. All profits deriving therefrom are turned over to the society's funds for charity.

To illustrate the activity of the German Society of New York it may be stated, that it distributed in 1915 to deserving people $16,911 in cash; 5565 meal-tickets; 2312 tickets for lodgings and 632 half tons of coal. The physicians of the Society made 3347 free calls to sick people, to whom also $2241 in free medical stimulants were distributed. 2297 men were provided with work; and $23,000 as profit of the business departments were turned over to charity.

As one single grain of seed often bears many fruits so the German Society of New York further created the German

Savings Bank, the German Hospital, the German Rechts-schutzverein, and, through the latter, the Legal Aid Society of New York.

The establishment of the two latter institutions resulted from the desire, to assist immigrants who had been wronged and were too poor to pay for legal assistance. To procure justice for them the Rechtsschutzverein was founded in March 1876, with its own bureau and lawyers, to hear and right the complaints of German immigrants.

But immigrants of other nationalities came also, suffering from bitter wrongs. To send them away would have been cruel, impossible. Therefore it was decided in 1890, that the bureau should give assistance to all who might ask legal help without considering their nationalities. But as such liberality threatened the means of the Society with exhaustion, it was suggested to invite the help of the general public for the good work. At the same time it was resolved to change the name of the institution to **Legal Aid Society,** to indicate its general character.

Under the able leadership of **Arthur von Briesen,** who remained at the helm of the Legal Aid Society from the beginning until 1916, a period of 26 years, the business of the Society increased tremendously.

Taking the Legal Aid Society of New York as a model, similar institutions have been established in Boston, Philadelphia, Washington, Newark, Pittsburgh, Cincinnati, Chicago, San Francisco and Atlanta; also in Berlin, Hamburg, Kopenhagen and many other European cities. When in October 1913 in Nuernberg, Germany, the first international convention of Legal Aid Societies was held, it appeared, that in Germany alone 312 of such corporations had been organized, all after the model of the New York society.

Thus we see that since the Christmas meeting at the Lutheran schoolhouse in Philadelphia untold millions of people profited by the earnest work, begun by that small band of Germans, who had the welfare of their poor countrymen so much at heart, and who showed what genuine Christmas spirit can do for humanity, if only put to proper purpose.

* * * *

German charity is responsible also for many splendid hospitals, orphan asylums, homes for aged people and similar institutions.

Reverend **William Augustus Mühlenberg,** belonging to the famous Mühlenberg family, was the founder of the beautiful St. Luke's Hospital in New York and was in charge of it as superintendent until his death in 1877. He also was originator of St. John's Land on Long Island, with homes for old men and crippled children. Similar institutions were founded by **Johann D. Lankenau** and **Peter Schem** in Philadelphia; by

Georg Ellwanger in Rochester; by Anna Woerishoffer, **Edward Uhl, Henry Villard, Georg H. Schrader, H. O. Havemeyer** in New York, **Louis Zettler** in Columbus, Ohio, and many others. German charity directed its attention also to the proper care of dumb animals. The organization in 1866 of the **Society for the Prevention of Cruelty to Animals** in New York is due to **Henry Bergh**, born in 1823 in New York of German ancestry. Through his efforts cock- and dog fights were prohibited, and also the transportation and killing of cattle, the care of the horse and other beasts of burden greatly improved. By inventing clay-pigeons he found a substitute for live pigeons in shooting-matches, and to him is due also the erection of watering places for animals in large cities. Making frequent lecture tours throughout the country, he implored also the clergymen to preach at least once a year in the behalf of those, "who could not speak for themselves." The splendid results, obtained by this society, encouraged Bergh, to organize also the **Society for the Prevention of Cruelty to Children.**"

Noted as an indefatigable organizer of charity institutions is also **Louis Klopsch,** a journalist born in 1852 in Germany. Through his magazine The Christian Herald he conducted large philanthropies, raising and distributing over 4,000,000 dollars, including the Russian famine relief, the Indian famine relief, and the relief of the starving reconcentrados in Cuba. Enormous sums were also raised for famine sufferers in Italy, Sweden, Finland, China, Japan and elsewhere. —

The Germans' great regard for science and learning manifested itself in many gifts to public libraries, museums, schools, universities and similar institutions. One of the first and most significant donations of this kind in America was that of the famous Astor Library to the City of New York by **Johann Jacob Astor,** the founder of the American Fur Company. This library had several hundred thousand volumes. Opened on February 1, 1854, it has been to many millions of people a never failing source of edification. For its maintainance and increase it was endowed by Astor and his descendents to an amount of $1,700,000. In 1895 this library was merged with the famous Lenox and Tilden Libraries to the New York Public Library, which since May 23, 1911, is housed in the beautiful marble palace at 42d Street and 5th Avenue.

Oswald Ottendorfer made a similar gift to New York in 1899 in the form of a Germanistic Library, which mediates to students the rich treasures of ancient and modern German literatvre.

In Philadelphia **William Wagner,** an enthusiastic friend of natural history, founded in 1855 the Wagner Free Institute of Science, which besides containing priceless collections, employs an able corps of lecturers, who give free instrutions in natural science.

The Germans also contributed freely to the University of Pennsylvania. General Isaac Wistar (Wüster) presented not only the building for the Wistar Institute of Anatomy and Biology, but provided it also with a liberal endowment. Anthony J. Drexel, son of Franz Martin Drexel of Tirol, founded the Drexel Institute of Art, Science and Industry. The cost of the beautiful building was about $4,500,000. The institute is devoted to the education of young men and women in arts, technics and craftsmanship.

Jacob Tome, born in Manheim, Pa., as the son of a German Lutheran family, left about 3,000,000 dollars for the establishment of the Tome Institute at Exeter and Andover, Pa., which is a preparatory school for poor children for college.

The heirs of Johann Kraus in Syracuse donated in his memory the beautiful Crouse Building, the home of the musical department of the Syracuse University.

Louis Miller, the son of a Maryland German, born in 1829 in Greentown, Ohio, conceived and organized the famous Chautauqua institution, located at Chautauqua in Western New York and devoted to educational, religious and social work. There has been established a Summer School, which is noted for its lectures, classes and summer recreations and was the incentive for the founding of sister institutions in many parts of the United States.

Richard Hermann founded in Dubuque the Hermann Museum of Natural History. Adolf Sutro gave to San Francisco a public reference library of 200,000 volumes, a large collection of paintings, a public park, public baths and a replica of Bartholdi's Statue of Liberty. Claus Spreckels, the Sugar king of California, supported liberally all benevolent enterprises and donated to the Golden Gate Park of San Francisco a beautiful music pavillion, costing 100,000 dollars.

Adolphus Busch, the late president of the Anheuser-Busch Brewing Association in St. Louis, contributed 250,000 dollars to the Germanistic Museum at Harvard University in Cambridge, Mass., and gave a similar amount to the Washington University at St. Louis; also many hundred thousands of dollars to charity. To the generosity of Friedrich Pabst and Joseph Schlitz the inhabitants of Milwaukee are indebted for a beautiful theatre and a public park.

John Fritz of Bethlehem gave the Lehigh University a thoroughly equipped engineering laboratory, valued at over $50,000. Other Germans of Pennsylvania made gifts to the Franklin and Marshall College at Lancaster.

C. A. Ficke in Davenport made very valuable donations in money as well as in archæological and ethnological collections to the Davenport Academy of Science.

Henry Villard provided the means for several scientific expeditions to Peru and Bolivia, which were under supervision

216

of the famous archæologist Adolf Bandelier and enriched the American Museum of Natural History.

William Ziegler, the organizer of the Royal Baking Powder Company, furnished the money for an exploration expedition which penetrated the Arctic regions by way of Franz Joseph Land. Through the same source Lieutenant Peary was enabled to make in 1906 one of his memorable expeditions toward the North Pole.

John D. Rockefeller, a descendant of Johann Peter Rockefeller of Germany, gave untold millions to the General Education Board, the University of Chicago, the Rockefeller Institute for Medical Research in New York, to Yale, Brown, Johns Hopkins, Cornell, Vassar Universities and other institutions. **James Lick,** descendant of a Pennsylvania German family **Lück,** left to California several million dollars for scientific and benevolent purposes. Among these donations were those for the construction of the Lick-Observatorium on the summit of Mount Hamilton, California, which is world-famous for its magnificent discoveries in astronomy.

The National German American Alliance and its Purposes.

The beginning of the 20th century marks also for the German element of the United States the beginning of a new and promising era. Alive to the great advantages of centralization a small number of representative citizens of various States of the Union assembled on October 6, 1901, in Philadelphia, the old stronghold of German effort in America, to organize the **National German American Alliance,** not for the purpose of forming a State within the States, but to consolidate the enormous forces of the German American population for the

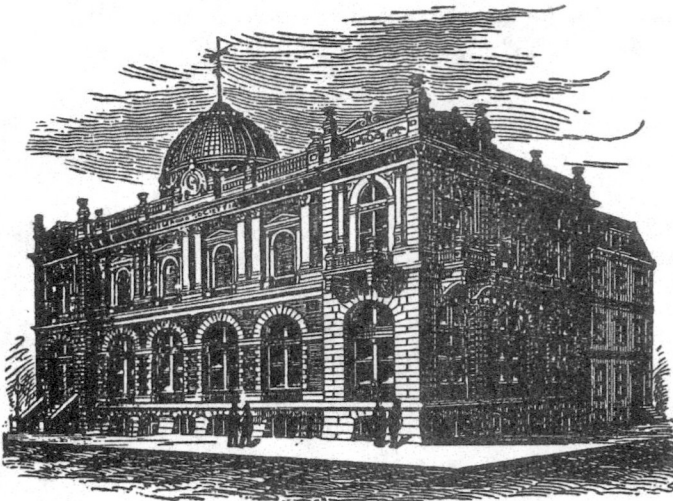

BUILDING OF THE GERMAN SOCIETY OF PENNSYLVANIA, THE BIRTHPLACE OF THE NATIONAL GERMAN AMERICAN ALLIANCE.

sole purpose of promoting everything that is good in German character and culture and that might be to the benefit and welfare of the whole American nation.

The constituting convention took place in the hall of the German Society of Pennsylvania and was combined with a celebration of the "German Day," in commemoration of the landing of the German Pilgrims in Philadelphia on October 6, 1683.

218

The platform adopted by the National German American Alliance in this convention sets forth and explains its purposes. It reads as follows:

Principles of the National German American Alliance of the United States of America.

The National German American Alliance aims to awaken and strengthen the sense of unity among the people of German origin in America with a view to promote useful and healthy development of the power inherent in them as a united body for the mutual energetic protection of such legitimate desires and interests not inconsistent with the common good of the country and the rights and duties of good citizens; to check nativistic encroachments; to maintain and safeguard the good friendly relations existing between America and the old German fatherland. To read the history of German immigration is to be convinced how much it has contributed to the advancement of the spiritual and economic development of this country, and to realize what it is still destined to contribute, and how the German immigrant has at all times stood by his adopted country in weal or in woe.

The Alliance demands therefore the full honest recognition of these merits and opposes every attempt to belittle them. Always true to the adopted country, ever ready to risk all for its welfare, sincere and unselfish in the exercise of the duties of citizenship, respecting the law — still remains the watchword! It has no exclusive interests in view, nor the founding of a State within a State, but sees in the centralization of the inhabitants of German origin the shortest road and the surest guarantee for the attainment of the aims set forth in this constitution. It calls therefore on all German organizations — as the organized representatives of the German spirit and manners — to co-operate with it for their development, and recommends further the formation of Societies in all the States of the Union for the preservation of the interest of German Americans, looking toward an eventual centralization of these societies into a great German American Alliance, and would have all German societies consider it a duty and an honor to join the organization in their respective States. The Alliance engages to labor firmly and at all times with all the legal means at its command for the maintenance and propagation of its principles, and to defend them energetically wherever and whenever they are in danger. Its purposes are the following platform:

1. The Alliance, as such, refrains from all interference in party politics reserving, however, the right and duty to defend its principles also in the political field, in case these should be

219

attacked or endangered by political measures. The Alliance will inaugurate and support all legislation for the common good that is sure to find unanimous approval of its members.

2. Questions and matters of religion are strictly excluded.

3. It recommends the introduction of the study of German into the public schools on the following broad basis:

Along with English, German is a world language; wherever the pioneers of civilization, trade and commerce have penetrated, we find the people of both languages represented; wherever real knowledge of another language prevails more generally, there an independent, clear and unprejudiced understanding is more easily formed and mutual friendly relations promoted.

4. We live in an age of progress and invention; the pace of our time is rapid, and the demands on the individual are inexorable; the physical exertion involved increases the demand on the bodily force; a healthy mind should live in a healthy body. For these reasons the alliance will labor for the introduction of systematic and practical gymnastic (physical culture) instruction in the public schools.

5. It further declares in favor of taking the school out of politics, for only a system of education that is free from political influence can offer the people real and satisfactory schools.

6. It calls on all Germans to acquire the right of citizenship as soon as they are legally entitled to it, to take an active part in public life, and to exercise their right at the polls fearlessly and according to their own judgment.

7. It recommends either a liberal and modern interpretation or the abolition of laws, that put unnecessary difficulties in the way of acquiring the right of citizenship, and frequently entirely prevent it. Good character, unblamable upright life, obedience to laws should decide, and not the answering or non-answering of arbitrarily selected political or historical questions, which easily confuse the applicant.

8. It opposes any and every restriction of immigration of healthy persons from Europe, exclusive of convicted criminals and anarchists.

9. It favors the abolition of antiquated laws no longer in accordance with the spirit of the times, which check free intercourse and restrict the personal freedom of the citizen, and recommends a sane regulation of the liquor traffic in conformity with good common sense and high ethical principles.

10. It recommends the founding of educational societies

which will foster the German language and literature, teach those anxious to learn, and arrange courses of lectures on art and science and questions of general interest.

11. It recommends a systematic investigation of the share Germans have had in the development of their adopted country, in war and in peace, in all kinds of German American activity, from the earliest days, as the basis for the founding and continuance of a German American history.

12. The Alliance advocates all legal and economically correct measures for the protection of the forests of the United States.

13. We deem it our duty to assist as much as possible original ideas and inventions of Americans of German birth or descent for the common good of our country.

14. It reserves the right to extend or supplement this platform when new conditions within the scope of its time and aims make it desirable or necessary.

This platform contains nothing whatever that is not in full accord with good citizenship and to the best interests of the whole country. In recognition of this fact the Alliance was, after a very painstaking investigation of its aims and purposes, incorporated on February 27, 1907, by an Act of Congress.

The Alliance was fortunate enough to find in **Dr. Charles John Hexamer** an enthusiastic leader, who since the founding of the organization has kept it in the right channel. That the movement met the enthusiastic response from the whole German American population, is seen by the rapid extension of the Alliance, which now has organizations in every State of the Union, even in Hawaii.

Its whole membership amounts to about 2½ to 3 millions. The national conventions are held biannually and have taken place as follows: 1903 at Baltimore; 1905 at Indianapolis; 1907 at New York; 1909 at Cincinnati; 1911 at Washington; 1913 at St. Louis; and 1915 at San Francisco.

One of the first acts of the constitutional convention of October 6, 1901, was the adoption of a motion made by Rudolf Cronau, the delegate from New York, that a monument be erected to the memory of Franz Daniel Pastorius and the Founders of Germantown. For this purpose the Alliance collected from its members $30,000, to which the U. S. Congress in recognition of the great contributions of the German element to American culture granted an additional sum of $25,000. The monument, executed by Albert Jaegers in New York, has been described in another chapter.

In like manner the memory of the Major-Generals von Steuben and Mühlenberg has been honored by the erection of beautiful statues in Washington, D. C., in the Valley Forge National Park, in Utica, N. Y., and in Philadelphia. The Johnstown branch of the Pennsylvania Organization erected a monumental fountain with the bust of Joseph Schantz, the first settler of that city, a German. The United Societies of New York City did homage to the memory of Jakob Leisler by planting an oak tree in City Hall Park. In response to its advocacy the name of a public park bordering on East River was changed to Carl Schurz Park. The New York State organization succeeded in having a bill passed in legislature by

DR. CHARLES JOHN HEXAMER.

which the old homestead of Nicolas Herchheimer was purchased and made a historic museum, containing relics on the General and the war for independence. To Major-General Peter Osterhaus and to the widow of Franz Sigel pensions were secured. Large sums were collected and distributed to the San Francisco Earthquake Sufferers and to the wounded, and the war-widows and orphans in Germany and Austro-Hungary. The sums raised for these humanitarian purposes amount to many hundreds of thousands of dollars.

In accordance with its principles the German American Alliance promotes the culture of gymnastics, song, music, art and the study of German language and literature in public schools. By pointing out the great achievements of the German element in America it seeks to secure a proper respect and fair regard for this element. By founding a Junior Order in 1908 it seeks to inspire the younger generation to continue in the works of their fathers, and to endeavor the same industriousness, enterprise and patriotism. By lifting its members from the narrow limits of club-life, it induces them to participate as true citizens of the Republic in all public affairs. Through its committees it makes practical recommendations for the preservation and wise utilization of all natural resources of our country.

And so it strives in many directions to win recognition for its motto: "Always true to our adopted country; ever ready to risk all for its welfare; sincere and unselfish in the duties of citizenship; respecting the law — is and always shall remain the watchword."

EMBLEM OF THE NATIONAL GERMAN AMERICAN ALLIANCE.

The Future Mission of the German Element in the United States.

When the National German American Alliance held its sixth convention at Washington, D. C., in October 1911, the delegates were welcomed in hearty editorials by all papers of our Capital. One of these editorials read as follows:

"The German Americans.

Throughout American history runs testimony bearing on the value and high character of the Germans who have made the new world their home. It is beyond the powers of estimation for even the shrewdest judge of historical values to determine how great has been the benefit bestowed upon the western republic by the sturdy sons of the Fatherland who have come here to settle, to build, to prosper and to become an integral part of our nation. The fact that they maintain "German American" societies and institutions in no wise lessens their value to this country or their loyalty to it in all its activities. The "German American" is first the American, and it is to his credit that he retains an affection for the land of his birth or of the origin of his parents, and preserves its traditions and continues the use of its language.

The sessions of the National German American Alliance now in progress in this city are attended by men who command unqualified respect for their character, their progress, their influence in their communities and the constructive work that they have been and are doing in the upbuilding of the nation. They are what are known as "good citizens," law abiding, charitable, considerate and patriotic. Such men as these were of the most substantial service to this government fifty years ago, when it was menaced with destruction. In statesmanship, in science, in business, in the professions, the trades and the arts the German Americans have contributed many leaders and have written a record of great achievments.

Washington welcomes these men, who stand for so large a part of the American life of to-day, and trusts that their visit to the capital will make them appreciate the fact that they are citizens of a country which offers more of opportunity than the land whose memory they honor and to which America feels grateful for contributing them to it."

224

This appreciation of the German element of the United States was received by all delegates to the Convention of the National German American Alliance with great satisfaction. Recognizing that the aims and efforts of the Alliance were well understood and valued, the delegates were inspired to continue in their work as well as in the resolution, never to relax in the duties owed by them to this country as loyal citizens.

Of these obligations the most sacred is to guard for all future generations that precious gift derived from our ancestors, won with their blood and the sacrifice of their lives:

The Independence of our Country.

To keep this country free and independent is a duty equally incumbent on German Americans as on all other loyal citizens. This task needs constant vigilance, as danger is ahead!

All who have eyes to see and ears to hear must be aware, that as was pointed out in 1914 by the author of this work in the pamphlet: "Do we need a third War for Independence?" another struggle for the freedom of our United States is impending. It may become the most difficult and desperate of all, as for many years mighty powers and numerous shrewd men have been at work, to deliver our republic back into the hands of that country which since the days of our Declaration of Independence has been the worst and unscrupulous enemy of our United States: England.

The origin of the conspiracy to reunite the destiny of our republic with that of Great Britain dates back to September 19, 1877, when Cecil Rhodes, the "Diamond King of South Africa," and the intellectual originator of the infamous Jameson-Raid and the war of conquest against the South African Republics, made in the first draft of his will provisions for the following purpose:

> "To and for the establishment, promotion and development of a SECRET SOCIETY, the true aim of which and object whereof shall be the extension of BRITISH RULE THROUGHOUT THE WORLD. ... and especially THE ULTIMATE RECOVERY OF THE UNITED STATES OF AMERICA AS AN INTEGRATE PART OF THE BRITISH EMPIRE."

Rhodes, possessing all the ingenuity, audacity and unscrupulousness of his prototypes Robert Clive, Warren Hastings and other transgressors who were so instrumental in the extension of the British Empire, was driven by a passionate desire to make himself a great name in history. With this aim in view he grasped the idea to make England and the Anglo-Saxon race the dominating powers of the world.

To bring about the union of all English speaking people, Rhodes established, in the conviction that educational relations make the strongest tie, the so-called **"Rhodes Scholarships,"** for which he set aside a fund of several million pounds.

This institution provides the election of three to nine scholars from each of the British Colonies, and two from each State and Territory of the United States, or one hundred in all. Each scholarship covers a three years' course at the University of Oxford, and each student receives an allowance of 300 pounds a year, which is equivalent to $1500. In awarding the scholarships account shall be taken of various qualities, among them the desire to serve in public affairs.

On July 1, 1899, Rhodes dictated another draft of his last will, in which the provisions for the scholarships are more specified. In January, 1901, he added the following codicil:

> "I note the German Emperor has made instruction in English compulsory in German schools. I leave five yearly scholarships at Oxford of 250 pounds per annum to students of German birth, the scholars to be nominated by the German Emperor for the time being."

That these dispositions are not fully approved at Oxford, appears from an article "The American Rhodes Scholars at Oxford" in the "Educational Review" of February 1905. On page 117 it says:

> "Oxford is carrying out the Rhodes bequest without being in sympathy with the Anglo-Saxon ideal. When the Dons think aloud they blurt out the truth that in their estimation the Colossus of South Africa made a gigantic mistake in undertaking to educate Germans, Americans, and even Colonials, at Oxford on terms of equality with Englishmen. They do not hesitate to say that it would have been better if he had left his fortune to the university itself, which is not well endowed, although the colleges themselves are rich. They consider it a misfortune that the Rhodes' Scholarship Trust is diverted from the education of Englishmen, Welshmen and Scotsmen, and possibly Irishmen as well, to a missionary enterprise **for converting Germans, Americans, and Colonials into good Anglo-Saxons.** They would certainly have dropped the Germans, if they could have had their way; for they do not believe that the students nominated from the palace in Berlin will ever be good Anglo-Saxons. Some of them say outright that the Rhodes' Scholarship Trust will enable the German Emperor to give candidates for the diplomatic service a good training in English studies without expense; and that when they leave Oxford they will be more uncompromising Germans than ever. **The Americans are regarded as more hopeful subjects of Anglo-Saxon missionary effort than the Germans."**

These last remarks indicate clearly the object of the Rhodes' Scholarships.

‹By taking from their native country in every year such large numbers of American students and by placing them for so long a time under the strong influence of British students and Professors at a British university, such an institution clearly aims at nothing less than to form, in time, from the recipients of these scholarships a vast army of active agents, who may be counted upon to carry out in the United States England's fond hopes, as they become influential citizens or leaders and official representatives of the American people.

The great danger to the freedom of the United States from this institution becomes clear when it is shown to us that Rhodes' idea of a World Empire under control of Great Britain is endorsed and furthered by Andrew Carnegie and many other men of great influence. An article, published over Carnegie's signature in the North American Review of June 1893, under the heading "A Look Ahead" contains the following passage:

> **"Let men say what they will, I say that as surely as the sun in the heavens once shone upon Britain and America united, so surely is it one morning to rise, shine upon and greet again the "RE-UNITED STATES," THE BRITISH AMERICAN UNION."**

The purpose of this union Carnegie set forth in the same article as follows:

> "The advantages of a race confederation are so numerous and so obvious that one scarcely knows how to begin their enumeration. Consider its defensive power. A reunion of the Anglo-Americans, consisting to-day of one-hundred and eight millions, which fifty years hence will number more than two hundred millions, would be unassailable upon land by any power or combination of powers that it is possible to create. We need not, therefore, take into account attacks upon the land; as for the water, the combined fleets would sweep the seas. **The new nation would dominate the world** and banish from the earth its greatest stain — the murder of men by men. It would be the arbiter between nations, and enforce the peaceful settlement of all quarrels. Such a giant among pigmies as the Re-United States would never need to exert its power, but only intimate its wishes and decisions."

And at another place Carnagie says:

> **"Were Britain part of the Re-United States all that she would be interested about in Europe would be**

fully secured; namely the protection of her own soil and the command of the seas. No balance of power or any similar question would be of the slightest importance. The re-united nation would be prompt to repel any assault upon the soil or the rights of any of its parts."

We leave it to those readers acquainted with the history of England to imagine the consequences, which such a union, under the leadership of the unscrupulous diplomats of England, would have for all other nations.

Carnegie not only expressed his resolution to bring about this reunion in the words: "Whatever obstructs reunion, I oppose; whatever promotes it, I favor!" but he also spent many million dollars for this same purpose. Numerous Americans believe that the establishment of a discretionary endowment pension fund of almost $20,000,000 for American college- and university professors has been made with no other design, than to influence these professors to lend their great moral assistance to Carnegie's aims, just as such help is expected from that army of men, who received the "benefits" of Rhodes' Scholarships.

Surmise is rife also, that Carnegie's endowment of $10,000,000 for "International Peace," has no other end, than to proclaim through its large staff of well paid orators and lecturers to the people of our republic the blessings they are to get when they will forget the evil doings of Jefferson, Franklin, Henry, Washington, Herchheimer, Mühlenberg and all the other foolish mutineers of the "War of Rebellion," and will return to their original vassalage of England.

To discredit these "rebels," numerous orators and authors are constantly at work. Harvard professors have explained in public lectures, that George Washington had an unexampled temper and did neither possess large brain power nor education; that Benjamin Franklin was a liar and dressed freakishly to be a social lion; and that Patrick Henry, Jeremiah Belknap, and Noah Webster speculated on inside tips received from Congressmen. It fell to the lot of Poultney Bigelow to besmirch the memory of Steuben by publishing in the New York Sun of May 2, 1915, that "the famous Steuben obtained his rank in the American Army by a pious Prussian fraud," and that "he was one of the alleged patriots, who came to Washington with bogus titles to rank, and sought for the triumph of American liberty only in so far as a salary followed in its wake." —

The gradual elimination from our public school histories of all reference to the nefarious part played by England in American history; the movement to ignore the celebration of the Fourth of July and substitute the signing of the British Magna Charta to be celebrated by American youth as the true origin of our independence, as proposed by Carnegie, are so many indications, whither currents are carrying our people.

Distrust in the real objects of the "International Peace Society" grows, when we note that its president is Elihu Root, England's solicitor in America; and that among its vice-presidents are men like Dr. Charles W. Eliot, President Emeritus of Harvard, and Joseph H. Choate, U. S. Ambassador to Great Britain. The former is the man, who in 1913 at a banquet in New York lauded German civilization to the skies, stating that to no other country America is so deeply indebted as to Germany. Since the outbreak of the European Conflict this same person has become notorious for expressing diametrically opposite views and for suggesting urgently that the United States should prepare to enter the war in aid of the Allies and help in the destruction of Germany. Ex-Ambassador Choate startled in January 1916 his hearers, when at a banquet of the "Pilgrims Society" he addressed the guests in the words: "I now ask you all to rise and drink a good old loyal toast to the President and King George of England!

Hand in hand with such "Patriots" works a powerful pro-British press, influenced and controlled by Lord Northcliffe, publisher of the London Times, and by J. P. Morgan, the American financial and munition agent for Great Britain.

By displaying an exceedingly hostile attitude toward everything German; by accusing the German element in the United States of disloyalty toward the land of its adoption; by working up a strong anti-German sentiment; by supplementing their abusive language with drawings and cartoons of the most insulting and abominable character; and last but not least, by their incessant efforts to force the United States into war with Germany, this un-American press has not only degraded itself but made evident its bondage to British dictations.

Inveigled into this dangerous conspiracy are the owners and presidents of hundreds of factories making arms and ammunition; Senators and Representatives, interested in the stocks of those establishments, which provide "things to kill" or are needed to bring our country in the state of "preparedness;" furthermore university professors, ministers, authors and many other American citizens of prominence.*)

What havoc and dreadful demoralization has already been caused by this pro-British propaganda among our people, appears from the fact, that an "American Legion" has been

---

*)For full information about this subject we refer to Carnegie's article in the "North American Review" of June 1893; to the publication "The Conquest of the United States," distributed by the "American Truth Society" in New York; to the well documented disclosures appearing in the "Fatherland" of March 22, and April 26, 1916; to S. Ivor Stephen's booklet "Neutrality," New York, 1916; to "Issues and Events," "Fair Play" of 1916, etc.

formed, to fight in British uniforms in Flanders against that country which since the birth of our Republic has been a true friend of our United States: Germany.

To give the reader an idea of the demoralization that has taken place among our people, we quote here verbally from a lengthy article, which under the heading:

"First of American Legion off for Flanders"

appeared in the Magazine Section of the New York Times of May 28, 1916. Approving the formation of the "American Legion," this paper states, that the legion consists of American citizens and that they adopted **"as their brigade badge the coat of arms of George Washington (1)** on the Canadian maple leaf. The recruiting station of the legion is Toronto, and here have assembled representatives of forty-five States and Territories of the United States, and here, without renouncing American citizenship, they have made oath, each of them, as follows:

"I will be faithful and bear true allegiance to his Majesty King George V. and I will, as in duty bound, honestly and faithfully defend his Majesty in person, crown, and dignity against all enemies and will observe and obey all orders of his Majesty and of all the Generals and Officers set over me."

"The leader of all these men who have taken that oath is a Unitarian clergyman and a citizen of the United States in the uniform of a British Lieutenant-Colonel, Seymour Bullock, formerly a United States chaplain."

About this founder of the legion the Times states that he was formerly a cadet at West Point. "But when he heard Moody and Sankey, he was convinced that he should be an evangelist and not a fighter. He was that until he went to Northwestern University, graduating as a clergyman in 1889. He got his next chance at the army when he went out as a chaplain in the Spanish war. Then he experienced a change of faith and became a Unitarian clergyman." In 1914 he was the preacher at the Unitarian Church in Ottawa, although still an American citizen. When hostilities among the European nations began, Bullock, according to the Times, "was mulling over the idea that he should do something besides preaching and talking for the cause of the Allies, and then was born the idea of the American Legion. Sir Sam Hughes was enthusiastic and authorized the project immediately. The Rev. Dr. Bullock became captain and chaplain. The legion soon became too big for a captain to handle, so Sir Sam Hughes made him a major. His organization outgrew that, so he was made a Lieutenant-Colonel, with supervising authority over all the American battalions."

The article states, that the members of the legion "feel very keenly about their American citizenship and take it for granted that there will be some to question it. In fact, the American Consul at Vancouver told Americans that their enlistment in the British battalion of the American Legion will cancel their citizenship."

Eager to dispel such scruples, the Times states "that the American Consul at Winnipeg takes the opposite view." Continuing it says: "That the opinion of the members of the legion regarding the worthiness of their project is shared by their friends in the United States, and friends in high places at that, is indicated by many letters which have become a part of the archives of the organization. Some of the letters to the officers and men of the legion congratulating them on the step they have taken. Incidentally, Dr. Charles W. Eliot, President Emeritus of Harvard University, has promised Colonel Bullock that he will write a preface for the book used by the men at the religious services in the field. And the American Legion March is being composed by Sousa."

Furthermore it is said, that, when Bullock "got his appointment he received a letter from ex-President William Howard Taft congratulating him on his promotion and expressing the hope that it would be permanent."

The same article contains also the interesting notes, that "at every meal in the mess room, decorated, by the way, with both the United States and British flags, the American officers rise and drink the toast "The King" and that the Ninety-Seventh Batalion before leaving for the front, appeared in review with 15,000 other troops before Sir Sam Hughes, and was greeted along the line as "the Yankees." —

Much ado has been made in our histories about the poor Hessian soldiers, who, having no free will, during the 18th century by their rulers were hired out to King George III. to fight his battles and suppress the Americans in their heroic struggle for liberty. It was left to our 20th century to witness the much more shameful spectacle, that free American citizens voluntarily hire themselves to King George V., to fight his mercenary battles and help to crush a friendly nation, which is struggling heroically for its existence.

And these men wear a badge showing the coat of arms of George Washington!

Against this profanation of the coat of arms of the "Father of our Country," and against the gross offence committed by these Americans against the spirit of neutrality, neither President Wilson nor Theodore Roosevelt have raised one single word of protest. While they strived to excell one another in baseless insinuations and unjustified attacks upon the character of the German element, they remained singularly silent in face of the pro-British propaganda carried on in our country to verify the dreams of Rhodes and Carnegie of the "Re-United States." Shall we assume that these acts have their consent?

231

To frustrate this sinister plot against the independence of our United States is the end German Americans must strive for with might and main. In conjunction with other loyal citizens they must demand that the noble heroes of our two wars for independence shall not have fought in vain and that the achievements of Jefferson, Franklin, Washington, Herchheimer, Steuben and all the other patriotic men of those great times shall not become obliterated. They must insist, that our republic has a higher destiny than that of becoming satrap of a country the history of which is made up of the most abominable crimes against liberty and of incessant outrages against every country and island too feeble to offer resistance.

Now is the time, when every citizen should take to heart the admonition of Carl Schurz:

"MY COUNTRY! WHEN RIGHT, KEEP IT RIGHT; WHEN WRONG, SET IT RIGHT!" which far surpasses the saying "My Country right or wrong!"

The German Americans, on whom falls again an important rôle in the coming struggle, must continue to use the effective weapon **Truth** against misrepresentation and deception. They must undo the Anglo-Saxon propaganda and the machinations to plunge our United States into the present European Conflict or in any other that may follow.

Only by adhering to the excellent advice given by George Washington in his Farewell Address, to avoid all entanglements with foreign nations, our citizens can maintain this country as "the Land of the Free," and enable it **to become a model for other nations by virtue of Impartiality, Love of Justice and Sincerity of Efforts to restore to mankind the blessings of Peace.**

Selective Bibliography

For a recent concise essay on German-American history, see Willi Paul Adams, **The German-Americans: An Ethnic Experience**. Translated and Adapted by LaVern J. Rippley and Eberhard Reichmann. (Indianapolis: Max Kade German-American Center, Indiana University-Purdue University at Indianapolis, 1993). For a more in-depth study, see LaVern J. Rippley, **The German-Americans**. (Boston: Twayne, 1976).

For bibliographical references to German-American history, see Don Heinrich Tolzmann, **German-Americana: A Bibliography**. (Metuchen, NJ: Scarecrow Pr., 1975).

Other Heritage Books by Don Heinrich Tolzmann:

*Amana: William Rufus Perkins' and Barthinius L. Wick's
History of the Amana Society, or Community of True Inspiration*

*Americana Germanica: Paul Ben Baginsky's Bibliography of
German Works Relating to America, 1493–1800*

*Biography of Baron Von Steuben, the Army of the American Revolution and
Its Organizer: Rudolf Cronau's Biography of Baron von Steuben*

CD: German-American Biographical Index (Midwest Families)

CD: Germans, Volume 2

CD: The German Colonial Era (four volumes)

Cincinnati's German Heritage

Covington's German Heritage

*Custer: Frederick Whittaker's Complete Life of General George A. Custer,
Major General of Volunteers, Brevet Major General U.S. Army
and Lieutenant-Colonel Seventh U.S. Cavalry*

*Dayton's German Heritage: Karl Karstaedt's Golden Jubilee History of the
German Pioneer Society of Dayton, Ohio*

Early German-American Newspapers: Daniel Miller's History

German Achievements in America: Rudolf Cronau's Survey History

German Americans in the Revolution

German Immigration to America: The First Wave

German Pioneer Life and Domestic Customs

German Pioneer Lifestyle

German Pioneers in Early California: Erwin G. Gudde's History

German-American Achievements: 400 Years of Contributions to America

German-Americana: A Bibliography

Germany and America, 1450–1700

Kentucky's German Pioneers: H. A. Rattermann's History

*Lives and Exploits of the Daring Frank and Jesse James: Thaddeus Thorndike's
Graphic and Realistic Description of Their Many Deeds of Unparalleled
Daring in the Robbing of Banks and Railroad Trains*

Louisiana's German Heritage: Louis Voss' Introductory History

Maryland's German Heritage: Daniel Wunderlich Nead's History

*Memories of the Battle of New Ulm: Personal Accounts of the Sioux Uprising.
L. A. Fritsche's History of Brown County, Minnesota (1916)*

*Michigan's German Heritage: John Andrew Russell's History of the
German Influence in the Making of Michigan*

Ohio's German Heritage

Outbreak and Massacre by the Dakota Indians in Minnesota in 1862: Marion P. Satterlee's Minute Account of the Outbreak, with Exact Locations, Names of All Victims, Prisoners at Camp Release, Refugees at Fort Ridgely, etc. Complete List of Indians Killed in Battle and Those Hung, and Those Pardoned at Rock Island, Iowa

The German Element in Virginia: Herrmann Schuricht's History

The German Immigrant in America

The Pennsylvania Germans: James Owen Knauss, Jr.'s Social History

The Pennsylvania Germans: Jesse Leonard Rosenberger's Sketch of Their History and Life

www.ingramcontent.com/pod-product-compliance
Lightning Source LLC
Chambersburg PA
CBHW070904270326
41927CB00011B/2450